Networking

FOR

DUMMIES®

7TH EDITION

Networking
FOR
DUMMIES®
7TH EDITION

by Doug Lowe

WILEY

Wiley Publishing, Inc.

Networking For Dummies®, 7th Edition

Published by
Wiley Publishing, Inc.
111 River Street
Hoboken, NJ 07030-5774

Copyright © 2005 by Wiley Publishing, Inc., Indianapolis, Indiana

Published by Wiley Publishing, Inc., Indianapolis, Indiana

Published simultaneously in Canada

For general information on our other products and services or to obtain technical support, please contact our Customer Care Department within the U.S. at 800-762-2974, outside the U.S. at 317-572-3993, or fax 317-572-4002.

Wiley also publishes its books in a variety of electronic formats. Some content that appears in print may not be available in electronic books.

Library of Congress Control Number: 2004107904

ISBN: 0-7645-7583-X

Manufactured in the United States of America

10 9 8 7 6 5 4 3 2 1

7O/SQ/RQ/QU/IN

WILEY

About the Author

Doug Lowe has written a whole bunch of computer books, including more than 35 *For Dummies* books (such as *PowerPoint 2003 For Dummies*, *Word 2003 All-In-One Desk Reference For Dummies*, *Networking All-In-One Desk Reference For Dummies,* and *Internet Explorer 6 For Dummies*). He lives in that sunny All-American City of Fresno, California, which isn't nearly as close to San Francisco as most people think, with his wife and two of his daughters (the other one's away at college). He's one of those obsessive-compulsive decorating nuts who puts up tens of thousands of lights at Christmas and creates computer-controlled Halloween decorations that rival Disney's Haunted Mansion. Maybe his next book should be *Tacky Holiday Decorations For Dummies.* (For pictures, check out his Web site at www.LoweWriter.com.)

Dedication

To Debbie, Rebecca, Sarah, and Bethany.

Author's Acknowledgments

The list of thank-yous for this book is long and goes back several years. I'd like to first thank John Kilcullen, David Solomon, Janna Custer, Erik Fafforn, Grag Robertson, and Ray Marshall for all of their help with the first edition. Those who worked on subsequent editions include Tim Gallan, Mary Goodwin, Joe Salmeri, Jennifer Ehrlich, Constance Carlisle, and Jamey L. Marcum, Jeanne S. Criswell, Ted Cains, Jamey L. Marcum, Danna Lesh, Rebekah Mancilla, Becky Huehls, Amy Pettinella, Suzanne Thomas, Garret Pease, and Andrea Boucher. Each of these people made valuable contributions to the content, readability, and accuracy that have paved the way for the current edition.

Now, for the seventh edition, I'd like to thank project editor Christopher Morris, who did a great job overseeing all the editorial work that was required to put this book together. I'd also like to thank Dan DiNicolo, who once again gave the entire manuscript a thorough technical look-through and offered many excellent suggestions, and copy editor Barry Childs-Helton, who maid sure there whir know spelling hair ores. And, as always, thanks to all the behind-the-scenes people who chipped in with help I'm not even aware of.

Oh, and I'd also like to thank Becca Freeman. She didn't have anything to do with this book, but I thought it would make her happy to see her name in print.

Publisher's Acknowledgments

We're proud of this book; please send us your comments through our online registration form located at www.dummies.com/register/.

Some of the people who helped bring this book to market include the following:

Acquisitions, Editorial, and Media Development

Project Editor: Christopher Morris

Acquisitions Editor: Melody Layne

Senior Copy Editor: Barry Childs-Helton

Technical Editor: Dan DiNicolo

Editorial Manager: Kevin Kirschner

Media Development Specialist: Angela Denny

Media Development Manager: Laura VanWinkle

Media Development Supervisor: Richard Graves

Editorial Assistant: Amanda Foxworth

Cartoons: Rich Tennant, www.the5thwave.com

Composition

Project Coordinator: Erin Smith

Layout and Graphics: Andrea Dahl, Lauren Goddard, Denny Hager, Joyce Haughey, Michael Kruzil, Heather Ryan, Rashell Smith, Julie Trippetti

Proofreaders: Laura Albert, John Greenough, Carl William Pierce, TECHBOOKS Production Services

Indexer: TECHBOOKS Production Services

Publishing and Editorial for Technology Dummies

Richard Swadley, Vice President and Executive Group Publisher

Andy Cummings, Vice President and Publisher

Mary Bednarek, Executive Editorial Director

Mary C. Corder, Editorial Director

Publishing for Consumer Dummies

Diane Graves Steele, Vice President and Publisher

Joyce Pepple, Acquisitions Director

Composition Services

Gerry Fahey, Vice President of Production Services

Debbie Stailey, Director of Composition Services

Contents at a Glance

Table of Contents

Introduction

*W*elcome to the seventh edition of *Networking For Dummies,* the book that's written especially for people who have this nagging feeling in the back of their minds that they should network their computers but haven't a clue as to how to start or where to begin.

Do you often copy a spreadsheet file to a floppy disk and give it to the person in the next office so that he or she can look at it? Are you frustrated because you can't use the fancy laser printer that's on the financial secretary's computer? Do you wait in line to use the computer that has the customer database? You need a network!

Or maybe you already have a network, but you have just one problem: They promised that the network would make your life easier, but instead, it's turned your computing life upside down. Just when you had this computer thing figured out, someone popped into your office, hooked up a cable, and said, "Happy networking!" Makes you want to scream.

Either way, you've found the right book. Help is here, within these humble pages.

This book talks about networks in everyday — and often irreverent — terms. The language is friendly; you don't need a graduate education to get through it. And the occasional potshot will help unseat the hallowed and sacred traditions of networkdom, bringing just a bit of fun to an otherwise dry subject. The goal is to bring the lofty precepts of networking down to earth where you can touch them and squeeze them and say, "What's the big deal? I can do this!"

About This Book

This isn't the kind of book you pick up and read from start to finish, as if it were a cheap novel. If I ever see you reading it at the beach, I'll kick sand in your face. This book is more like a reference, the kind of book you can pick up, turn to just about any page, and start reading. It has 30 chapters, each one covering a specific aspect of networking — such as printing on the network, hooking up network cables, or setting up security so that bad guys can't break in. Just turn to the chapter you're interested in and start reading.

Each chapter is divided into self-contained chunks, all related to the major theme of the chapter. For example, the chapter on hooking up the network cable contains nuggets like these:

- ✔ What Is Ethernet?
- ✔ All About Cabling and Stuff
- ✔ Attaching Connectors to UTP Cable
- ✔ Hubs and Switches
- ✔ Wall Jacks and Patch Panels

You don't have to memorize anything in this book. It's a "need-to-know" book: You pick it up when you need to know something. Need to know what 100BaseT is? Pick up the book. Need to know how to create good passwords? Pick up the book. Otherwise, put it down and get on with your life.

How to Use This Book

This book works like a reference. Start with the topic you want to find out about. Look for it in the table of contents or in the index to get going. The table of contents is detailed enough that you should be able to find most of the topics you're looking for. If not, turn to the index, where you can find even more detail.

After you've found your topic in the table of contents or the index, turn to the area of interest and read as much as you need or want. Then close the book and get on with it.

Of course, the book is loaded with information, so if you want to take a brief excursion into your topic, you're more than welcome. If you want to know the big security picture, read the whole chapter on security. If you just want to know how to make a decent password, read just the section on passwords. You get the idea.

If you need to type something, you'll see the text you need to type like this: **Type this stuff**. In this example, you type **Type this stuff** at the keyboard and press Enter. An explanation usually follows, just in case you're scratching your head and grunting, "Huh?"

Whenever I describe a message or information that you see on the screen, I present it as follows:

```
A message from your friendly network
```

This book rarely directs you elsewhere for information — just about everything that you need to know about networks is right here. But if you do find the need for additional information, there are plenty of other *For Dummies* books that can help. If you have a networking question that isn't covered in this book, allow me to suggest my own *Networking All-in-One Desk Reference For Dummies* — it's a much-expanded reference book that goes deeper into specific network operating systems and TCP/IP protocols. You can also find plenty of other *For Dummies* books that cover just about every operating system and application program known to humanity.

What You Don't Need to Read

Aside from the topics you can use right away, much of this book is skippable. I've carefully placed extra-technical information in self-contained sidebars and clearly marked them so you can steer clear of them. Don't read this stuff unless you're really into technical explanations and want to know a little of what's going on behind the scenes. Don't worry; my feelings won't be hurt if you don't read every word.

Foolish Assumptions

I'm going to make only two assumptions about who you are: (1) You're someone who works with a PC, and (2) you either have a network or you're thinking about getting one. I hope you know (and are on speaking terms with) someone who knows more about computers than you do. My goal is to decrease your reliance on that person, but don't throw away his or her phone number quite yet.

Is this book useful for Macintosh users? Absolutely. Although the bulk of this book is devoted to showing you how to link Windows-based computers to form a network, you can find information about how to network Macintosh computers as well.

How This Book Is Organized

Inside this book, you find chapters arranged in six parts. Each chapter breaks down into sections that cover various aspects of the chapter's main subject. The chapters are in a logical sequence, so reading them in order (if you want to read the whole thing) makes sense. But the book is modular enough that you can pick it up and start reading at any point.

Here's the lowdown on what's in each of the six parts.

Part I: Getting Started with Networking

The chapters in this part present a layperson's introduction to what networking is all about. This is a good place to start if you're clueless about what a network is and why you're suddenly expected to use one. It's also a great place to start if you're a hapless network user who doesn't give a whit about "optimizing network performance," but you want to know what the network is and how to get the most out of it.

The best thing about this part is that it focuses on how to use a network without getting into the technical details of setting up a network or maintaining a network server. In other words, this part is aimed at ordinary network users who have to learn how to get along with a network.

Part II: Building Your Own Network

Uh-oh. The boss just gave you an ultimatum: Get a network up and running by Friday or pack your things. The chapters in this section cover everything you need to know to build a network, from picking the network operating system to installing the cable.

Part III: Network Management For Dummies

I hope that the job of managing the network doesn't fall on your shoulders, but in case it does, the chapters in this part can help you out. You find out all about backup, security, performance, dusting, mopping, changing the oil, and all the other stuff network managers have to do.

Part IV: Network Operating Systems

This part has some specific information about the most common network operating systems — Windows Server 2003, NetWare 6, and Linux — to help you get started managing your network's servers. Note that much of the information in the Windows Server 2003 chapter applies to Windows 2000 as well, since the two are similar. Though the specific details may vary, the concepts are the same.

This part also has a chapter on Macintosh networking, explaining the subtle nuances of incorporating Macintosh computers into your network.

Part V: TCP/IP and the Internet

TCP/IP is the most common protocol used for networking today, so the chapters in this part show you how to use it. First, you'll learn how to safely connect your network to the Internet. Then you'll learn the ugly details of how IP addresses work so you'll be able to understand what an IP address such as 192.168.168.30 means and how a subnet mask such as 255.255.255.0 works. Finally, you'll learn how to set up one of the most important TCP/IP services: DHCP, which automatically assigns IP addresses to the computers on your network.

Part VI: The Part of Tens

This wouldn't be a *For Dummies* book without a collection of lists of interesting snippets: ten network commandments, ten network gizmos only big networks need, ten big network mistakes, and more!

Icons Used in This Book

Those nifty little pictures in the margin aren't just there to pretty up the place. They also have practical functions:

Hold it — technical details lurk just around the corner. Read on only if you have your pocket protector.

Pay special attention to this icon; it lets you know that some particularly useful tidbit is at hand — perhaps a shortcut or a little-used command that pays off big.

Did I tell you about the memory course I took?

Danger, Will Robinson! This icon highlights information that may help you avert disaster.

Where to Go from Here

Yes, you can get there from here. With this book in hand, you're ready to plow right through the rugged networking terrain. Browse through the table of contents and decide where you want to start. Be bold! Be courageous! Be adventurous! And above all, have fun!

Part I
Getting Started with Networking

The 5th Wave   By Rich Tennant

"I like getting complaint letters by e-mail. It's easier to delete than to shred."

In this part . . .

One day the Network Thugs barge into your office and shove a gun in your face. "Don't move until we've hooked you up to the network!" one of them says while the other one connects one end of a suspicious-looking cable to the back of your computer and shoves the other end into a hole in the wall. "It's done," they say as they start to leave. "Now . . . don't you say nuttin' to nobody . . . or we'll be back!"

If this has happened to you, you'll appreciate the chapters in this part. They provide a gentle introduction to computer networks written especially for the reluctant network user.

What if you don't have a network yet, and you're the one who's supposed to do the installing? Then the chapters in this part clue you in to what a network is all about. That way, you're prepared for the (unfortunately more technical) chapters contained in Parts II and beyond.

Chapter 1

Networks Will Not Take Over the World, and Other Network Basics

Computer networks get a bad rap in the movies. In the *Terminator* movies, a computer network of the future called Skynet takes over the planet, builds deadly terminator robots, and sends them back through time to kill everyone unfortunate enough to have the name Sarah Connor. In *The Matrix* movies, a vast and powerful computer network enslaves humans and keeps them trapped in a simulation of the real world. And in one of Matthew Broderick's first movies, *War Games,* a computer whiz kid nearly starts World War III by connecting to a Defense Department network and playing a game called Global Thermonuclear War.

Fear not. These bad networks exist only in the dreams of science-fiction writers. Real-world networks are much more calm and predictable. They don't think for themselves, they can't evolve into something you don't want them to be, and they won't hurt you — even if your name is Sarah Connor.

Now that you're over your fear of networks, you're ready to breeze through this chapter. It's a gentle, even superficial, introduction to computer networks, with a slant toward the concepts that can help you use a computer that's attached to a network. This chapter goes easy on the details; the really detailed and boring stuff comes later.

What Is a Network?

A *network* is nothing more than two or more computers connected by a cable (or in some cases, by a wireless connection) so that they can exchange information.

Of course, computers can exchange information in other ways besides networks. Most of us have used what computer nerds call the *sneakernet.* That's where you copy a file to a diskette and then walk the disk over to someone else's computer. (The term *sneakernet* is typical of computer nerds' feeble attempts at humor, and why not? As a way to transfer information, sneakernet *was* pretty feeble.)

The whole problem with the sneakernet is that it's slow — plus, it wears a trail in your carpet. One day, some penny-pinching computer geeks discovered that connecting computers together with cables was actually cheaper than replacing the carpet every six months. Thus the modern computer network was born.

You can create a computer network by hooking all the computers in your office together with cables and installing a special *network interface card* (an electronic circuit card that goes inside your computer — ouch!) in each computer so you have a place to plug in the cable. Then you set up your computer's operating-system software to make the network *work,* and — voilà — you have a working network. That's all there is to it.

If you don't want to mess with cables, you can create a *wireless network* instead. In a wireless network, each computer is equipped with a special wireless network adapter that has little rabbit-ear antennas. Thus, the computers can communicate with each other without the need for cables.

Figure 1-1 shows a typical network with four computers. You can see that all four computers are connected with a network cable to a central network device called a *hub.* You can also see that Ward's computer has a fancy laser printer attached to it. Because of the network, June, Wally, and the Beaver can also use this laser printer. (Also, you can see that the Beaver has stuck yesterday's bubble gum to the back of his computer. Although not recommended, the bubble gum shouldn't adversely affect the network.)

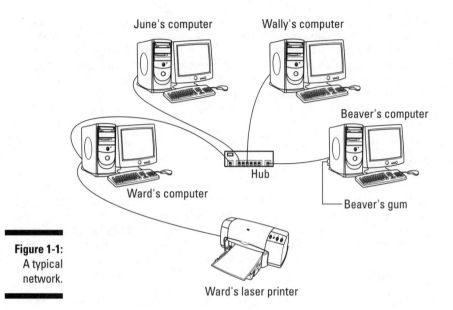

June's computer   Wally's computer

Beaver's computer

Ward's computer   Hub

Beaver's gum

Figure 1-1:
A typical
network.

Ward's laser printer

Computer networking has its own strange vocabulary. Fortunately, you don't have to know every esoteric networking term. Here are a few basic buzzwords to get you by:

- Networks are often called LANs. *LAN* is an acronym that stands for *local-area network*. It's the first *TLA*, or *three-letter acronym*, that you see in this book. You don't really need to remember it, or any of the many TLAs that follow. In fact, the only three-letter acronym you need to remember is TLA.

- You may guess that a four-letter acronym is called an *FLA*. Wrong! A four-letter acronym is called an *ETLA*, which stands for *extended three-letter acronym*. (After all, it just wouldn't be right if the acronym for *four-letter acronym* had only three letters.)

- Every computer connected to the network is said to be *on the network*. The technical term (which you can forget) for a computer that's on the network is a *node*.

- When a computer is turned on and can access the network, the computer is said to be *online*. When a computer can't access the network, it's *offline*. A computer can be offline for several reasons. The computer can be turned off, the user may have disabled the network connection, the computer may be broken, the cable that connects it to the network can be unplugged, or a wad of gum can be jammed into the disk drive.

- When a computer is turned on and working properly, it's said to be *up*. When a computer is turned off, broken, or being serviced, it's said to be *down*. Turning off a computer is sometimes called *taking it down*. Turning it back on is sometimes called *bringing it up*.

✔ Don't confuse local-area networks with the Internet. The *Internet* is a huge amalgamation of computer networks strewn about the entire planet. Networking the computers in your home or office so they can share information with one another and connecting your computer to the worldwide Internet are two entirely separate things. If you want to use your local-area network to connect your computers to the Internet, you can consult Chapter 18 for instructions.

Why Bother?

Frankly, computer networks are a bit of a pain to set up. So why bother? Because the benefits of having a network make the pain of setting one up bearable. You don't have to be a PhD to understand the benefits of networking. In fact, you learned everything you need to know in kindergarten: Networks are all about sharing. Specifically, networks are about sharing three things: files, resources, and programs.

✔ **Sharing files:** Networks enable you to share information with other computers on the network. Depending on how you set up your network, you can share files with your network friends in several different ways. You can send a file from your computer directly to a friend's computer by attaching the file to an e-mail message and then mailing it. Or, you can let your friend access your computer over the network so that your friend can retrieve the file directly from your hard drive. Yet another method is to copy the file to a disk on another computer, and then tell your friend where you put the file so that he or she can retrieve it later. One way or the other, the data travels to your friend's computer over the network cable, and not on a floppy disk as it would in a sneakernet.

✔ **Sharing resources:** You can set up certain computer resources — such as a hard drive or a printer — so all the computers on the network can access them. For example, the laser printer attached to Ward's computer in Figure 1-1 is a shared resource, which means that anyone on the network can use it. Without the network, June, Wally, and the Beaver would have to buy their own laser printers.

Hard drives can be shared resources, too. In fact, you must set up a hard drive as a shared resource in order to share files with other users. Suppose Wally wants to share a file with the Beaver, and a shared hard drive has been set up on June's computer. All Wally has to do is copy his file to the shared hard drive in June's computer and tell the Beaver where he put it. Then, when the Beaver gets around to it, he can copy the file from June's computer to his own. (Unless, of course, Eddie Haskell deletes the file first.)

You can share other resources, too, such as an Internet connection. In fact, sharing an Internet connection is one of the main reasons many networks are set up.

↙ **Sharing programs:** Rather than keeping separate copies of programs on each person's computer, sometimes putting programs on a drive that everyone shares is best. For example, if you have ten computer users who all use a particular program, you can purchase and install ten copies of the program — one for each computer. Or you can purchase a ten-user license for the program and then install just one copy of the program on a shared drive. Each of the ten users can then access the program from the shared hard drive.

In most cases, however, running a shared copy of a program over the network is unacceptably slow. A more common way of using a network to share programs is to copy the program's installation disks or CDs to a shared network drive. Then you can use that copy to install a separate copy of the program onto each user's local hard drive. For example, Microsoft Office enables you to do this, if you purchase a license from Microsoft for each computer on which you install Office.

The advantage of installing Office from a shared network drive is that you don't have to lug around the installation disks or CDs to each user's computer. And the system administrator can customize the network installation so that the software is installed the same way on each user's computer. (However, these benefits are significant only for larger networks. If your network has fewer than about ten computers, you're probably better off installing the program separately on each computer directly from the installation disks or CDs.)

Remember that purchasing a single-user copy of a program and then putting it on a shared network drive — so that everyone on the network can access it — is illegal. If you have five people who use the program, you need to either purchase five copies of the program or purchase a *network license* that specifically allows five or more users.

Another benefit of networking is that networks enable computer users to communicate with one another over the network. The most obvious way networks allow computer users to communicate is by passing messages back and forth, using e-mail or instant-messaging programs. But networks also offer other ways to communicate: For example, you can hold online meetings over the network. Network users who have inexpensive video cameras (webcams) attached to their computers can have video conferences. You can even play a friendly game of Hearts over a network — during your lunch break, of course.

Servers and Clients

The network computer that contains the hard drives, printers, and other resources that are shared with other network computers is called a *server*. This term comes up repeatedly, so you have to remember it. Write it on the back of your left hand.

Any computer that's not a server is called a *client.* You have to remember this term, too. Write it on the back of your right hand.

Only two kinds of computers are on a network: servers and clients. Look at your left hand and then look at your right hand. Don't wash your hands until you have these terms memorized.

The distinction between servers and clients in a network has parallels in sociology — in effect, a sort of class distinction between the "haves" and "have-nots" of computer resources:

- ✔ Usually, the most powerful and expensive computers in a network are the servers. There's a good technical reason: Every user on the network shares the server's resources.

- ✔ The cheaper and less powerful computers in a network are the clients. Clients are the computers used by individual users for everyday work. Because clients' resources don't have to be shared, they don't have to be as fancy.

- ✔ Most networks have more clients than servers. For example, a network with ten clients can probably get by with one server.

- ✔ In many networks, a clean line of demarcation exists between servers and clients. In other words, a computer functions as either a server or a client, and not both. For the sake of an efficient network, a server can't become a client, nor can a client become a server.

- ✔ Other (usually smaller) networks can be more even-handed, allowing any computer in the network to be a server and allowing any computer to be both server and client at the same time.

Dedicated Servers and Peers

In some networks, a server computer is a server computer and nothing else. It's dedicated to the sole task of providing shared resources, such as hard drives and printers, to be accessed by the network client computers. Such a server is referred to as a *dedicated server* because it can perform no other task besides network services.

Other networks take an alternative approach, enabling any computer on the network to function as both a client and a server. Thus, any computer can share its printers and hard drives with other computers on the network. And while a computer is working as a server, you can still use that same computer for other functions such as word processing. This type of network is called a *peer-to-peer network,* because all the computers are thought of as *peers,* or equals.

Here are some points to ponder concerning the difference between dedicated server networks and peer-to-peer networks while you're walking the dog tomorrow morning:

✔ Peer-to-peer networking features are built into Windows. Thus, if your computer runs Windows, you don't have to buy any additional software to turn your computer into a server. All you have to do is enable the Windows server features.

✔ The network server features that are built into desktop versions of Windows (such as Windows XP) aren't very efficient because these versions of Windows were not designed primarily to be network servers. If you're going to dedicate a computer to the task of being a full-time server, you should use a special network operating system instead of the standard Windows operating system. A *network operating system,* also known as a *NOS,* is specially designed to handle networking functions efficiently. The two most commonly used network operating systems are the server version of Windows — which, depending on the version you use, is known as Windows Server 2003, Windows 2000 Server, or Windows NT Server — and Novell NetWare. I describe these alternatives briefly in the next section, "The NOS Choice."

✔ Many networks are both peer-to-peer *and* dedicated-server networks at the same time. These networks have one or more server computers that run a NOS such as Windows Server 2003, as well as client computers that use the server features of Windows to share their resources with the network.

✔ Besides being dedicated, it's helpful if your servers are also sincere.

The NOS Choice

Most dedicated network servers do not run a desktop version of Windows (such as Windows XP, ME, or 98). Instead, they usually run a network operating system (NOS) designed to efficiently carry out the tasks that coordinate access to shared network resources among the network client computers.

Although you have several network operating systems to choose from, the two most popular are NetWare and Windows 2000 Server. Here's a bird's-eye view of what's out there:

✔ One of the most popular network operating systems is NetWare, from a company called Novell. NetWare is very advanced but also very complicated. So complicated, in fact, that it has an intensive certification program that rivals the bar exam. The lucky ones that pass the test are awarded the coveted title *Certified Novell Engineer,* or *CNE,* and a lifetime supply of pocket protectors. Fortunately, a CNE is really required only for large networks to which dozens (even hundreds) of computers are attached. Building a NetWare network with just a few computers isn't too difficult.

✔ Microsoft makes a special server version of its popular Windows operating system. The latest and greatest version is called Windows Server 2003. Its predecessor, Windows 2000 Server, is still widely used. In addition, many networks still use an even older version called Windows NT Server. (Throughout this book, I'll use the term *Windows Server* to refer to the various server versions of Windows.)

Not wanting to be left out, Microsoft has its own certification program for Windows server specialists. If you pass the full battery of certification tests, you get to wear an MCSE badge, which lets the whole world know that you are a *Microsoft Certified Systems Engineer.*

✔ Other network-operating-system choices include Unix and Linux. Apple also makes its own network server operating system called Mac OS X Server, designed specially for Macintosh computers.

You get a closer look at these NOS options in Chapter 8.

What Makes a Network Tick?

To use a network, you don't really have to know much about how it works. Still, you may feel a little bit better about using the network if you realize that it doesn't work by voodoo. A network may seem like magic, but it isn't. The following is a list of the inner workings of a typical network:

✔ **Network interface cards:** Inside any computer attached to a network is a special electronic circuit card called a *network interface card.* The TLA for network interface card is *NIC.*

Using your network late into the evening is not the same as watching NIC at night. If the network is set up to use that time to update software and back up data, the NIC has to be robust enough to handle all-day-all-night use.

Although it's also possible to use an external network interface that connects to the computer via the computer's USB port, most networked computers use a built-in network interface card.

✔ **Network cable:** The network cable is what physically connects the computers together. It plugs into the network interface card at the back of your computer.

The most common type of network cable looks something like telephone cable. However, appearances can be deceiving. Most phone systems are wired using a lower grade of cable that won't work for networks. For a computer network, each pair of wires in the cable must be twisted in a certain way. That's why this type of cable is called a *twisted-pair cable.* (Standard phone cable doesn't do the twist.)

Older networks often use another type of cable, called *coaxial cable* or just *coax*. Coax is similar to the cable used to bring Nick at Nite to your TV. The cable used for cable TV is not the same as the cable used for computer networks, though. So don't try to replace a length of broken network cable with TV cable. It won't work. Networks require a higher grade of cable than is used for cable TV.

Of the two cable types, twisted-pair cable is the best kind to use for new networks. Coax cable is found in plenty of older networks, but if you are building a new network, use twisted-pair cable. For the complete lowdown on networking cables, refer to Chapter 9.

You can do away with network cable by creating a wireless network, though that option has some challenges of its own. For more information about wireless networking, see Chapter 10.

✔ **Network hub:** If your network is set up using twisted-pair cable, your network also needs a network hub. A *hub* is a small box with a bunch of cable connectors. Each computer on the network is connected by cable to the hub. The hub, in turn, connects all the computers to each other. If your network uses coax cable, the cable goes directly from computer to computer; no network hub is used.

Instead of hubs, most newer networks use a faster device known as a *switch.* The term *hub* is often used to refer to both true hubs and switches.

✔ **Network software:** Of course, the software really makes the network work. To make any network work, a whole bunch of software has to be set up just right. For peer-to-peer networking with Windows, you have to play with the Control Panel to get networking to work. And network operating systems such as Windows Server 2003 or Novell's NetWare require a substantial amount of tweaking to get them to work just right. For more information about choosing which network software to use for your network, refer to Chapter 8. To find out what you need to know to configure the software so that your network runs smoothly, refer to Chapters 19 through 22.

It's Not a Personal Computer Anymore!

If I had to choose one point that I want you to remember from this chapter more than anything else, it's this: After you hook up your personal computer (PC) to a network, it's not a "personal" computer anymore. You are now part of a network of computers, and in a way, you've given up one of the key things that made PCs so successful in the first place: independence.

I got my start in computers back in the days when mainframe computers ruled the roost. *Mainframe computers* are big, complex machines that used to fill entire rooms and had to be cooled with chilled water. My first computer was a water-cooled Binford Power-Proc Model 2000. Argh, argh, argh. (I'm not making up the part about the water. A plumber was frequently required to install a mainframe computer. In fact, the really big ones were cooled by liquid nitrogen. I *am* making up the part about the Binford 2000.)

Mainframe computers required staffs of programmers and operators in white lab coats just to keep them going. They had to be carefully managed. A whole bureaucracy grew up around managing mainframes.

Mainframe computers used to be the dominant computers in the workplace. Personal computers changed all that. Personal computers took the computing power out of the big computer room and put it on the user's desktop, where it belongs. PCs severed the tie to the centralized control of the mainframe computer. With a PC, a user could look at the computer and say, "This is mine . . . all mine!" Mainframes still exist, but they're not nearly as popular as they once were.

Networks are changing everything all over again. In a way, it's a change back to the mainframe-computer way of thinking: central location, distributed resources. True, the network isn't housed in the basement and doesn't have to be installed by a plumber. But you can no longer think of "your" PC as your own. You're part of a network — and, like the mainframe, the network has to be carefully managed.

Here are a few ways in which a network robs you of your independence:

- ✔ You can't just indiscriminately delete files from the network. They may not be yours.

- ✔ The network forces you to be concerned about security. For example, a server computer has to know who you are before it will let you access its files. So you'll have to know your user ID and password to access the network. This is to prevent some 15-year-old kid from hacking his way into your office network via its Internet connection and stealing all your computer games.

- ✔ Just because Wally sends something to Ward's printer doesn't mean it immediately starts to print. The Beave may have sent a two-hour print job before that. Wally just has to wait.

- ✔ You may try to retrieve an Excel spreadsheet file from a network drive, only to discover that someone else is using it. Like Wally, you just have to wait.

- ✔ If you copy a 600MB database file to a server's drive, you may get calls later from angry coworkers complaining that no room is left on the server's drive for their important files.

- ✔ Someone may pass a virus to you over the network. You may then accidentally infect other network users.

✔ You have to be careful about saving sensitive files on the server. If you write an angry note about your boss and save it on the server's hard drive, your boss may find the memo and read it.

✔ If you want to access a file on Ward's computer but Ward hasn't come in and turned his computer on yet, you have to go into his office and turn it on yourself. To add insult to injury, you have to know Ward's password if Ward decided to password-protect his computer. (Of course, if you're the Beave, you probably already know Ward's password and everyone else's too, for that matter. If you don't, you can always ask Eddie Haskell.)

✔ If your computer is a server, you can't just turn it off when you're finished using it. Someone else may be accessing a file on your hard drive or printing on your printer.

✔ Why does Ward always get the best printer? If *Leave It to Beaver* were made today, I bet the good printer would be on June's computer.

The Network Manager

Because so much can go wrong — even with a simple network — designating one person as the *network manager* (sometimes also called the *network administrator*) is important. This way, someone is responsible for making sure that the network doesn't fall apart or get out of control.

The network manager doesn't have to be a technical genius. In fact, some of the best network managers are complete idiots when it comes to technical stuff. What's important is that the manager be organized. The manager's job is to make sure that plenty of space is available on the file server, that the file server is backed up regularly, that new employees can access the network, and so on.

The network manager's job also includes solving basic problems that the users themselves can't solve — and knowing when to call in an expert when something really bad happens. It's a tough job, but somebody's got to do it.

✔ Part III of this book is devoted entirely to the hapless network manager. So if you're nominated, read that section. If you're lucky enough that someone *else* is nominated, celebrate by buying him or her a copy of this book.

✔ In small companies, picking the network manager by drawing straws is common. The person who draws the shortest straw loses and becomes manager.

✔ Of course, the network manager can't really be a *complete* technical idiot. I was lying about that. (For those of you in Congress, the word is *testifying*.) I exaggerated to make the point that organizational skills are more important than technical skills. The network manager needs to know how to do various maintenance tasks. This knowledge requires at least a little technical know-how, but the organizational skills are more important.

What Have They Got That You Don't Got?

With all this stuff to worry about, you may begin to wonder if you're smart enough to use your computer after it's attached to the network. Let me assure you that you are. If you're smart enough to buy this book because you know that you need a network, you're more than smart enough to use the network after it's put in. You're also smart enough to install and manage a network yourself. This isn't rocket science.

I know people who use networks all the time. And they're no smarter than you are. But they do have one thing that you don't have: a certificate. And so, by the powers vested in me by the International Society for the Computer Impaired, I present you with the certificate in Figure 1-2, confirming that you've earned the coveted title, *Certified Network Dummy,* better known as *CND.* This title is considered much more prestigious in certain circles than the more stodgy CNE or MCSE badges worn by real network experts.

Congratulations, and go in peace.

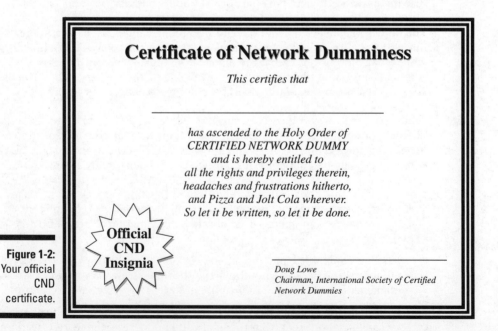

Figure 1-2: Your official CND certificate.

Certificate of Network Dumminess

This certifies that

_____

has ascended to the Holy Order of
CERTIFIED NETWORK DUMMY
and is hereby entitled to
all the rights and privileges therein,
headaches and frustrations hitherto,
and Pizza and Jolt Cola wherever.
So let it be written, so let it be done.

Official CND Insignia

_____
Doug Lowe
Chairman, International Society of Certified
Network Dummies

Chapter 2

Life on the Network

After you hook up your PC to a network, it's not an island anymore — separated from the rest of the world like some kind of isolationist fanatic waving a "Don't tread on me" flag. The network connection changes your PC forever. Now your computer is part of a system, connected to other computers on the network. You have to worry about annoying network details, such as using local and shared resources, logging in and accessing network drives, using network printers, logging off, and who knows what else.

Oh, bother.

This chapter brings you up to speed on what living with a computer network is like. Unfortunately, this chapter gets a little technical at times, so you may need your pocket protector.

Distinguishing between Local Resources and Network Resources

In case you didn't catch this in Chapter 1, one of the most important differences between using an isolated computer and using a network computer lies in the distinction between local resources and network resources. *Local resources* are things such as hard drives, printers, modems, and CD-ROM drives that are connected directly to your computer. You can use local resources whether you're connected to the network or not. *Network resources,* on the other hand, are the hard drives, printers, modems, and CD-ROM drives that are connected to the network's server computers. You can use network resources only after your computer is connected to the network.

The whole trick to using a computer network is to know which resources are local resources (those that belong to you) and which are network resources (those that belong to the network). In most networks, your C drive is a local drive. And if a printer is sitting next to your PC, it's probably a local printer. You can do anything you want with these resources without affecting the network or other users on the network (as long as the local resources aren't shared on the network).

- ✔ You can't tell just by looking at a resource whether it's a local resource or a network resource. The printer that sits right next to your computer is probably your local printer, but then again, it may be a network printer. The same holds for hard drives: The hard drive in your PC is probably your own, but it may be a network drive, which can be used by others on the network.

- ✔ Because dedicated network servers are full of resources, you may say that not only are they dedicated (and sincere) but also resourceful. (Groan. Sorry, this is yet another in a tireless series of bad computer-nerd puns.)

What's in a Name?

Just about everything on a computer network has a name: The computers themselves have names, the people that use the computers have names, and the hard drives and printers that can be shared on the network have names. Knowing all the names used on your network isn't essential, but you do need to know some of them.

- ✔ Every person who can use the network has a *user identification* (*user ID* for short). You need to know your user ID in order to log on to the network. You also need to know the user IDs of your buddies, especially if you want to steal their files or send them nasty notes. You can find more information about user IDs and logging on in the section "Logging On to the Network" later in this chapter.

- ✔ Letting the folks on the network use their first names as their user IDs is tempting, but not a good idea. Even in a small office, you eventually run into a conflict. (And what about that Mrs. McCave — made famous by Dr. Seuss — who had 23 children and named them all Dave?) I suggest that you come up with some kind of consistent way of creating user IDs. For example, you may use your first name plus the first two letters of your last name. Then Wally's user ID would be `wallycl` and Beaver's would be `beavercl`. Or you may use the first letter of your first name followed by your complete last name. Then Wally's user ID would be `wcleaver` and Beaver's would be `bcleaver`. (Note that in most networks, capitalization doesn't matter in the user name. Thus, `bcleaver` is the same as `BCleaver`.)

✔ Every computer on the network must have a unique computer name. You don't have to know the names of all the computers on the network, but it helps if you know your own computer's name and the names of any server computers you need to access. The computer's name is often the user ID of the person who uses the computer most often. Sometimes the names indicate the physical location of the computer, such as `office-12` or `back-room`. Server computers often have names that reflect the group that uses the server most, like `acctng-server` or `cad-server`.

Then again, some network nerds like to assign techie-sounding names like `BL3K5-87a`. And some like to use names from science fiction movies — `HAL`, `Colossus`, `M5`, and `Data` come to mind. Cute names like `Herbie` are not allowed. (However, `Tigger` and `Pooh` are entirely acceptable. Recommended, in fact. Tiggers like networks.)

✔ Network resources such as hard drives and printers have names, too. For example, a network server may have two printers, named `laser` and `inkjet` (to indicate the type of printer), and two hard drives, named `C drive` and `D drive`.

✔ In NetWare, names of hard drives are called *volume names*. Often they are names such as `SYS1`, `SYS2`, and so on. (NetWare administrators frequently lack sufficient creativity to come up with snazzy volume names.)

✔ Networks that use a network operating system such as Windows Server or Novell's NetWare have a user ID for the network administrator. If you log on using the administrator's user ID, you can do anything you want — add new users, define new network resources, change Wally's password — anything. The supervisor's user ID is usually something very clever, such as `ADMINISTRATOR`.

Logging On to the Network

To use network resources, you must connect your computer to the network, and you must go through a super-secret process called *logging on.* The purpose of logging on is to let the network know who you are so it can decide whether you're one of the good guys.

Logging on is a little bit like cashing a check: The process requires two forms of identification. The first form is your *user ID,* the name by which the network knows you. Your user ID is usually some variation of your real name, like "Beave" for "The Beaver." Everyone who uses the network must have a user ID.

Your *password* is a secret word that only you and the network know. If you type the correct password, the network believes you are who you say you are. Every user has a different password, and the password should remain a secret.

In the early days of computer networking, you had to type a logon command at a stark MS-DOS prompt and then supply your user ID and password. Nowadays, the glory of Windows is that you get to log on to the network through a special network logon dialog box, which appears when you start your computer, as shown in Figure 2-1.

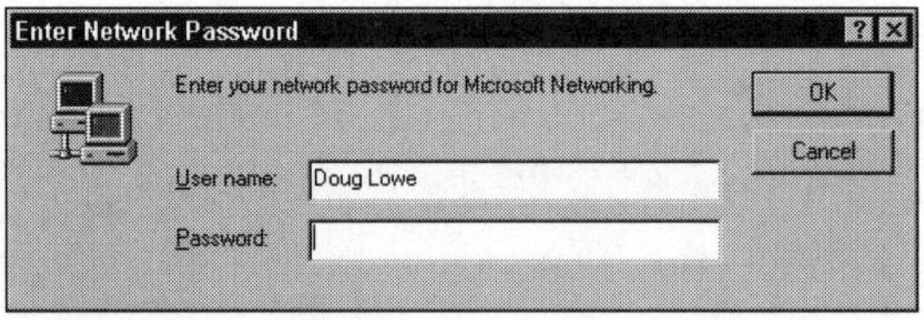

Figure 2-1:
You have to
enter your
user ID and
password to
access the
network.

Here are some more logon points to ponder:

✔ The terms *user name* and *logon name* are sometimes used instead of *user ID.* They mean the same thing.

✔ As long as we're talking about words that mean the same thing, *log in* and *log on* mean the same thing, as do (respectively) *log out* and *log off* as ways of saying, "I'm outta here." Although you'll see both out there in the world, this book uses *log on* and *log off* throughout — and if there's any exception, the book will say why and grouse about it a bit.

✔ As far as the network is concerned, you and your computer aren't the same thing. Your user ID refers to you, not to your computer. That's why you have a user ID, and your computer has a computer name. You can log on to the network using your user ID from any computer that's attached to the network. And other users can log on at your computer using their own user IDs.

When others log on at your computer using their own user IDs, they can't access any of your network files that are protected by your password. However, they *can* access any local files that you haven't protected. So be careful which people you allow to use your computer.

✔ Windows XP has a cool feature that displays icons for each of the users registered on your computer. When this feature is enabled, you can log on by clicking your name's icon and then typing your password.

✔ If you are logging on to a Windows Server network, the Logon dialog box includes a field in which you can enter the domain name you want to log on to. Hopefully, a suitable default value appears for the domain name so you can safely ignore this field. If not, your network administrator will be happy to tell you how to enter this information.

✔ For NetWare networks, the Logon dialog box may indicate the tree and context you are using to log on. Hopefully, your network administrator already configured the tree and context to the correct values. If not, he or she will tell you how to set the correct tree and context values. (On older NetWare networks, you may be asked to enter the name of the NetWare Login Server. Again, your network administrator will tell you what name to enter.)

✔ Your computer may be set up so that it logs you on automatically whenever you turn it on. In that case, you don't have to type your user ID and password. This setup makes the task of logging on more convenient but takes the sport out of it. And it's a terrible idea if you're the least bit worried about bad guys' getting into your network or personal files.

✔ Guard your password with your life. I'd tell you mine, but then I'd have to shoot you.

Understanding Shared Folders

Long ago, in the days Before Network (B.N.), your computer probably had just one hard drive, known as C: drive. Maybe it had two — C: and D:. The second drive might be another hard disk, or possibly a CD-ROM or DVD-ROM drive. And even to this day, the descendants of those drives are physically located inside your PC. They are your *local drives*.

Now that you're on a network, however, you probably have access to drives that aren't located inside your PC but are located instead in one of the other computers on the network. These network drives can be located on a dedicated server computer or, in the case of a peer-to-peer network, on another client computer.

In some cases, you can access an entire network drive over the network. But in most cases, you can't access the entire drive. Instead, you can access only certain folders (*directories,* in old MS-DOS lingo) on the network drives. Either way, the shared drives or folders are known in Windows terminology as *shared folders.*

Shared folders can be set up with restrictions on how you may use them. For example, you may be granted full access to some shared folders so that you can copy files to or from them, delete files on them, create or remove folders on them, and so on. On other shared folders, your access may be limited in certain ways. For example, you may be able to copy files to or from the shared folder but not delete files, edit files, or create new folders. You may also be asked to enter a password before you can access a protected folder. The amount of disk space you are allowed to use on a shared folder may also be limited. For more information about file-sharing restrictions, refer to Chapter 13.

Keep in mind that in addition to accessing shared folders that reside on other people's computers, you can also designate your computer as a server to enable other network users to access folders that you share. To learn how to share folders on your computer with other network users, refer to Chapter 4.

Oh, the Network Places You'll Go

Windows enables you to access network resources, such as shared folders, by opening the My Network Places icon that resides on your desktop. When you first open My Network Places, you're greeted by icons that represent the shared resources you can access from your computer, as shown in Figure 2-2.

As you can see from Figure 2-2, each of the four computers on the network has been set up with a shared folder. You can open any of these shared folders and access the files they contain as if they were on your local computer. (Network computers that don't have shared folders won't appear in My Network Places.)

You can summon a list of all the computers that are available on your network by clicking View Workgroup Computers in the Network Tasks section of the My Network Places window. This action displays an icon for each computer on your network. (If your computer is on a large network, you may not have a View Workgroup Computers link. In that case, your network administrator can set up shortcuts to the network resources you need or tell you how to set up the shortcuts yourself.)

You can also access My Network Places from any Windows application program. For example, suppose that you're working with Microsoft Word and would like to open a document file that has been stored in a shared folder on your network. All you have to do is choose the File➪Open command to bring up an Open dialog box. Near the top of the Open dialog box is a list box labeled *Look In.* From this list, choose the My Network Places icon. This displays a list of shared network resources you can access. Then locate the document file that you want to open on the network.

If you are using Windows 95 or 98, My Network Places is referred to as the Network Neighborhood. When you call up the Network Neighborhood in Windows 95 or 98, you are immediately greeted by a list of the computers available on your network. You can then click one of the computers to access its shared drives and folders.

Figure 2-2:
My Network
Places lists
the shared
resources
on your
network.

Here are a few points to ponder concerning My Network Places:

✔ Viewing the resources that are available on the network by way of My Network Places is also known as *browsing the network*. Unfortunately, browsing the network through My Network Places may be painfully slow if a large number of computers is connected to your local network workgroup.

✔ If your network has fewer than 32 computers, Windows automatically displays icons for each shared network resource when you open My Network Places. If you are on a larger network, you may need to set up icons for the network resources you use. You can do so by clicking Add a Network Place in the My Network Places window. Contact your network guru for details about how to use the Add a Network Place wizard to set up your network places.

✔ A trick known as *mapping* lets you access your favorite shared network folders quickly without having to browse the entire network. For more information, see the next section, titled "Mapping Network Drives."

Mapping Network Drives

If you find yourself accessing a particular shared folder frequently, you may want to use a special trick called *mapping* to access the shared folder more efficiently. Mapping assigns a drive letter to a shared folder. Then you can use the drive letter to access the shared folder as if it were a local drive. In this way, you can access the shared folder from any Windows program without having to navigate through My Network Places.

For example, you can map a shared folder named \Wal's Files to drive G on your computer. Then, to access files stored in the shared \Wal's Files folder, you would look on drive G.

To map a shared folder to a drive letter, follow these steps:

1. **Open a My Computer window by double-clicking the My Computer icon on your desktop.**

2. **Choose Tools⇨Map Network Drive.**

   This action summons the Map Network Drive dialog box.

3. **Change the drive letter in the Drive drop-down list, if you want to.**

   You probably don't have to change the drive letter that Windows selects (in Figure 2-5, drive Z). But if you're picky, you can select the drive letter from the Drive drop-down list.

4. **Click the Browse button. Then use the Browse For Folder dialog box to find the shared folder you want to use. When you find the folder, select it and click OK.**

5. **If you want this network drive to be automatically mapped each time you log on to the network, check the Reconnect at Logon option.**

   If you leave the Reconnect at Logon option unchecked, the drive letter is available only until you shut Windows down or log off the network. If you check this option, the network drive automatically reconnects each time you log on to the network.

   Be sure to check the Reconnect at Logon option if you use the network drive often.

6. **Click OK.**

   That's it! You're done.

Your network administrator may have already set up your computer with one or more mapped network drives. If so, you can ask him or her to tell you which network drives have been mapped. Or you can just open My Computer and have a look. (Mapped network drives are listed in My Computer using the icon shown in the margin.) For another method of mapping network drives, see Chapter 6.

✔ Assigning a drive letter to a network drive is called *mapping the drive,* or *linking the drive* by network nerds. "Drive H is mapped to a network drive," they say.

✔ The drive letter that you use to map a drive on a network server doesn't have to be the same drive letter that the server uses to access the file. For example, suppose that you use drive H to link to the server's C drive. (This is confusing, so have another cup of coffee.) In this scenario, drive H on your computer is the same drive as drive C on the server computer. This shell game is necessary for one simple reason: You can't access the server's C drive as drive C, because your computer has its own drive C! You have to pick an unused drive letter and map or link it to the server's C drive.

✔ Network drive letters don't have to be assigned the same way for every computer on the network. For example, a network drive that is assigned drive letter H on your computer may be assigned drive letter Q on someone else's computer. In that case, your drive H and the other computer's drive Q are really the same drive. This can be very confusing. If your network is set up this way, put pepper in your network administrator's coffee.

✔ Accessing a shared network folder through a mapped network drive is much faster than accessing the same folder via My Network Places. That's because Windows has to browse the entire network to list all available computers whenever you open My Network Places. In contrast, Windows does not have to browse the network at all to access a mapped network drive.

✔ If you choose the Reconnect at Logon option for a mapped drive, you receive a warning message if the drive is not available when you log on. In most cases, the problem is that the server computer isn't turned on. Sometimes, however, this message is caused by a broken network connection. For more information about fixing network problems such as this, refer to Chapter 6.

Four Good Uses for a Shared Folder

After you know which shared network folders are available, you may wonder what you're supposed to do with them. Here are four good uses for a network folder.

Use it to store files that everybody needs

A shared network folder is a good place to store files that more than one user needs to access. Without a network, you have to store a copy of the file on everyone's computer, and you have to worry about keeping the copies synchronized (which you can't do, no matter how hard you try). Or you can keep the file on a disk and pass it around. Or you can keep the file on one computer and play musical chairs — whenever someone needs to use the file, he or she goes to the computer that contains the file.

With a network, you can keep one copy of the file in a shared folder on the network, and everyone can access it.

Use it to store your own files

You can also use a shared network folder as an extension of your own hard drive storage. For example, if you've filled up all the free space on your hard drive with pictures, sounds, and movies that you've downloaded from the Internet, but the network server has billions and billions of gigabytes of free space, you have all the drive space you need. Just store your files on the network drive!

Here are a few guidelines for storing files on network drives:

- ✔ Using the network drive for your own files works best if the network drive is set up for private storage that other users can't access. That way, you don't have to worry about the nosy guy down in Accounting who likes to poke around in other people's files.

- ✔ Don't overuse the network drive. Remember that other users have probably filled up their own hard drives, so they want to use the space on the network drive, too.

- ✔ Before you store personal files on a network drive, make sure that you have permission. A note from your mom will do.

Use it as a pit stop for files on their way to other users

"Hey, Wally, could you send me a copy of last month's baseball stats?"

"Sure, Beave." But how? If the baseball stats file resides on Wally's local drive, how does Wally send a copy of the file to Beaver's computer? Wally can do this by copying the file to a network folder. Then Beaver can copy the file to his local hard drive.

Here are some tips to keep in mind when you use a network drive to exchange files with other network users:

✔ Don't forget to delete files that you've saved to the network folder after they've been picked up! Otherwise, the network folder quickly fills up with unnecessary files.

✔ Creating a directory on the network drive specifically intended for holding files en route to other users is a good idea. Call this directory `PITSTOP` or something similar to suggest its function.

In many cases, it's easier to send files to other network users via e-mail. Just send a message to the other network user and attach the file you want to share. The advantage of sending a file via e-mail is that you don't have to worry about details like where to leave the file on the server and who's responsible for deleting the file.

Use it to back up your local hard drive

If enough drive space is available on the file server, you can use it to store backup copies of the files on your hard drive. Just copy the files that you want to back up to a shared network folder.

Obviously, if you copy *all* your data files to the network drive — and everybody else follows suit — it can quickly fill up. You'd better check with the network manager before you start storing backup copies of your files on the server. The manager may have already set up a special network drive that is designed just for backups. And, if you're lucky, your network manager may be able to set up an automatic backup schedule for your important data so you don't have to remember to back it up manually.

Hopefully, your network administrator also routinely backs up the contents of the network server's disk to tape (yes, *tape* — see Chapter 15 for details). That way, if something happens to the network server, the data can be recovered from the backup tapes.

Using a Network Printer

Using a network printer is much like using a network hard drive: You can print to a network printer from any Windows program by choosing File➪Print to call up a Print dialog box from any program and choosing a network printer from the list of available printers.

Keep in mind, however, that printing on a network printer isn't exactly the same as printing on a local printer — you have to take turns. When you print on a local printer, you're the only one using it. But when you print to a network printer, you are (in effect) standing in line behind other network users, waiting to share the printer. This complicates things in several ways:

✔ If several users print to the network printer at the same time, the network has to keep the print jobs separate from one another. If it didn't, the result would be a jumbled mess, with your 168-page report getting mixed up with the payroll checks. That would be bad. Fortunately, the network takes care of this situation by using a fancy feature called *print spooling*.

✔ Invariably, when I get in line at the hardware store, the person in front of me is trying to buy something that doesn't have a product code on it. I end up standing there for hours waiting for someone in Plumbing to pick up the phone for a price check. Network printing can be like that. If someone sends a two-hour print job to the printer before you send your half-page memo, you have to wait. Network printing works on a first-come, first-served basis, unless you know some of the tricks that I discuss in Chapter 3.

✔ Before you were forced to use the network, your computer probably had just one printer attached to it. Now you may have access to a local printer and several network printers. You may want to print some documents on your cheap (oops, I mean *local*) inkjet printer but use the network laser printer for really important stuff. To do that, you have to find out how to use your programs' functions for switching printers.

✔ Network printing is really too important a subject to squeeze into this chapter. So Chapter 3 goes into this topic in more detail.

Logging Off the Network

After you finish using the network, you should log off. Logging off the network makes the network drives and printers unavailable. Your computer is still physically connected to the network (unless you cut the network cable with pruning shears — bad idea! Don't do it!), but the network and its resources are unavailable to you.

✔ After you turn off your computer, you're automatically logged off the network. After you start your computer, you have to log in again. Logging off the network is a good idea if you're going to leave your computer unattended for a while. As long as your computer is logged in to the network, anyone can use it to access the network. And because unauthorized users can access it under your user ID, you get the blame for any damage they do.

✔ In Windows, you can log off the network by clicking the Start button and choosing the Log Off command. This process logs you off the network without restarting Windows. (In some versions of Windows 95, you must choose the Start➪Shut Down command to log off the network.)

Chapter 3

Using a Network Printer

*I*f you come to hate anything about using a network, it's likely to be using a network printer. Oh, for the good ol' days when your slow (but simple) dot-matrix printer sat on your desk right next to your computer for you, and nobody else but you, to use. Now you have to share the printer down the hall. It may be a neat printer, but now you can't watch it all the time to make sure it's working.

Now you have to send your 80-page report to the network printer, and when you go check on it 20 minutes later, you discover that it hasn't printed yet because someone else sent an 800-page report before you. Or the printer's been sitting idle for 20 minutes because it ran out of paper. Or all 80 pages of your report printed on the company letterhead that someone accidentally left in the paper tray. Or your report just disappeared into Network-Network Land.

What a pain. This chapter can help you out. It clues you in to the secrets of network printing and gives you some Network Pixie Dust (NPD) to help you find those lost print jobs. (This chapter may also convince you to spend $69 of your own money to buy your own little inkjet printer so you won't have to mess around with the network printer!)

What's So Special about Network Printing?

Why is network printing such a big deal? In Chapter 4, I talk about sharing network drives and folders and show that sharing is really pretty simple. After everything is set up right, using a network drive is hardly different from using a local drive.

The situation would be great if sharing a printer were just as easy. But it isn't. The problem with network printing is that printers are slow and finicky devices. They run out of paper. They eat paper. They run out of toner or ink. And sometimes they just croak. Dealing with all these problems is hard enough when the printer is right next to the computer on your desk, but using the printer that's accessed remotely via a network is even harder.

A printer in every port

Before I delve into the details of network printing, I want to review some printing basics. A *port* is a connection on the back of your computer. You use ports to connect devices to the computer. You plug one end of a cable into the port and plug the other end of the cable into a connector on the back of the device that you want to connect. Nearly all computers have at least two devices connected to ports: a keyboard and a mouse. Many computers also have a printer attached to a port, and some computers have other devices, such as a modem or a scanner.

There are two types of ports you can attach printers to: *parallel* and *USB*. Certain types of older printers used serial port connections, but most of these printers have long since been used to make beehives. The serial port is mostly used nowadays to connect a mouse or a modem to the computer. (Actually, USB ports are updated, improved versions of that old standby, the serial port — and they're becoming very popular for connecting printers. For more information about USB, see the sidebar "Hop on the Universal Serial Bus.")

Another type of port that your computer may or may not have is a SCSI port. *SCSI* (pronounced *skuzzy*), which stands for *Small Computer System Interface*, is a special type of high-speed parallel port that's used mostly to connect disk drives, tape drives, CD-ROM drives, and other devices (such as scanners) to your computer. Because you don't use the SCSI port to connect a printer, you can ignore it for now.

Here are some additional points to ponder concerning the mysteries of printer ports:

- ✔ After the introduction of the first IBM Personal Computer in A.D.1260 (kidding, but it seems that long ago), the names LPT1, LPT2, and LPT3 were assigned to the parallel ports (*LPT* stands for *Line Printer*). The first parallel port (and the only parallel port on most computers) is LPT1. LPT2 and LPT3 are the second and third parallel ports. Even today, Windows uses these same names.

- ✔ LPT1 has a pseudonym: PRN. The names LPT1 and PRN both refer to the first parallel port and are used interchangeably.

- ✔ COM1, COM2, COM3, and COM4 are the names used for the four serial ports. (*COM* stands for *communications,* a subject that the people who came up with names like LPT1 and COM1 needed to study more closely.)

- ✔ With any luck, the name assigned to each port on your computer is printed next to the port's connector on the back of your computer. If not, you have to check your computer's manual to find out which port is which.

Some network printers don't connect to a port on a computer at all. Instead, these printers have an Ethernet port and connect directly to the network.

Printer configuration

All you have to do to use a printer is plug it into the parallel port (or the USB port) on the back of your computer, right? Nope. You must also configure Windows to work with the printer. To do this, you must install a special piece of software called a *printer driver,* which tells Windows how to print to your printer.

Each type of printer has its own type of printer driver. Drivers for the most common printers come with Windows. For printers that are more exotic — or for newer printers that weren't available at the time you purchased Windows — the printer manufacturer supplies the driver on a disk that comes with the printer.

To find out what printers are already configured in Windows XP, click the Start button and open the Control Panel. Then, double-click the Printers and Faxes icon. The Printers and Faxes folder appears, as shown in Figure 3-1. (To call up this folder in Windows 98, Windows Me, or Windows 2000, choose Start➪Settings➪Printers.)

Hop on the Universal Serial Bus

Newer computers have one or more ports called USB ports. *USB,* which stands for *Universal Serial Bus,* is designed to eventually replace most, if not all, external connections required by your computer.

Think about all the external devices that you may have to connect to a typical computer: keyboard, monitor, mouse, printer, and perhaps a scanner, video camera, speakers, and maybe even an external CD-ROM or tape drive. Each of these devices needs its own type of cable, and it's up to you to figure out which of the many receptacles on the back of your computer to plug each cable into.

Now, with USB, you can replace all these components (except the monitor and speakers) with USB-compatible devices and plug them all into USB ports. Most recent computers have two or more USB ports (usually in back) for hooking up your keyboard, mouse, and printer, and a couple of USB ports on the front for connecting devices such as digital cameras. And many USB keyboards also have one or two USB connections. So if you use up all your computer's USB ports, you can plug additional USB devices into the

keyboard's USB port. If you still don't have enough USB ports for all your USB devices, you can purchase an inexpensive USB *hub,* a connector you can use to plug four or more USB devices into a single USB port.

Besides saving you the hassle of untangling a multitude of cables and connectors, USB devices also automatically reconfigure themselves after you attach them to your computer. You no longer have to fuss with detailed configuration settings such as IRQ numbers and DMA addresses. You can even add or remove USB devices without turning off your computer or restarting Windows. When you plug a USB device into your computer, Windows automatically recognizes the device and configures it for use.

You can also use the USB to connect to the network without having to install a separate network interface card inside your computer. The hardware that does this trick is called a *USB Ethernet adapter,* although that's not generally a very efficient route to go; its slower USB port slows down your network connection.

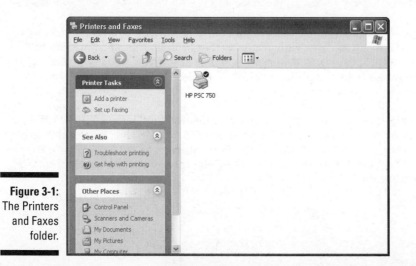

Figure 3-1:
The Printers
and Faxes
folder.

The Printers and Faxes folder shows an icon for each printer installed on your computer. In the case of Figure 3-1, only one printer has been installed: a Hewlett-Packard HP PSC-750. If you have more than one printer installed on your computer, you see a printer icon for each printer. In addition, the icon for the default printer will have a checkmark next to it.

Add a printer | You can configure a new printer for your computer by double-clicking the Add a Printer icon. Doing so starts the Add Printer wizard, which adds a printer driver for a new printer to your computer. For more information about using this wizard, see the "Adding a Network Printer" section, later in this chapter.

Spooling and the print queue

Printers are far and away the slowest part of any computer. As far as your computer's central processing unit (CPU) is concerned, the printer takes an eternity to print a single line of information. To keep the CPU from twiddling its microscopic thumbs, computer geeks invented *spooling*.

Spooling is really pretty simple. Suppose you use Microsoft Word to print a 200-page report. Without spooling, Word would send the report directly to the printer. You'd have to play Solitaire until the printer finished printing.

With spooling, Word doesn't send the report directly to the printer. Instead, Word sends the report to a disk file. Because the disk drives are so much faster than printers, you have to wait only a few seconds for the print job to finish. After your 200-page report is sent to the spool file, you can continue to use Word for other work, even though the printer hasn't actually finished your report yet.

Suppose you turn right around and send another 200-page report to the printer, while the printer is still busy printing the first 200-page report. The second report must wait for the printer to finish the first report. The place where the report waits is called the *print queue* — a computer-nerd term for the line in which your print job has to wait while other print jobs that reached the line sooner are printed. Your print job isn't actually printed until it gets to the front of the line — that is, until it gets to the front of the queue.

Here are a few more spooling tidbits:

- ✔ The people who invented network printing way back in the 1960s thought that calling the line that print jobs wait in a *line* would be uncool. The Beatles and anything British were popular back then, so they picked the British-sounding word *queue* instead.

- ✔ Although considered rude, cutting to the front of the queue is possible. You find out how to do that later in this chapter. This trick is good to know — especially if you're the only one who knows.

✔ Brits always use too many letters. They like to throw extra letters into words, like *colour*. The word *queue* is pronounced like "cue," not "cue-you." "Cue-you" is spelled "queueue" and is often used by Certified Network Dummies as an insult.

  ✔ Believe it or not, the word *spool* is actually an acronym — a five-letter acronym, or EETLA (Expanded Extended Three-Letter Acronym), to be precise. Brace yourself, because this acronym is really nerdy: *Spool* stands for *Simultaneous Peripheral Output On-Line*.

What is a print job?

I've used the term *print job* several times without explaining what it means, so you're probably already mad at me. I'd better explain before it's too late: A print job is a collection of printed pages that are kept together and treated as a set. If you print a 20-page document from Word, the entire 20-page printout is a single print job. Every time you use Word's Print command (or any other program's Print command), you create a print job.

How does the network know when one print job ends and the next one begins? Because the programs that do the printing send out a special code at the end of each Print command that says, "This is the end of the print job. Everything up to this point belongs together, and anything I print after this point belongs to my next print job."

Analogy alert! You can think of this code as the little stick you use at the grocery-store checkout stand to separate your groceries from the groceries that belong to the person in line behind you. The stick tells the clerk that all the groceries in front of the stick belong together, and the groceries behind the stick belong to the next customer.

When you print over a network, you can do lots of neat stuff with print jobs. You can tell the print server to print more than one copy of your job. You can tell it to print a full-page banner at the beginning of your job to make your job easy to find in a big stack. Or you can tell it to stop printing when your job gets to the front of the line so you can change from plain paper to preprinted invoices or checks. You handle these tricks from the standard Windows Print dialog boxes.

Adding a Network Printer

Before you can print to a network printer, you have to configure your computer to access the network printer that you want to use. From the Start menu, open the Control Panel and then double-click the Printers and Faxes icon. If your computer is already configured to work with a network printer, an icon for the network printer appears in the Printers folder (see the icon in the margin). You can tell a network printer from a local printer by the shape of the printer icon. Network printer icons have a pipe attached to the bottom of the printer.

If you don't have a network printer configured for your computer, you can add one by using the Add Printer wizard. Just follow these steps:

1. **Open the Add a Printer icon in the Printers folder to start the Add Printer wizard.**

   The wizard asks whether you want to add a local or a network printer.

2. **Choose Network.**

   The wizard asks you to specify a printer.

3. **Choose the Browse option and click the Next button.**

   A dialog box similar to the one in Figure 3-2 appears, showing the computers and shared resources available in My Network Places. Sniff around in this dialog box until you find the printer you want to use from your computer.

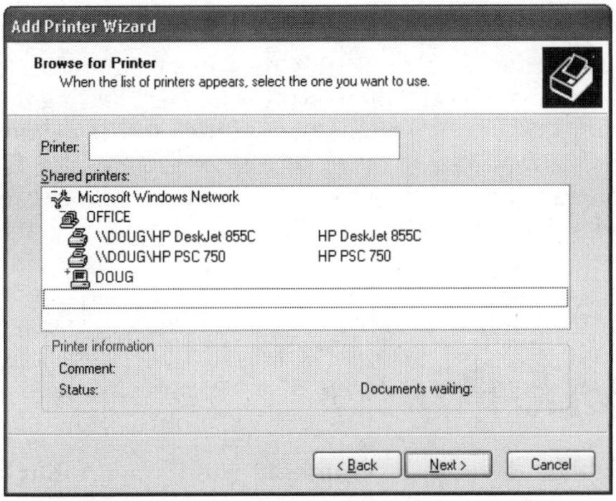

Figure 3-2:
The Add Printer wizard wants to know which network printer you want to use.

Add Printer Wizard

Browse for Printer
When the list of printers appears, select the one you want to use.

Printer:

Shared printers:

Microsoft Windows Network
  OFFICE
  \\DOUG\HP DeskJet 855C   HP DeskJet 855C
  \\DOUG\HP PSC 750   HP PSC 750
  DOUG

Printer information
Comment:
Status: Documents waiting:

< Back   Next >   Cancel

4. **Click the name of the printer you want to use.**

   If you can't find the printer you want to use, ask your network administrator for the printer's UNC path, which is the name used to identify the printer on the network. Then, instead of browsing for the printer, type the printer's UNC path when the Add Printer wizard asks you to specify a printer.

5. **Click OK to return to the Add Printer wizard.**

   The wizard copies the correct printer driver for the network printer to your computer.

6. **If your operating system asks you to insert your Windows CD-ROM so Windows can locate the driver files, do so.**

   In some cases, you may have to insert the driver disk that came with the printer. Typically, however, Windows copies the driver files directly from the server computer that the printer is attached to, so you won't have to bother with the Windows CD or the printer's driver disks.

7. **Designate a default printer.**

   To get you started, the Add Printer wizard asks whether you want to designate the currently highlighted printer as your default printer. You have two options:

   • Check Yes if this is the printer you expect to use most of the time.

   • Check No if (for example) you have a local printer that you use most of the time and are just creating a connection to a network printer that you will use only on special occasions.

8. **Click Next to continue and finish the wizard.**

Many network printers, especially newer ones, are connected directly to the network via a built-in Ethernet card. Setting up these printers can be tricky. You may need to ask the network administrator for help setting up this type of printer. (Some printers that are connected directly to the network have their own Web address, such as `Printer.CleaverFamily.com`. If that's the case, you can often set up the printer in a click or two: Use your Web browser to go to the printer's Web page, and then click a link that lets you install the printer.)

Using a Network Printer

After you have installed the network printer in Windows, printing to the network printer is a snap. You can print to the network printer from any Windows program by using the File➪Print command to summon the Print dialog box. For example, Figure 3-3 shows the Print dialog box for WordPad — the free text-editing program that comes with Windows. The available printers are listed near the top of this dialog box. Choose the network printer from this list and then click OK to print your document. That's all there is to it!

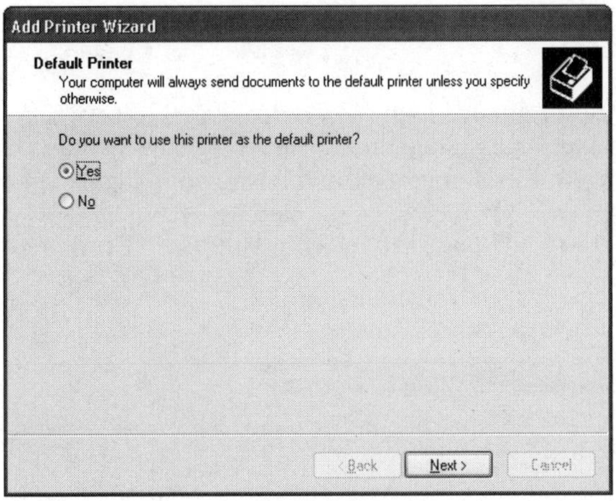

Add Printer Wizard

Default Printer
Your computer will always send documents to the default printer unless you specify otherwise.

Do you want to use this printer as the default printer?

⦿ Yes

○ No

‹ Back   Next ›   Cancel

Figure 3-3:
A typical
Print dialog
box.

Playing with the Print Queue

After you send your document to a network printer, you usually don't have to worry about it. You just go to the network printer, and — *voilà!* — your printed document is waiting for you.

That's what happens in the ideal world. In the real world where you and I live, all sorts of things can happen to your print job between the time you send it to the network printer and the time it actually prints:

- ✔ You discover that someone else already sent a 50-trillion-page report ahead of you that isn't expected to finish printing until the national debt is completely paid off.

- ✔ The price of framis valves suddenly goes up $2 each, rendering foolish the recommendations you made in your report.

- ✔ Your boss calls and tells you that his brother-in-law will be attending the meeting, so won't you please print an extra copy of the proposal for him. Oh, and a photocopy won't do. Originals only, please.

- ✔ You decide to take lunch, so you don't want the output to print until you get back.

Fortunately, your print job isn't totally beyond your control just because you've already sent it to the network printer. You can easily change the status of jobs that you've already sent. You can change the order in which jobs print, hold a job so that it won't print until you say so, or cancel a job altogether.

You can probably make your network print jobs do other tricks, too — such as shake hands, roll over, and play dead. But the basic tricks — hold, cancel, and change the print order — are enough to get you started.

Using Windows Print Queue Tricks

To play with the printer queue, open the Control Panel (Start⇨Control Panel) and click Printers and Faxes. Then, open the icon for the printer that you want to manage. A window similar to the one shown in Figure 3-4 appears. If you happen to be Wally, you can see the bad news: Some user named Beaver has slipped in a 145-page report from Microsoft Word before your little 1-page memo.

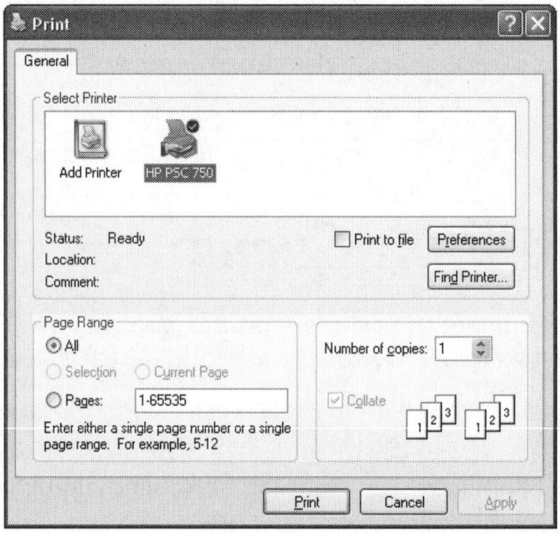

Figure 3-4: Managing a print queue.

To manipulate the print jobs that appear in the print queue or in the printer itself, use the following tricks:

✓ To temporarily stop a job from printing, select the job and choose the Document⇨Pause Printing command. Choose the same command again to release the job from its state of frustration and print it out, already.

✓ To delete a print job, select the job and choose the Document⇨ Cancel Printing command.

✓ To stop the printer, choose the Printer⇨Pause Printing command. To resume, choose the command again.

✓ To delete all print jobs, choose the Printer⇨Purge Print Documents command.

✓ To cut to the front of the line, drag the print job that you want to print to the top of the list.

✓ All of these tips apply only to your own print jobs. Unfortunately, you can't capriciously delete other people's print jobs.

The best thing about Windows printer management is that it shelters you from the details of working with different network operating systems. Whether you print on a NetWare printer, a Windows 2000 network printer, or a shared Windows XP printer, the Printer window icon manages all print jobs in the same way.

What to Do When the Printer Jams

The only three sure bets in life: The original *Star Wars* movies are better than the prequels, old actors like Harrison Ford always play opposite leading ladies who are 30 years younger, and the printer always jams shortly after your job reaches the front of the queue.

What do you do when you walk in on your network printer while it's printing all 133 pages of your report on the same line?

1. **Start by yelling, "Fire!"**

   Not really. But no one comes to your rescue if you yell, "Printer!"

2. **Find the printer's online button and press it.**

   This step takes the printer offline so the server stops sending information to it and the printer stops. This doesn't cure anything, but it stops the noise. If you must, turn the printer off.

3. **Pull out the jammed paper and reinsert the good paper into the printer. Nicely.**

4. **Press the online button so that the printer resumes printing.**

If the printer completely crumples up one or more pages of your document, you can reprint just the pages that were messed up. Just walk calmly to your computer, call up the Print dialog box from the program you used to print the document, select the pages you want to reprint, and choose the Print command. Of course, if the printer ate the entire print job, you'll have to reprint the entire thing. (If you're using Windows 2000, you can use the Print Queue to restart the print job from the first page.)

If you don't want to mess with clearing the printer jam, just cancel the print job. Then, print your document again using another printer. Then act surprised when you hear someone shouting that the first printer is full of crumpled paper.

Chapter 4

Sharing Your Files and Printers

As you probably know, networks consist of two types of computers: client computers and server computers. In the economy of computer networks, *client computers* are the consumers — the ones that use network resources such as shared printers and disk drives. *Servers* are the providers — the ones that offer their own printers and hard drives to the network so the client computers can use them.

This chapter shows you how to turn your humble Windows client computer into a server computer so other computers on your network can use your printer and any folders that you decide you want to share. In effect, your computer functions as both a client and a server at the same time. A couple of examples show how:

✔ It's a client when you send a print job to a network printer or when you access a file stored on another server's hard drive.

✔ It's a server when someone else sends a print job to your printer or accesses a file stored on your computer's hard drive.

Enabling File and Printer Sharing

Before you can share your files or your printer with other network users, you must set up a Windows feature known as *File and Printer Sharing*. Without this feature installed, your computer can be a network client but not a server.

If you're lucky, the File and Printer Sharing feature is already set up on your computer. To find out, double-click the My Computer icon on your desktop. Select the icon for your C drive and then click File in the menu bar to reveal the File menu. If the menu includes a Sharing command, then File and Printer Sharing is already set up, so you can skip the rest of this section. If you can't find a Sharing command in the File menu, then you have to install File and Printer Sharing before you can share a file or a printer with other network users.

File and Printer Sharing is usually installed on Windows XP systems. To install File and Printer Sharing on a Windows 9x/Me computer, follow these steps:

1. **From the Start menu, choose Settings⇨Control Panel.**

   The Control Panel comes to life.

2. **Double-click the Network icon.**

   The Network dialog box appears, as shown in Figure 4-1.

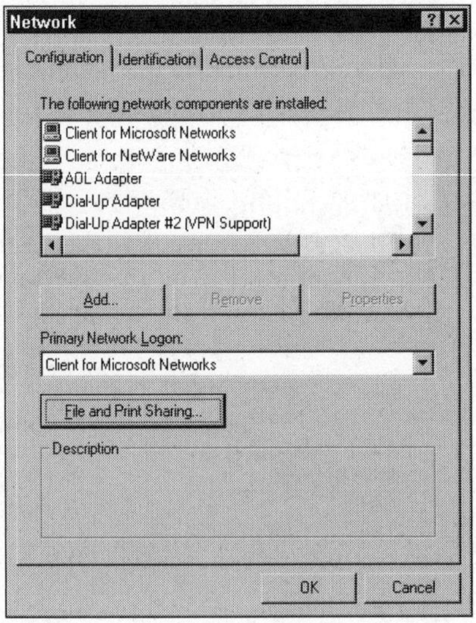

Figure 4-1:
The
Network
dialog box.

3. **Click the File and Print Sharing button.**

   This action summons the File and Print Sharing dialog box.

4. **Click the File and Print Sharing options you want to enable for your computer.**

   The first option enables you to share your files with other network users; the second allows you to share your printer. To share both your files and your printer, check both options.

5. Click OK to dismiss the File and Print Sharing dialog box.

You return to the Network dialog box.

6. Click OK to dismiss the Network dialog box.

The Network dialog box vanishes, and a Copy Progress dialog box appears and lets you know that Windows is copying the files required to enable File and Print Sharing. If you're prompted to insert the Windows CD-ROM, do so with a smile.

After all the necessary files have been copied, you see a dialog box informing you that you must restart your computer for the new settings to take effect.

7. Click Yes to restart your computer.

Your computer shuts down and then restarts. Your computer may take a minute or so to restart, so be patient. When your computer comes back to life, you're ready to share files or your printer.

While you are in the Network dialog box, do not mess around with any of the other network settings. You can safely change the File and Print Sharing options, but you should leave the rest of the settings on the Network dialog box well enough alone.

Sharing a Hard Drive or Folder

To enable other network users to access files that reside on your hard drive, you must designate either the entire drive or a folder on the drive as a _shared_ drive or folder. If you share an entire drive, other network users can access all the files and folders on the drive. If you share a folder, network users can access only those files that reside in the folder you share. (If the folder you share contains other folders, network users can access files in those folders, too.)

I recommend against sharing an entire hard drive, unless you want to grant _everyone on the network_ the freedom to sneak a peek at every file on your hard drive. Instead, you should share just the folder or folders containing the specific documents that you want others to be able to access. For example, if you store all your Word documents in the My Documents folder, you can share your My Documents folder so other network users can access your Word documents.

To share a folder on a Windows XP computer, follow these steps:

1. Double-click the My Computer icon on your desktop.

The My Computer window comes to center stage.

2. Select the folder that you want to share.

Click the icon for the drive that contains the folder that you want to share, and then find the folder itself and click it.

3. Choose the File⇨Sharing and Security command.

The Properties dialog box for the folder that you want to share appears. Notice that the sharing options are grayed out.

4. Click the Share This Folder on the Network option.

After you click this option, the rest of the sharing options come alive, as shown in Figure 4-2.

If you prefer, you can skip Steps 2 through 4. Instead, just right-click the folder you want to share and then choose Sharing and Security from the pop-up menu that appears.

5. Change the Share Name if you don't like the name that Windows proposes.

The *share name* is the name that other network users use to access the shared folder. You can give it any name you want, but the name can be no more than 12 characters long. Uppercase and lowercase letters are treated the same in a share name, so the name My Documents is the same as MY DOCUMENTS.

Windows proposes a share name for you, based on the actual folder name. If the folder name is 12 or fewer characters long, the proposed share name is the same as the folder name. But if the folder name is longer than 12 characters, Windows abbreviates it. For example, the name Multimedia Files becomes MULTIMEDIA F.

If the name that Windows chooses doesn't make sense or seems cryptic, you can change the share name to something better. For example, I would probably use MEDIA FILES instead of MULTIMEDIA F.

6. If you want to allow other network users to change the files in this folder, check the Allow Network Users to Change My Files option.

If you leave this option unchecked, other network users will be able to open your files, but they won't be able to save any changes they make.

7. Click OK.

The Properties dialog box vanishes, and a hand is added to the icon for the folder to show that the folder is shared (as shown in the margin here).

If you change your mind and decide that you want to stop sharing a folder, double-click the My Computer icon, select the folder or drive that you want to stop sharing, and choose the File⇨Sharing command to summon the Properties dialog box. Uncheck the Share This Folder on the Network option and then click OK.

The procedure for sharing folders in previous versions of Windows is similar, but the command is called Sharing instead of Sharing and Security.

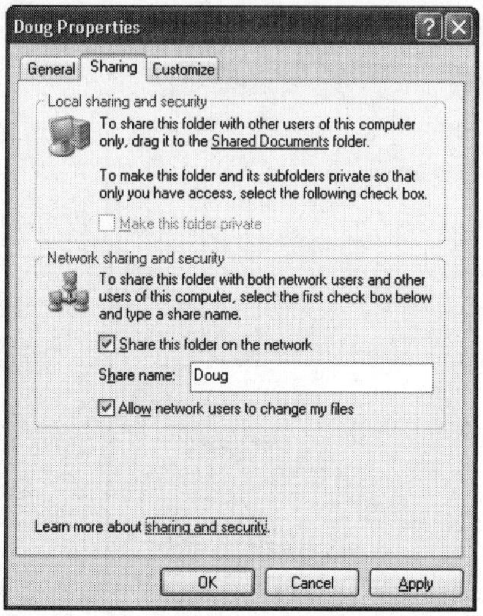

Figure 4-2:
The Sharing options come to life when you click the Share This Folder on the Network option.

Sharing a Printer

Sharing a printer is much more traumatic than sharing a hard drive. When you share a hard drive, other network users access your files from time to time. When they do, you hear your drive click a few times, and your computer may hesitate for a half-second or so. The interruptions caused by other users accessing your drive are sometimes noticeable, but rarely annoying.

But when you share a printer, you get to see Murphy's Law in action: Your coworker down the hall is liable to send a 40-page report to your printer just moments before you try to print a 1-page memo that has to be on the boss's desk in two minutes. The printer may run out of paper or, worse yet, it may jam during someone else's print job — and you'll be expected to attend to the problem.

Although these interruptions can be annoying, sharing your printer makes a lot of sense in some situations. If you have the only decent printer in your office or workgroup, everyone is going to bug you to let them use it anyway. You may as well share the printer on the network. At least this way, they won't be lining up at your door asking you to print their documents for them.

The following procedure shows you how to share a printer in Windows:

1. **From the Start menu, choose Control Panel⇨Printers and Faxes.**

   The Printers and Faxes folder appears, as shown in Figure 4-3. In this example, the Printers folder lists a single printer, named HP PSC 750.

Figure 4-3:
The Printers and Faxes folder.

2. **Select the printer that you want to share.**

   Click the icon for the printer to select the printer.

3. **Choose File⇨Sharing.**

   You're right: This doesn't make sense. You're sharing a *printer*, not a file, but the Sharing command is found under the File menu. Go figure.

   When you choose the File⇨Sharing command, the Properties dialog box for the printer appears.

4. **Select the Share This Printer option.**

5. **Change the Share Name if you don't like the name suggested by Windows.**

   Other computers use the share name to identify the shared printer, so choose a meaningful or descriptive name.

6. **Click OK.**

   You return to the Printers folder, where a hand is added to the printer icon, as shown in the margin, to show that the printer is now a shared network printer.

To take your shared printer off the network so other network users can't access it, follow the above procedure through Step 3 to call up the Printer Properties dialog box. Check Do Not Share This Printer, and then click OK. The hand disappears from the printer icon to indicate that the printer is no longer shared.

Chapter 5

Mr. McFeeley's Guide to E-mail

· ·

In This Chapter

▶ Using e-mail

▶ Reading and sending e-mail messages

▶ Scheduling and conferencing electronically

▶ Watching smileys and e-mail etiquette

· ·

*I*n ancient times B.P.C. (Before Personal Computers), a typical office worker often returned from a long lunch to find the desk covered with little pink "While You Were Out" notes. By the end of the old millennium, early computer screens were often plastered with stick-on notes — but even then, relief was in sight: electronic mail.

If you're a secret twentieth-century holdout, maybe the time has come for you to bite the bullet and find out how to use your computer network's electronic mail (*e-mail*) program. Most computer networks have one. If yours doesn't, hide the network manager's stone axe until he or she gets e-mail up and running.

This chapter introduces you to what's possible with a good e-mail program. So many e-mail programs are available that I can't possibly show you how to use all of them, so I'm focusing on Microsoft Outlook, the e-mail program that comes with Microsoft Office. Other e-mail programs are similar, and work in much the same way.

E-mail and Why It's So Cool

E-mail is nothing more than the computer-age equivalent of Mr. McFeeley, the postman from *Mr. Rogers' Neighborhood*. E-mail enables you to send messages to (and receive messages from) other users on the network. Instead of writing the messages on paper, sealing them in an envelope, and then giving them to Mr. McFeeley to deliver, e-mail messages are stored on disk and electronically delivered to the appropriate user.

Sending and receiving e-mail

Sending an e-mail message to another network user means doing several electronic chores. These used to be simple, but they're a bit more complex nowadays:

- **Activate the e-mail program.** Normally, this entails double-clicking the program's icon. If the program asks you for a password, you'll have to type one in before the program can do its thing. If you have no password, check with your network administrator to get one.

- **Compose the message.** You can, of course, work it up beforehand in a text editor (such as Notepad), but today's typical e-mail program provides you with a nice blank New Message screen for the purpose.

- **Type an address for the message to go to.** This is usually the network user ID of the user to whom you want the message sent. Most e-mail programs also require that you create a short comment *(subject line)* that identifies what the message is about.

- **Send the message when it's ready to go.** Normally, there's a handy, obvious Send button just waiting for you to click it.

When you receive a message from another user, the e-mail program copies the message to your computer and then displays it on-screen so you can read it. You can then delete the message, print it, save it to a disk file, or forward it to another user. You can also reply to the message by composing a new message to be sent back to the user who sent the original message.

Here are some additional thoughts about sending and receiving e-mail:

- When someone sends a message to you, most e-mail programs immediately display a message on your computer screen or make a sound to tell you to check your e-mail. If your computer isn't on the network or your e-mail program isn't running when the message is sent, then you're notified the next time that you log on to the network or start your e-mail program.

- E-mail programs can be set up to check for new e-mail automatically — when you log on to the network, and periodically throughout the day (say, every 10 or 15 minutes).

- You can easily attach files to your messages. You can use this feature to send a word-processing document, a spreadsheet, or a program file to another network user. (For details, see "Dealing with attachments," later in this chapter.)

Be careful about attachments other people send to you. E-mail attachments are how computer viruses are spread. So don't open an attachment you weren't expecting or from someone you don't know.

Also, realize that it's easy to fake the From address in an e-mail message. As a result, not all e-mails you receive are really from whom they claim to be from. So again, don't open attachments you weren't expecting.

✔ Most e-mail programs have a feature called an *address book* that lets you store the e-mail addresses you frequently use. That way you don't have to retype the user ID every time.

✔ You can address a message to more than one user — the electronic equivalent of a carbon copy. Some programs also enable you to create a list of users and assign a name to this list. Then you can send a message to each user in the list by addressing the message to the list name. For example, June may create a list including Ward, Wally, and Beaver, and call the list Boys. To send e-mail to all the boys on her family network, she simply addresses the message to Boys.

✔ Some e-mail programs can handle your Internet e-mail as well as your LAN e-mail. There are subtle differences between Internet and LAN e-mail, however. LAN e-mail is exchanged with other users on your local network. To send a message to another user on your network, you just specify that person's user name. In contrast, you can exchange Internet e-mail with anyone in the world who has an Internet connection and an Internet e-mail account. To send Internet e-mail, however, you must address the message to the recipient's Internet e-mail address. (Of course, you can store Internet e-mail addresses in your e-mail program's address book.)

Understanding the mail server

E-mail programs rely on a network server computer that is set up as a mail server, which works kind of like an electronic post office where messages are stored until they can be delivered to the recipient. A network server that functions as a mail server doesn't have to be dedicated to this purpose, although this is sometimes true for larger networks. In smaller networks, a network file and print server can also act as the mail server.

Here are some details that you should know about mail servers:

✔ The server versions of Windows and NetWare come with basic mail-server programs that let you set up an e-mail system for your network. For more advanced e-mail functions, you can purchase and install a separate mail-server program such as Microsoft Exchange Server.

✔ Disk space on a mail server is often at a premium. Be sure to delete unneeded messages after you read them.

✔ Managing the mail server can become one of the most time-consuming tasks of managing a network. Be prepared to spend time managing user accounts, fixing broken message folders, and tinkering with various settings and options.

Microsoft Outlook

Because it is a part of Microsoft Office, Microsoft Outlook is one of the most popular programs for accessing e-mail. Although many other e-mail programs are available, most of them work much like Outlook for the basic chores of reading and creating e-mail messages.

Internet Explorer (which comes with Windows) includes a scaled-back version of Outlook called *Outlook Express*. Outlook Express is designed to work only with e-mail that you send and receive over the Internet, not for e-mail that you exchange with other users over a local-area network. As a result, Outlook Express is generally not used as an e-mail program for network users. (However, if each network user has an Internet connection and an Internet e-mail account, Outlook Express works fine.)

The following sections describe some basic procedures for using Microsoft Outlook to send and receive e-mail.

Sending e-mail

Sending an e-mail message to another network user is pretty straightforward in Outlook. Just follow these steps:

1. **Start Microsoft Outlook by choosing Microsoft Outlook from the Start⇨ Programs menu.**

   Outlook appears in its own window, as shown in Figure 5-1.

2. **Create a message to send to another user.**

   You do so by clicking the New Mail Message button.

   A window appears in which you may type the e-mail address of the recipient (usually the recipient's network user ID), the subject of the message, and then the message itself. Figure 5-2 shows a message that has been composed and is now ready to be delivered.

3. **Type your message and click the Send button.**

   The message is delivered to the user listed in the To field.

Here are a few additional points about sending e-mail:

- ✔ The recipient must run Outlook or another e-mail program on his or her computer to check for incoming e-mail. When the recipient runs his or her e-mail program, your message is delivered.

- ✔ You can keep a personalized address list using the Address Book feature, which is available from the Tools menu in Outlook.

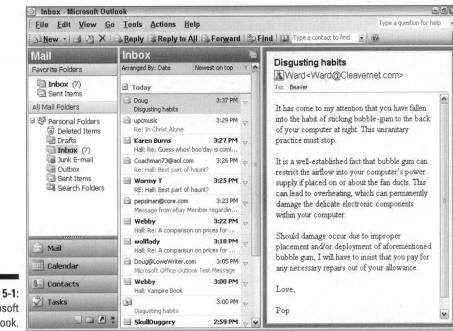

Figure 5-1:
Microsoft
Outlook.

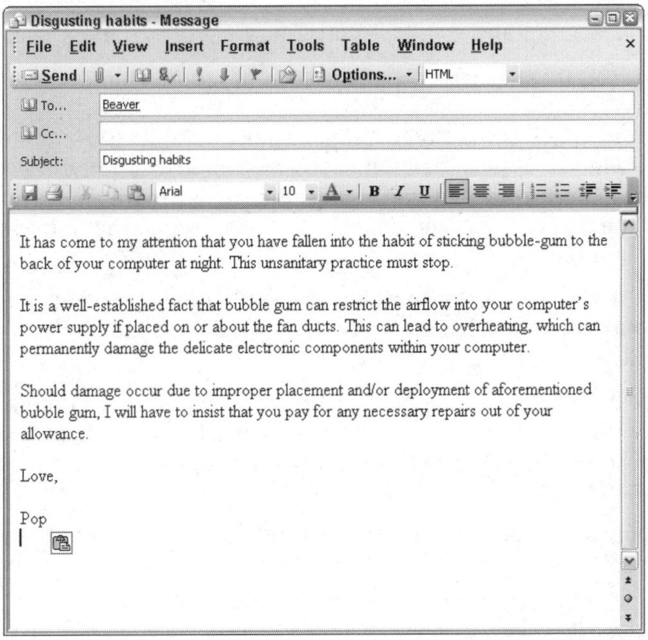

Figure 5-2:
Creating
an e-mail
message.

✔ You can send a copy of your message to another person by listing that person's e-mail address in the Cc field when you compose the message. (*Cc* stands for *Carbon Copy*, but e-mail programs don't actually use carbon paper to send copies.) If you don't want the main recipient to know that you sent a copy to someone else, you can use the Bcc field instead. (*Bcc* stands for *Blind Carbon Copy*.)

✔ You can use Outlook to send e-mail to other users of your local network and to send to and receive e-mail from Internet users. However, a modem or some other type of connection to the Internet is necessary to send e-mail to an Internet e-mail address.

Reading your e-mail

To read e-mail sent to you by other users, simply start Microsoft Outlook by choosing it from the Start⇨Programs menu. After you start Outlook, the program automatically checks to see if you have any new e-mail and automatically checks for new messages on a regular basis. Any new messages that you receive appear in the main Outlook window, highlighted with boldface type. In addition, Outlook plays a special sound to inform you whenever you receive new e-mail.

To read a message that has been sent to you, just double-click the message in the Outlook main window. The text of the message appears in a separate window.

After you read the message, you have several options for handling it:

✔ If the message is worthy of a reply, click the Reply button. A new message window appears, enabling you to compose a reply. The new message is automatically addressed to the sender of the original message, and the text of the original message is inserted at the bottom of the new message.

✔ If the message was addressed to more than one recipient, the Reply to All button lets you send a reply that is addressed to all the recipients listed on the original message.

✔ If the message was intended for someone else, or if you think that someone else should see it (maybe it contains a juicy bit of gossip), click the Forward button. A new message window appears, enabling you to type the name of the user that you want the message forwarded to.

✔ If you want a hard copy of the message, click the Print button.

✔ If the message is unworthy of even filing, click the Delete button. Poof! The message is whisked away to a folder called Deleted Items. (You can use the Edit⇨Empty "Deleted Items" Folder command to *permanently* delete everything in the Deleted Items folder.)

✔ If you have more than one message waiting, you can read the next message in line by clicking the Next button.

Dealing with attachments

An *attachment* is a file that is sent along with an e-mail message. An attachment can be any kind of file: a Word document, a spreadsheet, a program, a database file, or any other type of file.

To send an attachment as part of an outgoing message, just click the Insert File button (which looks like a paper clip) to summon the Insert File dialog box. Then select the file you want to attach and click OK.

If someone sends you e-mail with an attachment, a paper-clip icon appears next to the message in your Inbox — and you see an icon representing the attached file when you read the message. You can open the file by double-clicking that icon. However, before you do so, make sure you know who sent you the attachment and what the attachment is. Attachments are the main way computer viruses are spread, so be suspicious of any unexpected attachments.

To protect your computer (and your network) from e-mail viruses, consider installing an antivirus program such as Norton AntiVirus (`www.symantec.com`) or McAfee VirusScan (`www.mcafee.com`). If you're on a local-area network, check with your network administrator to make sure antivirus measures are in place.

E-mail Etiquette

Communicating with someone via e-mail is different from talking with that person face to face or over the telephone. You need to be aware of these differences, or you may end up insulting someone without meaning to. (Of course, if you *do* mean to insult someone, pay no attention to this section.)

The following paragraphs summarize the salient points of e-mail etiquette:

✔ Always remember that e-mail isn't as private as you'd like it to be. It's not that difficult for someone to electronically steam open your e-mail and read it. So be careful about what you say, to whom you say it, and about whom you say it.

✔ Don't forget that all the rules of social etiquette and office decorum apply to e-mail, too. If you wouldn't pick up the phone and call the CEO of the company, don't send him or her e-mail, either.

✔ When you reply to someone else's e-mail, keep in mind that the person you're replying to may not remember the details of the message that he or she sent to you. Providing some context for your reply is polite. Most e-mail systems (including Outlook) do this for you by automatically tacking on the original message at the end of the reply. If yours doesn't do this, be sure to provide some context, such as including a relevant snippet of the original message in quotation marks, so that the recipient knows what you're talking about.

✔ E-mail doesn't have the advantage of voice inflections. This limitation can lead to all kinds of misunderstandings. You have to make sure that people know when you're joking and when you mean it. E-mail nerds figured that out decades ago and developed a handy way to indicate tone of voice by using strings of symbols called *smileys*. Table 5-1 shows a few of the more commonly used (or abused) smileys.

Table 5-1	Commonly Used and Abused Smileys
Smiley	*What It Means*
: -)	Just kidding
; -)	Wink
: - (	Bummer
: - 0	Well, I never!
:-x	My lips are sealed.

If you don't get it, tilt your head to the left and look at the smiley sideways.

✔ E-mail nerds also like to use shorthand abbreviations for common words and phrases, like FYI (for "For Your Information") and that old corporate favorite ASAP (for "As Soon As Possible"). Table 5-2 lists some common ones.

Table 5-2	Common E-mail Abbreviations
Abbreviation	*What It Stands For*
BTW	By the Way
FWIW	For What It's Worth
IMO	In My Opinion

Abbreviation	What It Stands For
IMHO	In My Humble Opinion
IOW	In Other Words
PMJI	Pardon Me for Jumping In
ROFL	Rolling on the Floor, Laughing
ROFL,PP	Rolling on the Floor Laughing, Peeing My Pants
TIA	Thanks in Advance
TTFN	Ta Ta for Now (quoting Tigger)
TTYL	Talk to You Later
<g>	Grin
<bg>	Big Grin
<vbg>	Very Big Grin

Note that the abbreviations referring to gestures or facial expressions are typed between a less-than sign and a greater-than sign: <g>. Other gestures are spelled out, like <sniff>, <groan>, or <sigh>.

✔ You're not able to italicize or underline text on many e-mail programs (although you can do so in Exchange, Outlook, or Outlook Express). Type an asterisk before and after a word you *wish* you could italicize. Type an underscore _before_ and _after_ a word that you'd like to underline.

Be aware that if you do use italics, underlining, or any other formatting features that are available in Exchange, Outlook, or Outlook Express, the people receiving your mail may not be able to see the formatting if they're using other e-mail programs.

✔ Capital letters are the electronic equivalent of SHOUTING! TYPING AN ENTIRE MESSAGE IN CAPITAL LETTERS CAN BE VERY ANNOYING AND CAN CAUSE YOU TO GET THE ELECTRONIC EQUIVALENT OF LARYNGITIS.

✔ Don't be gullible about hoaxes and chain letters. If you receive an e-mail with a warning about some new virus that wipes out your hard drive if you sneeze near your computer or an e-mail that claims that you'll make eleven billion dollars if you forward the message to ten of your best friends, just delete the e-mail. Don't forward it.

✔ Frequently sending e-mail with large attachments can be annoying.

Chapter 6

Using Microsoft Office on a Network

Microsoft Office is far and away the most popular suite of application programs used on personal computers, and it includes the most common types of application programs used in an office: a word processing program (Word), a spreadsheet program (Excel), a presentation program (PowerPoint), and an excellent e-mail program (Outlook). Depending on the version of Office you purchase, you may also get a database program (Access), a Web-site development program (FrontPage), a desktop publishing program (Publisher), a set of Ginsu knives (KnifePoint), and a slicer and dicer (ActiveSalsa).

This chapter describes the networking features of Microsoft Office System 2003, the latest and greatest version of Office. Most of these features also work with previous versions of Office.

To get the most from using Office on a network, you should purchase the Microsoft Office Resource Kit. The Office Resource Kit, also known as *ORK*, contains information about installing and using Office on a network and comes with a CD that has valuable tools. If you don't want to purchase the ORK, you can view it online and download the ORK tools from Microsoft's TechNet Web site (www.microsoft.com/technet). Nanoo-nanoo, Earthling.

Installing Office on a Network — Some Options

You need to make some basic decisions when you prepare to install Microsoft Office on a network. In particular, here are some possible approaches to installing Microsoft Office on your network clients:

✔ You can simply ignore the fact that you have a network and purchase a separate copy of Office for each user on the network. Then, you can install Office from the CD on each computer. This option works well if your network is small, if each computer has ample disk space to hold the necessary Office files, and if each computer has its own CD-ROM drive.

✔ For a larger network, you can use the Office Setup program in Administrative Setup mode. This option lets you create a special type of setup on a network server disk from which you can install Office onto network computers. Administrative Setup enables you to control the custom features selected for each network computer and reduce the amount of user interaction required to install Office onto each computer.

If you choose to use Administrative Setup, you can use the Network Installation Wizard that comes with the Office Resource Kit. The Network Installation Wizard lets you customize settings for installing Office onto client computers. For example, you can choose which Office components to install, provide default answers to yes/no questions that Setup asks the user while installing Office, and select the amount of interaction you want the Setup program to have with the user while installing Office.

No matter which option you choose for installing Office on your network, you must purchase either a copy of Office or a license to install Office for every computer that uses Office. Purchasing a single copy of Office and installing it on more than one computer is illegal.

Accessing Network Files

Opening a file that resides on a network drive is almost as easy as opening a file on a local drive. All Office programs use the File⇨Open command to summon the Open dialog box, as shown in its Excel incarnation in Figure 6-1. (The Open dialog box is nearly identical in other Office programs.)

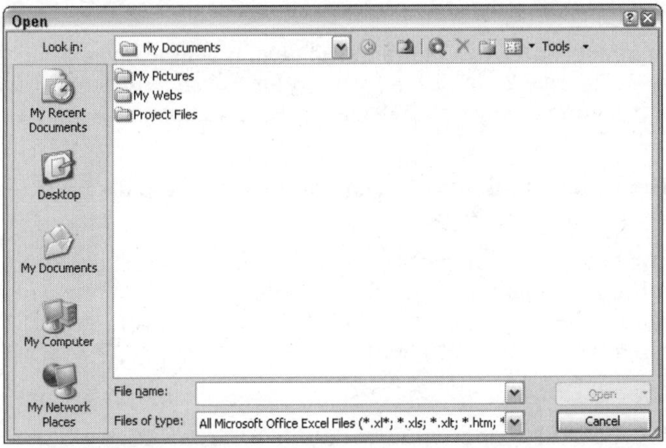

Figure 6-1:
The Open
dialog box
in Excel
2003.

To access a file that resides on a network volume that has been mapped to a drive letter, all you have to do is use the Look In drop-down list to select the network drive. If the network volume has not been mapped to a drive, click My Network Places near the bottom-left corner of the Open dialog box.

You can map a network drive directly from the Open dialog box by following these steps:

1. **Choose the File⇨Open command.**

   This summons the Open dialog box.

2. **Click Tools in the Open dialog box and then choose Map Network Drive.**

   The Map Network Drive dialog box appears, as shown in Figure 6-2.

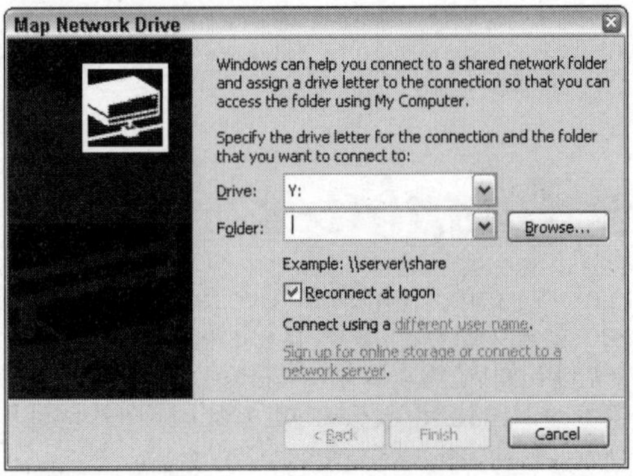

Figure 6-2:
Mapping a
network
drive.

3. **If you don't like the drive letter suggested in the Drive field, change it.**

   Map Network Drive defaults to the next available drive letter — in the case of Figure 6-2, drive Y:. If you prefer to use a different drive letter, you can choose any of the drive letters available in the Drive drop-down list.

4. **In the Folder field, type the complete network path for the shared drive you want to map.**

   In most cases, the network path is two backslashes, the server name, another backslash, and the shared volume's share name. For example, to map a shared volume named MYDOCS on a server named WALLY, type the following in the Path field:

   ```
   \\WALLY\MYDOCS
   ```

   This type of filename, with the double backslashes, the server name, and the share name, is known as a *UNC name*. (*UNC* stands for *Universal Naming Convention*.)

5. **If you want this drive to be mapped automatically each time you log on to the network, check the Reconnect at Logon option.**

   If you leave this option unchecked, the drive mapping vanishes when you log off the network.

6. **Click OK.**

   You return to the Open dialog box. The Look In field automatically shows the newly mapped network drive, so the Open dialog box lists the files and folders in the network drive.

If you try to open a file that another network user already has opened, Office tells you that the file is already in use and offers to let you open a read-only version of the file. You can read and edit the read-only version, but Office won't let you overwrite the existing version of the file. You'll have to use the Save As command instead to save your changes to a new file.

For more information about mapping network drives, refer to Chapter 2.

Using Workgroup Templates

A *template* is not a place of worship, though an occasional sacrifice to the Office gods may make your computing life a bit easier. Rather, a template is a special type of document file that holds formatting information, boilerplate text, and other customized settings that you can use as the basis for new documents.

Three Office programs — Word, Excel, and PowerPoint — enable you to specify a template whenever you create a new document. When you create a new document in Word, Excel, or PowerPoint by choosing the File⇨New command, you see a dialog box that lets you choose a template for the new document.

Office comes with a set of templates for the most common types of documents. These templates are grouped under the various tabs that appear across the top of the New dialog box.

In addition to the templates that come with Office, you can create your own templates in Word, Excel, and PowerPoint. Creating your own templates is especially useful if you want to establish a consistent look for documents prepared by your network users. For example, you can create a Letter template that includes your company's letterhead, or a Proposal template that includes a company logo.

Office enables you to store templates in two locations. Where you put them depends on what you want to do with them:

- ✔ **The User Templates folder on each user's local disk drive:** If a particular user needs a specialized template, here's where to put it.

- ✔ **The Workgroup Templates folder on a shared network drive:** If you have templates that you want to make available to all network users via the network server, put them here. This arrangement still allows each user to create templates that are not available to other network users.

When you use both a User Templates folder and a Workgroup Templates folder, Office combines the templates from both folders and lists them in alphabetical order in the New dialog box. For example, suppose that the User Templates folder contains templates called Blank Document and Web Page, and the Workgroup Templates folder contains a template called Company Letterhead. In this case, three templates appear in the New dialog box, in this order: Blank Document, Company Letterhead, and Web Page.

To set the location of the User Templates and Workgroup Templates folders, choose Tools⇨Options in Word to summon the Options dialog box. Then click the File Locations tab to display the file location options.

Although the User Templates and Workgroup Templates settings affect Word, Excel, and PowerPoint, you can change these settings only from Word. The Options dialog boxes in Excel and PowerPoint don't show the User Templates or Workgroup Templates options.

When you install Office, the standard templates that come with Office are copied into a folder on the computer's local disk drive, and the User Templates option is set to this folder. The Workgroup Templates option is left blank. You can set the Workgroup Templates folder to a shared network folder by click-ing Network Templates, clicking the Modify button, and specifying a shared network folder that contains your workgroup templates.

Networking an Access Database

If you want to share a Microsoft Access database among several network users, you should be aware of a few special considerations. Here are the more important ones:

- When you share a database, more than one user may try to access the same record at the same time. This situation can lead to problems if two or more users try to update the record. To handle this potential traffic snarl, Access locks the record so only one user at a time can update it. Access uses one of three methods to lock records:

    - **Edited Record:** Locks a record whenever a user begins to edit a record. For example, if a user retrieves a record in a form that allows the record to be updated, Access locks the record while the user edits it so that other users can't edit the record until the first record is finished.

    - **No Locks:** This doesn't really mean that the record isn't locked. Instead, No Locks means that the record is not locked until a user actually writes a change to the database. This method can be con-fusing to users because it enables one user to overwrite changes made by another user.

    - **All Records:** Locks an entire table whenever a user edits any record in the table.

- Access lets you split a database so the forms, queries, and reports are stored on each user's local disk drive, but the data itself is stored on a network drive. This feature can make the database run more efficiently on a network, but it's a little more difficult to set up. (To split a database, use the Tools⇨Database Utilities⇨Database Splitter command.)

- Access includes built-in security features that you should use if you share an Access database from a Windows client computer, such as one running Windows XP. If you store the database on a Windows NT/2000 server or on a NetWare server, you can use the server's security features to pro-tect the database.

- Access automatically refreshes forms and datasheets every 60 seconds. That way, if one user opens a form or datasheet and another user changes the data a few seconds later, the first user sees the changes within one minute. If 60 seconds is too long (or too short) an interval, you can change the refresh rate by using the Advanced tab of the Options dialog box.

Part II
Building Your Own Network

The 5th Wave   By Rich Tennant

"I guess you could say this is the hub of our network."

In this part . . .

You discover how to build a network yourself, which includes planning it and installing it. And you find out what choices are available for cable types, network operating systems, and all the other bits and pieces that you have to contend with.

Yes, some technical information is included in these chapters. But fear not! I bring you tidings of great joy! Lo, a working network is at hand, and you — yeah, even you — can design it and install it yourself.

Chapter 7

The Bad News: You Have to Plan Ahead

*O*kay, so you're convinced that you need to network your computers. What now? Do you stop by Computers-R-Us on the way to work, install the network before morning coffee, and expect the network to be fully operational by noon?

I don't think so.

Networking your computers is just like any other worthwhile endeavor: To do it right requires a bit of planning. This chapter helps you think through your network before you start spending money. It shows you how to come up with a networking plan that's every bit as good as the plan that a network consultant would charge $1,000 for. See? This book is already saving you money!

Making a Network Plan

Before you begin any networking project, whether it's a new network installation or an upgrade of an existing network, you should first make a detailed plan. If you make technical decisions too quickly, before studying all the issues that affect the project, you'll regret it. You'll discover too late that a key application won't run over the network, that the network has unacceptably slow performance, or that key components of the network don't work together.

Here are some general thoughts to keep in mind while you create your network plan:

- ✔ **Don't rush the plan.** The most costly networking mistakes are the ones you make *before* you install the network. Think things through and consider alternatives.

- ✔ **Write down the network plan.** The plan doesn't have to be a fancy, 500-page document. If you want to make it look good, pick up a ½-inch three-ring binder — big enough to hold your network plan with room to spare.

- ✔ **Ask someone else to read your network plan before you buy anything.** Preferably, ask someone who knows more about computers than you do.

- ✔ **Keep the plan up-to-date.** If you add to the network, dig up the plan, dust it off, and update it.

"The best-laid schemes of mice and men gang oft agley, and leave us not but grief and pain for promised joy." Robert Burns lived a couple hundred years before computer networks, but his famous words ring true. A network plan is not chiseled in stone. If you discover that something doesn't work the way you thought it would, that's okay. You can always adjust your plan for unforeseen circumstances.

Being Purposeful

One of the first steps in planning your network is making sure that you understand why you want the network in the first place. Here are some of the more common reasons for needing a network, all of them quite valid:

- ✔ My coworker and I exchange files using a floppy disk just about every day. With a network, we could trade files without using the floppies.

- ✔ I don't want to buy everyone a laser printer when I know the one we have now just sits there taking up space most of the day. So wouldn't buying a network be better than buying a laser printer for every computer?

- ✔ I want to provide an Internet connection for all my computers. Many networks, especially smaller ones, exist solely for the purpose of sharing an Internet connection.

- ✔ Someone figured out that we're destroying seven trees a day by printing interoffice memos on paper, so we want to give the rainforest a break by setting up an e-mail system and trying to print less of the routine stuff. (It won't work, however. One of the inescapable laws of business is that the more you try to eliminate paperwork, the more you end up creating.)

✔ Business is so good that one person typing in orders eight hours each day can't keep up. With a network, I can have two people entering orders, and I won't have to pay overtime to either person.

✔ My brother-in-law just put in a network at his office, and I don't want him to think that I'm behind the times.

Make sure that you identify all the reasons why you think you need a network, and then write them down. Don't worry about winning the Pulitzer Prize for your stunning prose. Just make sure that you write down what you expect a network to do for you.

If you were making a 500-page networking proposal, you'd place the description of why a network is needed in a tabbed section labeled "Justification." In your ½-inch network binder, file the description under "Purpose."

As you consider the reasons why you need a network, you may conclude that you don't need a network after all. That's okay. You can always use the binder for your stamp collection.

Taking Stock

One of the most challenging parts of planning a network is figuring out how to work with the computers you already have — how do you get from here to there? Before you can plan how to get "there," you have to know where "here" is: Take a thorough inventory of your current computers.

What you need to know

You need to know the following information about each of your computers:

✔ **The processor type and, if possible, its clock speed.** Hope that all your computers are 2GHz Pentium 4s or better. But in most cases, you find a mixture of computers, some new, some old, some borrowed, some blue. You might even find a few archaic pre-Pentium computers.

You can't usually tell what kind of processor a computer has just by looking at the computer's case. Most computers, however, display the processor type when you turn them on or reboot them. If the information on the startup screen scrolls too quickly for you to read it, try pressing the Pause key to freeze the information. After you finish reading it, press the Pause key again so that your computer can continue booting.

✔ **The size of the hard drive and the arrangement of its partitions.** In Windows, you can find out the size of your computer's hard drive by opening the My Computer window, right-clicking the drive icon, and choosing the Properties command from the shortcut menu that appears. Figure 7-1 shows the Properties dialog box for a 24.4GB hard drive that has 7.66GB of free space.

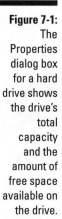

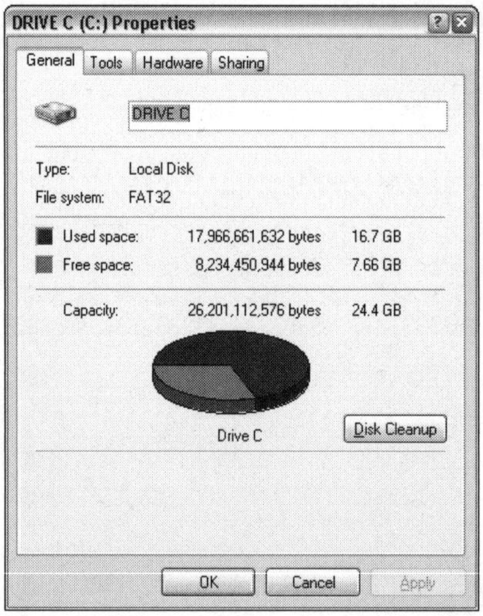

Figure 7-1: The Properties dialog box for a hard drive shows the drive's total capacity and the amount of free space available on the drive.

If your computer has more than one hard drive or partition, Windows lists an icon for each drive or partition in the My Computer window. Jot down the size and amount of free space available on each of the drives. (A *partition* is a section of a hard drive that's treated as if it were a separate drive. But that won't be on the test.)

✔ **The amount of memory.** In Windows, you can find out this information easily enough by right-clicking the My Computer desktop icon and choosing the Properties command. The amount of memory on your computer appears in the dialog box that appears. For example, Figure 7-2 shows the System Properties dialog box for a computer running Windows XP Professional with 512MB of RAM.

✔ **Which version of the operating system is installed?** If you are running Windows 95 or later, you can determine the version by checking the System Properties dialog box. For example, Figure 7-2 shows the System Properties dialog box for a computer running Windows XP Professional.

✔ **What type of network card, if any, is installed in the computer?** To find out the exact name of the card, open the Control Panel and double-click the System icon. Then, click the Hardware tab and then click the Device Manager button. This brings up the Device Manager dialog box, as shown in Figure 7-3. In this case, you can see that the computer's network card is a D-Link DFE-530TX+ PCI adapter.

The Device Manager is also useful for tracking down other hardware devices attached to the computer or for checking which device drivers are being used for the computer's devices.

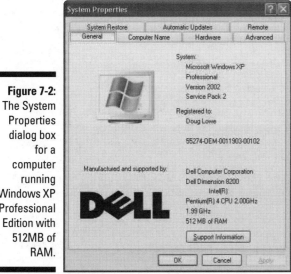

Figure 7-2:
The System Properties dialog box for a computer running Windows XP Professional Edition with 512MB of RAM.

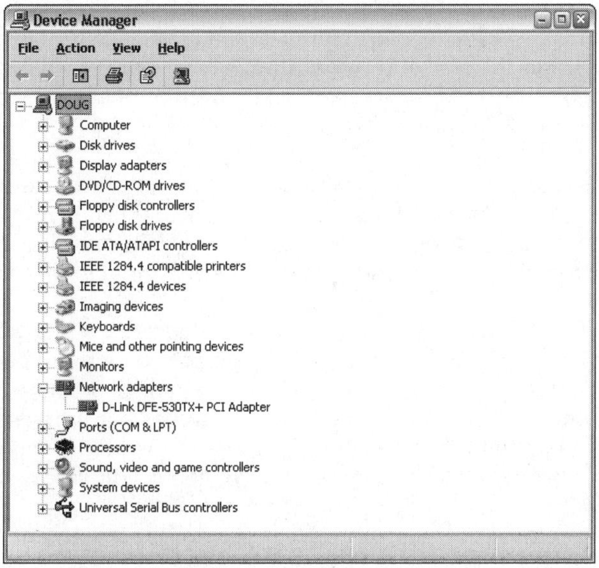

Figure 7-3:
Using the Device Manager to probe for hardware devices.

✔ **What network protocols are in use.** To determine this in Windows XP, open the Control Panel, double-click the Network Connections icon to open the Network Connections dialog box, and then right-click the network connection and choose the Properties command. (In previous versions of Windows, the drill was to double-click Network in the Control Panel.)

✔ **What kind of printer, if any, is attached to the computer?** Usually you can tell just by looking at the printer itself. You can also tell by examining the Printers and Faxes folder (in Windows XP, choose Start⇨Control Panel and then double-click Printers and Faxes).

✔ **Any other devices connected to the computer?** A CD, DVD, or CD-RW drive? Scanner? Zip or Jaz drive? Tape drive? Video camera? Battle droid? Hot tub?

✔ **Are driver and installation disks available?** Hopefully, you'll be able to locate the disks or CDs required by hardware devices such as the network card, printers, scanners, and so on. If not, you may be able to locate the drivers on the Internet.

✔ **What software is used on the computer?** Microsoft Office? WordPerfect? QuickBooks? Make a complete list, and include version numbers.

Programs that gather information for you

Gathering information about your computers is a lot of work if you have more than a few computers to network. Fortunately, several available software programs can automatically gather the information for you. These programs inspect various aspects of a computer, such as the CPU type and speed, amount of RAM, and the size of the computer's hard drives. Then they show the information on the screen and give you the option of saving the information to a hard drive file or printing it.

Windows comes with just such a program, which is called Microsoft System Information. Microsoft System Information gathers and prints information about your computer. You can start Microsoft System Information by choosing Start⇨Programs⇨Accessories⇨System Tools⇨System Information.

When you fire up Microsoft System Information, you see a window that initially displays basic information about your computer, such as your version of Microsoft Windows, the processor type, the amount of memory on the computer, and the free space on each of the computer's hard drives. You can obtain more detailed information by clicking any of the following in the left side of the window: Hardware Resources, Components, Software Environment, or Applications.

If you have Windows 95, don't panic. You may have Microsoft System Information anyway: Microsoft includes it with Office. To start Microsoft System Information from any of the Office programs (Word, Excel, or PowerPoint), choose the Help⇔About command. When the About dialog box appears, click the System Info button.

To Dedicate, or Not to Dedicate: That Is the Question

One of the most basic questions that a network plan must answer is whether the network will have one or more dedicated servers or whether it will rely completely on peer-to-peer networking, with no single computer acting as a dedicated server. If the only reason for purchasing your network is to share a printer and exchange an occasional file, then you may not need a dedicated server computer. In that case, you can create a peer-to-peer network by using the computers that you already have. However, all but the smallest networks will benefit from having a separate, dedicated server computer.

✔ Using a dedicated server computer makes the network faster, easier to work with, and more reliable. Consider what happens when the user of a server computer, which doubles as a workstation, decides to turn off the computer, not realizing that someone else is accessing files on his or her hard drive.

✔ You don't necessarily have to use your biggest and fastest computer as your server computer. I've seen networks where the slowest computer on the network is the server. This is especially true when the server is mostly used to share a printer or to store a small number of shared files. So if you need to buy a computer for your network, consider promoting one of your older computers to be the server and using the new computer as a client.

Types of Servers

Assuming your network will require one or more dedicated servers, you should next consider what types of servers the network will need. In some cases, a single server computer can fill one or more of these roles. Whenever possible, it's best to limit each server computer to a single server function.

File servers

File servers provide centralized disk storage that can be conveniently shared by client computers on the network. The most common task of a file server is to store shared files and programs. For example, the members of a small workgroup can use disk space on a file server to store their Microsoft Office documents.

File servers must ensure that two users don't try to update the same file at the same time. The file servers do this by *locking* a file while a user updates the file so that other users can't access the file until the first user finishes. For document files (for example, word-processing or spreadsheet files), the whole file is locked. For database files, the lock can be applied just to the portion of the file that contains the record or records being updated.

Print servers

Sharing printers is one of the main reasons that many small networks exist. Although it isn't often necessary to do so, you can dedicate a server computer for use as a *print server*, whose sole purpose is to collect information being sent to a shared printer by client computers and print it in an orderly fashion.

- ✔ A single computer may double as both a file server and a print server, but performance is better if you use separate print and file server computers.

- ✔ With inexpensive inkjet printers running about $100 or less each, just giving each user his or her own printer is tempting. However, you get what you pay for. Instead of buying a cheap inkjet printer for each user, you may be better off buying one really good laser printer and sharing it.

Web servers

A *Web server* is a server computer that runs software that enables the computer to host an Internet Web site. The two most popular Web server programs are Microsoft's IIS (Internet Information Services) and Apache, an open-source Web server program managed by the Apache Software Foundation.

Mail servers

A *mail server* is a server computer that handles the network's e-mail needs. It is configured with e-mail server software, such as Microsoft Exchange Server.

Your mail-server software must be compatible with your e-mail program; Exchange Server, for example, is designed to work with Microsoft Outlook, the e-mail client software that comes with Microsoft Office.

Most mail servers actually do much more than just send and receive electronic mail. For example, here are some of the features that Exchange Server 2000 offers beyond simple e-mail:

- Collaboration features that simplify the management of collaborative projects
- Audio and video conferencing
- Chat rooms and instant messaging (IM) services
- Microsoft Exchange Forms Designer, which lets you develop customized forms for applications (such as vacation requests or purchase orders)

Database servers

A *database server* is a server computer that runs database software, such as Microsoft's SQL Server 2000. Database servers are usually used along with customized business applications, such as accounting or marketing systems.

Choosing a Server Operating System

If you determine that your network needs one or more dedicated servers, the next step is to determine what network operating system those servers should use. If possible, all of the servers should use the same NOS so you don't find yourself awash in the conflicting requirements of different operating systems.

Although you can choose from many network operating systems, from a practical point of view, your choices are limited to the following:

- Windows 2000 Server or Windows Server 2003
- Novell NetWare
- Linux or another version of UNIX

For more information, refer to Chapter 8.

Planning the Infrastructure

You also need to plan the details of how you will connect the computers in the network. This includes determining which network topology that the network will use, what type of cable will be used, where the cable will be routed, and what other devices, such as repeaters, bridges, hubs, switches, and routers, will be needed.

Although you have many cabling options to choose from, you'll probably use Cat5 or better UTP for most — if not all — of the desktop client computers on the network. However, you have many decisions to make beyond this basic choice:

✔ Will you use hubs, which are cheaper, or switches, which are faster but more expensive?

✔ Where will you place workgroup hubs or switches — on a desktop somewhere within the group or in a central wiring closet?

✔ How many client computers will you place on each hub or switch, and how many hubs or switches will you need?

✔ If you need more than one hub or switch, what type of cabling will you use to connect the hubs and switches to one another?

For more information about network cabling, see Chapter 9.

If you are installing new network cable, don't scrimp on the cable itself. Because installing network cable is a labor-intensive task, the cost of the cable itself is a small part of the total cable-installation cost. And if you spend a little extra to install higher-grade cable now, you won't have to replace the cable in a few years when it's time to upgrade the network.

Drawing Diagrams

One of the most helpful techniques for creating a network plan is to draw a picture of it. The diagram can be a detailed floor plan, showing the actual location of each network component. This type of diagram is sometimes called a *physical map*. If you prefer, the diagram can be a *logical map*, which is more abstract and Picasso-like. Any time you change the network layout, update the diagram. Also include a detailed description of the change, the date that the change was made, and the reason for the change.

You can diagram very small networks on the back of a napkin, but if the network has more than a few computers, you'll want to use a drawing program to help you create the diagram. One of the best programs for this purpose is Microsoft Visio, shown in Figure 7-4. Here is a rundown of some of the features that make Visio so useful:

✔ Smart shapes and connectors maintain the connections you've drawn between network components, even if you rearrange the layout of the components on the page.

✔ Stencils provide dozens of useful shapes for common network components — not just client and server computers, but routers, hubs, switches, and just about anything else you can imagine. If you're really picky about the diagrams, you can even purchase stencil sets that have accurate drawings of specific devices, such as Cisco routers or IBM mainframe computers.

✔ You can add information to each computer or device in the diagram, such as the serial number or physical location. Then, you can quickly print an inventory that lists this information for each device in the diagram.

✔ You can easily create large diagrams that span multiple pages.

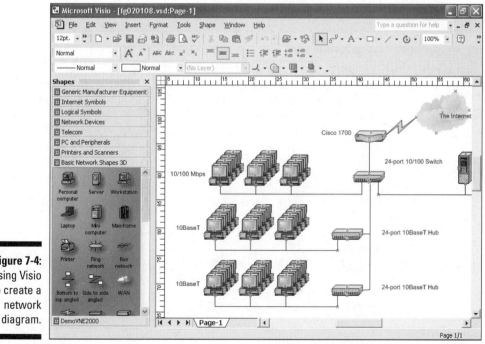

Figure 7-4:
Using Visio to create a network diagram.

Sample Network Plans

In what's left of this chapter, I present some network plans drawn from real-life situations. These examples will illustrate many of the network-design issues I've covered so far in this chapter. The stories you are about to read are true. The names have been changed to protect the innocent.

Building a small network: California Sport Surface, Inc.

California Sport Surface, Inc. (CSS) is a small company specializing in the installation of outdoor sports surfaces, such as tennis courts, running tracks, and football fields. CSS has an administrative staff of just four employees who work out of a home office. The company currently has three computers:

- A brand-new Dell desktop computer running Windows XP Home Edition, shared by the president (Mark) and vice-president (Julie) to prepare proposals and marketing brochures, to handle correspondence, and to do other miscellaneous chores. This computer has a built-in 10/100Mbps Ethernet network port.

- An older Gateway computer running Windows 98 Second Edition, used by the bookkeeper (Erin), who uses QuickBooks to handle the company's accounting needs. This computer doesn't have a network port.

- A notebook that runs Windows 2000, used by the company's chief engineer (Daniel), who often takes it to job sites to help with engineering needs. This computer has a built-in 10Mbps Ethernet port.

The company owns just one printer, a moderately priced ink-jet printer that's connected to Erin's computer. The computers are not networked, so whenever Mark, Julie, or Daniel need to print something, they must copy the file to a diskette and give it to Erin, who then prints the document. The computer shared by Mark and Julie is connected to the Internet via a residential DSL connection.

The company wants to install a network to support these three computers. Here are the primary goals of the network:

- Provide shared access to the printer so that users don't have to exchange diskettes to print their documents.

- Provide shared access to the Internet connection so that users can access the Internet from any of the computers.

- Allow for the addition of another desktop computer, which the company expects to purchase within the next six months, and potentially another notebook computer (if business is good, the company hopes to hire another engineer).

✔ The network should be intuitive to the users and should not require any extensive upkeep.

CSS's networking needs can be met with the simple peer-to-peer network diagrammed in Figure 7-5. Here's what the network will require:

✔ A 10/100Mbps Ethernet adapter card for the Gateway computer, which is the only computer that doesn't currently have a network port.

✔ A combination DSL router and four-port 10/100Mbps switch, such as the LinkSys BEFSR41W or the Belkin F5D5231-4. The company may outgrow this device when it adds an additional laptop, but if and when that happens, another 4- or 8-port 10/100Mbps switch can be added then.

✔ The firewall features of the DSL router will need to be enabled to protect the network from Internet hackers.

✔ File and printer sharing will need to be activated on Erin's computer and the printer will need to be shared.

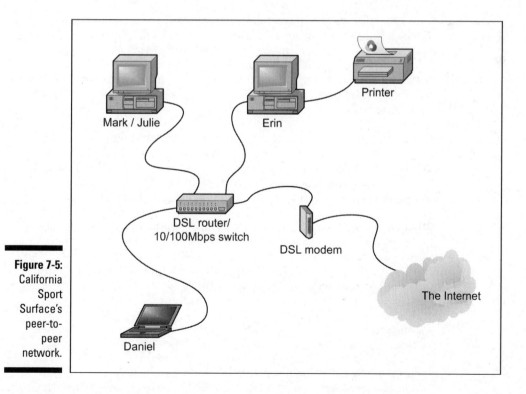

Figure 7-5:
California
Sport
Surface's
peer-to-
peer
network.

Connecting two networks: Creative Course Development, Inc.

Creative Course Development, Inc. (CCD) is a small educational publisher located in central California that specializes in integrated math and science curriculum for primary and secondary grades. They publish a variety of course materials, including textbooks, puzzle books, and CD-ROM software.

CCD leases two adjacent office buildings, separated only by a small court-yard. The creative staff, which consists of a dozen writers and educators, works in Building A. The sales, marketing, and administrative staff — all six employees of it — works in Building B.

The product development and marketing staff has 14 relatively new personal computers, all running Windows XP Professional, and a server computer run-ning Windows 2000 Server. These computers are networked by a 100Mbps UTP network, which utilizes a single 24-port 100Mbps switch. A fractional T1 line that's connected to the network through a small Cisco router provides Internet access.

The administrative staff has a hodgepodge of computers, some running Windows 98 Second Edition, some running Windows XP, and one still running Windows 95. They have a small Windows NT server that meets their needs. The older computers have 10BaseT network cards; the newer ones have 10/100Mbps cards. However, the computers are all connected to a fairly old 10Mbps Ethernet hub with 12 ports. Internet access is provided by an ISDN connection.

Both groups are happy with their computers and networks. The problem is that the networks can't communicate with each other. For example, the mar-keting team in Building A relies on daily printed reports from the sales system in Building B to keep track of sales, and they frequently go to the other build-ing to follow up on important sales or to look into sales trends.

Although several solutions to this problem exist, the easiest is to bridge the networks with a pair of wireless switches. To do this, CCD will purchase two wireless access points. One will be plugged into the 100Mbps switch in Building A, and the other will be plugged into the hub in Building B. After the access points are configured, the two networks will function as a single net-work. Figure 7-6 shows a logical diagram for the completed network.

Although the wireless solution to this problem sounds simple, a number of complications still need to be dealt with. Specifically:

  ✓ Depending on the environment, the wireless access points may have trouble establishing a link between the buildings. It may be necessary to locate the devices on the roof. In that case, CCD will have to spend a little extra money for weatherproof enclosures.

✔ Because the wireless access point in Building A will be connected to a switch rather than a hub, the switch will provide some degree of isolation between the networks. As a result, overall network performance shouldn't be affected.

✔ Before the networks were connected, each network had its own DHCP server to assign IP addresses to users as needed. Unfortunately, both DHCP servers have the same local IP address (192.168.0.1). When the networks are combined, one of these DHCP servers will have to be disabled.

✔ In addition, both networks had their own Internet connections. With the networks bridged, CCD can eliminate the ISDN connection altogether. Users in both buildings can get their Internet access via the shared T1 connection.

✔ The network administrator will also have to determine how to handle directory services for the network. Previously, each network had its own domain. With the networks bridged, CCD may opt to keep these domains separate, or they may decide to merge them into a single domain. (Doing so will require considerable work, so they'll probably leave the domains separate.)

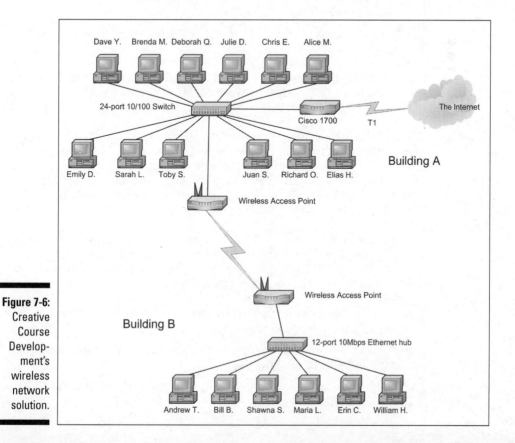

Figure 7-6: Creative Course Development's wireless network solution.

Improving network performance: DCH Accounting

DCH Accounting is an accounting firm that has grown in two years from 15 employees to 35, all located in one building. Here's the lowdown on the existing network:

- ✔ The network consists of 35 client computers and three servers running Windows 2000 Server.

- ✔ The 35 client computers run a variety of Windows operating systems. About a third (a total of 11) run Windows XP Professional. The rest run Windows 98 and a few still run Windows 95.

- ✔ The Windows XP computers all have 10/100Mbps Ethernet cards. The older computers have 10Mbps cards.

- ✔ The servers have 10Mbps cards.

- ✔ All of the offices in the building are wired with Category 5 wiring to a central wiring closet, where a small equipment rack holds two 24-port 10BaseT hubs.

- ✔ Internet access is provided through a T1 connection with a Cisco 1700 router.

Lately, network performance has been noticeably slow, particularly Internet access and large file transfers between client computers and the servers. Users have started to complain that sometimes the network seems to crawl.

The problem is most likely that the network has outgrown the old 10BaseT hubs. All network traffic must flow through them, and they are limited to the speed of 10Mbps. As a result, the new computers with the 10/100Mbps Ethernet cards are connecting to the network at 10Mbps, and not 100Mbps. In addition, the hubs treat the entire network as a single Ethernet segment. With 35 users, the network is saturated.

The performance of this network can be dramatically improved in two steps. The first step is to replace the 10Mbps network interface cards in the three servers with 10/100Mbps cards. Second, add a 24-port 10/100Mbps switch to the equipment rack. The equipment rack can be rewired as shown in Figure 7-7.

- ✔ Connect the servers, the Cisco router, and the 100Mbps clients to the switch. This will use 15 of the 24 ports.

- ✔ Connect the two hubs to the switch. This will use two more ports, leaving 7 ports for future growth.

- ✔ Divide the remaining clients between the two hubs. Each hub will have 12 computers connected.

This arrangement connects all of the 100Mbps clients to 100Mbps switch ports and groups the remaining 24 slower computers into two groups of 12, each with its own hub.

For even better performance, DCH could simply replace both hubs with 24-port switches.

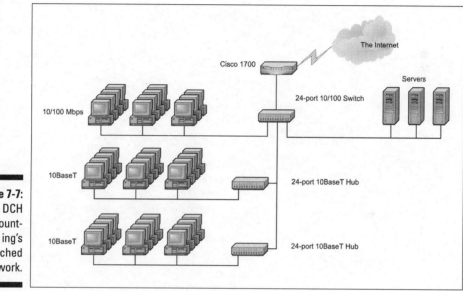

Figure 7-7:
DCH
Account-
ing's
switched
network.

Chapter 8

Understanding Network Operating Systems

*O*ne of the basic choices that you must make before you proceed any further is to decide which *network operating system* (NOS) to use as the foundation for your network. This chapter begins with a description of several important features found in all network operating systems. Next, it provides an overview of the advantages and disadvantages of the most popular network operating systems.

Network Operating System Features

All network operating systems, from the simplest (such as Windows XP Home Edition) to the most complex (such as Windows Server 2003 Datacenter Edition), must provide certain core functions, such as connecting to other computers on the network, sharing files and other resources, providing for security, and so on. In the following sections, I describe some core NOS features in general terms.

Network support

It goes without saying that a network operating system should support networks. (I can picture Mike Myers in his classic *Saturday Night Live* role as Linda Richman, host of *Coffee Talk,* saying, "I'm getting a little *verklempt* . . . talk amongst yourselves . . . I'll give you a topic: Network operating systems do not network, nor do they operate. Discuss.")

A network operating system must support a wide variety of networking protocols in order to meet the needs of its users. That's because a large network typically consists of a mixture of various versions of Windows, as well as Macintosh and Linux computers. As a result, the server may need to simultaneously support TCP/IP, NetBIOS, and AppleTalk protocols.

Many servers have more than one network interface card installed. In that case, the NOS must be able to support multiple network connections. Ideally, the NOS should have the ability to balance the network load among its network interfaces. In addition, in the event that one of the connections fails, the NOS should be able to seamlessly switch to the other connection.

Finally, most network operating systems include a built-in capability to function as a router that connects two networks. The NOS router functions should also include firewall features to keep unauthorized packets from entering the local network.

File-sharing services

One of the most important functions of a network operating system is to share resources with other network users. The most common resource that's shared is the server's *file system* — organized disk space that a network server must be able to share (in whole or in part) with other users. In effect, those users can treat the server's disk space as an extension of their own computers' disk space.

The NOS allows the system administrator to determine which portions of the server's file system to share. Although an entire hard drive can be shared, it is not commonly done. Instead, individual directories or folders are shared. The administrator can control which users are allowed to access each shared folder.

Because file sharing is the reason many network servers exist, network operating systems have more sophisticated disk-management features than are found in desktop operating systems. For example, most network operating systems can manage two or more hard drives as if they were a single drive. In addition, most can create a *mirror* — an automatic backup copy of a drive — on a second drive.

Multitasking

Only one user at a time uses a desktop computer; however, multiple users simultaneously use server computers. As a result, a network operating system must provide support for multiple users who access the server remotely via the network.

At the heart of multiuser support is *multitasking* — a technique that slices processing time microthin and juggles the pieces lighting-fast among running programs It's how an operating system can execute more than one program (called a *task* or a *process*) at a time. Multitasking operating systems are like the guy that used to spin plates balanced on sticks on the old *Ed Sullivan Show*. He'd run from plate to plate, trying to keep them all spinning so they wouldn't fall off the sticks. To make it challenging, he'd do it blindfolded or riding on a unicycle. Substitute programs for the plates and file management for the unicycle, and there you are.

Although multitasking creates the *appearance* that two or more programs are executing on the computer at the same time, in reality, a computer with a single processor can execute only one program at a time. The operating system switches the CPU from one program to another to create the appearance that several programs are executing simultaneously, but at any given moment, only one of the programs is actually processing commands. The others are patiently waiting their turns. (However, if the computer has more than one CPU, the CPUs *can* execute programs simultaneously — but that's another kettle of fish.)

To see multitasking in operation on a Windows XP computer, press Ctrl+Alt+Delete to bring up the Windows Task Manager and then click the Processes tab. This displays all tasks currently active on the computer, as shown in Figure 8-1.

Directory services

Directories are everywhere — and were, even in the days when they were all hard copy. When you needed to make a phone call, you looked up the number in a phone directory. When you needed to find the address of a client, you looked up him or her in your Rolodex. And then there were the non-book versions: when you needed to find the Sam Goody store at a shopping mall (for example), you looked for the mall directory — usually a lighted sign showing what was where.

Networks have directories, too, providing information about the resources that are available on the network — such as users, computers, printers, shared folders, and files. Directories are an essential part of any network operating system.

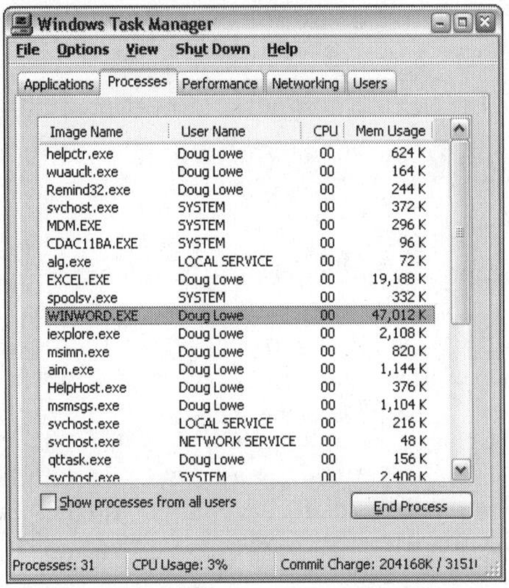

Figure 8-1:
Displaying
active
tasks on a
Windows
XP
computer.

In early network operating systems (such as Windows NT 3.1 and NetWare 3.*x*), each server computer maintained its own *directory database* — a file that contained an organized list of the resources available just on that server. The problem with that approach was that network administrators had to maintain each directory database separately. That wasn't too bad for networks with just a few servers, but maintaining the directory on a network with dozens or even hundreds of servers was next to impossible.

In addition, early *directory services* (programs that made the directory databases usable) were application-specific. For example, a server would have one directory database for user logins, another for file sharing, and yet another for e-mail addresses. Each directory had its own tools for adding, updating, and deleting directory entries.

Security services

All network operating systems must provide some measure of security to protect the network from unauthorized access. Hacking seems to be the national pastime these days. With most computer networks connected to the Internet, anyone anywhere in the world can — and probably will — try to break into your network.

The most basic type of security is handled through *user accounts,* which grant individual users the right to access the network resources and govern what resources the user can access. User accounts are secured by passwords;

therefore, good password policy is a cornerstone of any security system. Most network operating systems give you some standard tools for maintaining network security:

- ✔ **You can establish password policies,** such as requiring that passwords have a minimum length and include a mix of letters and numerals.

- ✔ **You can set passwords to expire after a certain number of days.** Doing so forces network users to change their passwords frequently.

- ✔ **You can encrypt network data.** A data-encryption capability scrambles data before it is sent over the network or saved on disk, making unauthorized use a lot more difficult. Good encryption is the key to setting up a *Virtual Private Network,* or *VPN,* which enables network users to securely access a network from a remote location by using an Internet connection.

- ✔ **You can issue digital certificates.** These special codes are used to ensure that users are who they say they are and files are what they claim to be.

Microsoft's Server Operating Systems

Microsoft currently supports three versions of its flagship server operating system: Windows NT Server 4, Windows 2000 Server, and Windows Server 2003. Windows Server 2003 is the newest version. It's so new, in fact, that few people are using it. So Windows 2000 Server is the Windows server application you're most likely to find in the field. Although Microsoft still supports Windows NT Server 4, it no longer sells this operating system. Still, plenty of networks are chugging along just fine with good old NT.

Windows NT 4 Server

Windows NT Server was the last in a long series of Windows server applications dubbed *NT,* which most likely stood for *New Technology,* though Microsoft never officially said so. The "new technology" that got everyone so excited about Windows NT in the first place was (drum roll, please) 32-bit processing — yep, the current standard that's about to make way for 64-bit — at the time, a huge step up from the 16-bit processing of earlier Windows versions. Windows NT was the first Microsoft operating system that was reliable enough to work as a network server on large networks. Version 4.0 shipped in July of 1996, so it is now more than 8 years old. That's a lifetime in operating-system years, which are kind of like dog years.

Probably the most important feature of Windows NT is its directory model, which is based on the concept of domains. A *domain* is a group of computers that are managed by a single directory database. To access shared resources within a domain, you must have a valid user account within the domain and be granted rights to access the resources in which you're interested. The domain system uses 15-character NetBIOS names to access individual computers within a domain and to name the domain itself.

Here's a summary of the other features of NT:

- ✔ Officially, Microsoft still claims that NT Server will run on any 486 processor with at least 16MB of memory. But I wouldn't try it on anything less than a 200MHz Pentium with 64MB of RAM. Of course, these days, 200MHz Pentiums with 64MB of RAM are given away as prizes in Cracker Jack boxes.

- ✔ Windows NT 4 uses the same user interface that was designed for Windows 95. In fact, the main difference between NT 4 and its predecessor (Windows NT 3.51) was this new user interface.

- ✔ Some of the limitations of the NT file system are worth considering:

  - • Max number of users: Unlimited (but you *do* have to make sure every one of them is covered under the software license)

  - • Number of disk volumes: 25

  - • Max size of a volume: 17,000GB

  - • Max hard drive space for server: 408,000GB

  - • Largest file: 17 billion GB (Wow! That's more than the maximum hard drive space for a server, which is impossible. So far.)

  - • Max amount of RAM in server: 4GB

  - • Max number of open files: Unlimited

Windows 2000 Server

Although Windows Server 2003 is newer, Windows 2000 Server is currently the most popular server operating system from Microsoft. As a product, Windows 2000 Server built on the strengths of Windows NT Server 4, adding new features and becoming faster, easier to manage, more reliable, and easier to use — for large and small networks alike.

The most significant new feature offered by Windows 2000 Server is called *Active Directory,* which provides a single directory of all network resources that program developers can incorporate into their programs. Active Directory drops the 15-character domain and computer names in favor of Internet-style DNS names, such as `Marketing.MyCompany.com` or `Sales.YourCompany.com`. (However, it still supports the old-style names for older client applications that don't deal well with DNS names.)

Windows 2000 Server comes in three versions:

- ✔ **Windows 2000 Server** is the basic server application, designed for small- to medium-sized networks. It includes all the basic server features, including file and printer sharing, and acts as a Web and e-mail server.

- ✔ **Windows 2000 Advanced Server** is the next step up, designed for larger networks. Advanced Server can support server computers that have up to 8GB of memory (not hard drive — RAM!) and four integrated processors instead of the single processor that desktop computers and most server computers have.

- ✔ **Windows 2000 Datacenter Server** is supports servers that have as many as 32 processors with up to 64GB of RAM. It's specially designed for large database applications.

For small networks with 50 or fewer computers, Microsoft offers a special bundle called the Small Business Server, which includes the following components for one low, low price:

- ✔ Windows 2000 Server, the operating system for your network server

- ✔ Exchange Server 2000, for e-mail and instant messaging

- ✔ Internet Security and Acceleration Server 2000, which provides improved security and performance for your Web applications

- ✔ SQL Server 2000, a database server

- ✔ FrontPage 2000, for building Web sites

- ✔ Outlook 2000, for reading and sending e-mail

The pricing for Windows 2000 Server is based on the number of clients that will use each server. Each server must have a server license — *and* an appropriate number of client licenses. When you buy Windows 2000 Server, you get a server license and (depending on the size of your network) a bundle of 5, 10, or 25 client licenses. You can then purchase additional client licenses 5 or 20 at a time. Table 8-1 lists the prices for the various types of Windows 2000 Server and client licenses.

Table 8-1	Windows 2000 Server Pricing
Product	*Price*
Windows 2000 Server, 5 clients	$999
Windows 2000 Server, 10 clients	$1,199
Windows 2000 Server, 25 clients	$1,799
Windows 2000 Advanced Server, 25 clients	$3,999
Client license 5-pack	$199
Client license 20-pack	$799

One of the best features of Windows 2000 Server is *Microsoft Management Console* (also known as *MMC*), which provides a single program for managing just about all aspects of server administration. With Windows NT, you had to use different programs for different server management functions, such as managing users or managing disk settings. MMC lets you perform almost all server management functions from within a single program.

Windows Server 2003

By mid-2003, Microsoft had released a new version of Windows Server called (ta-daaa!) Windows Server 2003. For several years prior to its release, this new version was called Windows .NET Server. (*.NET* is pronounced *dot-net.*) Windows Server 2003 builds on Windows 2000 Server, with many new features. Here are but a few of the additions:

✔ A new and improved version of Active Directory with tighter security, an easier-to-use interface, and better performance.

✔ A better and easier-to-use system-management interface called the Manage My Server window. On the flip side — for those who prefer brute-force commands — Windows Server 2003 includes a more comprehensive set of command-line management tools than is offered by Windows 2000 Server. Of course, the familiar Microsoft Management Console tools from Windows 2000 Server are still there.

✔ A built-in Internet firewall to secure your Internet connection.

✔ A new version of the Microsoft Web server, Internet Information Services (IIS) 6.0.

Like its predecessor, Windows Server 2003 comes in several versions. Four, to be specific:

- **Windows Server 2003, Standard Edition:** This is the basic version of Windows 2003. If you're using Windows Server 2003 as a file server or to provide other basic network services, this is the version you'll use. Standard Edition can support servers with up to four processors and 4GB of RAM.

- **Windows Server 2003, Web Edition:** A version of Windows 2003 optimized for use as a Web server.

- **Windows Server 2003, Enterprise Edition:** Designed for larger networks, this version can support servers with up to eight processors, 32GB of RAM, server clusters, and advanced features designed for high performance and reliability.

- **Windows Server 2003, Datacenter Edition:** The most powerful version of Windows 2003, with support for servers with 64 processors, 64GB of RAM, and server clusters, as well as advanced fault-tolerance features designed to keep the server running for mission-critical applications.

Table 8-2 lists the pricing for Windows Server 2003, which is similar to the pricing for Windows 2000 Server (with the exception of the Web Edition).

Table 8-2	Windows 2003 Server Pricing
Product	*Price*
Windows Server 2003, 5 clients	$999
Windows Server 2003, 10 clients	$1,199
Windows Server 2003 Enterprise Edition, 25 clients	$3,999
Client license 5-pack	$199
Client license 20-pack	$799
Windows Server 2003, Web Edition	$399

Novell NetWare

NetWare is one of the most popular network operating systems, especially for large networks. NetWare has an excellent reputation for reliability. In fact, some network administrators swear that they have NetWare servers on their networks that have been running continuously, without a single reboot, since Teddy Roosevelt was president.

NetWare versions

NetWare released the first version of NetWare in 1983, two years before the first version of Windows and four years before Microsoft's first network operating system, the now-defunct LAN Manager. Over the years, NetWare has gone through many versions. These are the versions you're most likely to encounter still in use today:

- NetWare version 3.*x*, the version that made NetWare famous. NetWare 3.*x* used a now outdated directory scheme called the *bindery*. Each NetWare 3.*x* server had a bindery file that contains information about the resources on that particular server. With the bindery, you had to log on separately to each server that contained resources you wanted to use.

- NetWare 4.*x*, in which NetWare Directory Service, or NDS, replaced the bindery. NDS is similar to Active Directory. It provides a single directory for the entire network rather than separate directories for each server.

- NetWare 5.*x* was the next step. It introduced a new user interface based on Java for easier administration, improved support for Internet protocols, multiprocessing with up to 32 processors, and many other features.

- The most popular version today is NetWare 6, described in more detail later in this section.

- Novell released its newest version, NetWare 6.5, in the summer of (surprise!) 2003.

NetWare 6 features

The most popular version of NetWare is version 6. Here are a few of the most important new features of NetWare 6:

- An improved disk-management system called Novell Storage Services that can manage billions of files on a single volume. (Whether storing billions of files on a single volume is a good idea is a separate question; if you decide to do it, NetWare 6 will let you.)

- Web-based access to network folders and printers.

- Built-in support for Windows, Linux, Unix, and Macintosh file systems so you can access data on the server from these operating systems without installing special client software.

✔ iFolder, a feature that automatically keeps your files synchronized between your work computer and your home computer (or a traveling laptop computer).

NetWare 6 is also available in a special Small Business edition, which includes the basic NetWare 6 operating system plus a collection of goodies designed to make networking easier for small businesses. Among the extras you get with NetWare for Small Business are the following:

✔ GroupWise 6, an e-mail and group-scheduling program that is similar to Microsoft Outlook and Exchange.

✔ ZENWorks, a tool for managing software and hardware on your network.

✔ BorderManager, a suite of security programs for safeguarding your network's Internet access.

✔ A basketful of programs for accessing the Internet and creating a Web server.

Unlike Windows Server 2003, NetWare's pricing is based only on the number of clients that the server supports. Novell doesn't charge for the basic server license. Table 8-3 summarizes the pricing structure for NetWare 6. Note that Novell offers competitive upgrade prices as an incentive for users to switch from Microsoft or other servers.

Table 8-3	NetWare 6 Server Pricing	
Product	*Full Price*	*Upgrade Price*
NetWare 6, 5 clients	$995	$530
NetWare 6, 10 clients	$1,840	$975
NetWare 6, 25 clients	$4,600	$2,440

NetWare 6.5

Novell's newest version of NetWare, version 6.5, builds on Version 6.0 with a number of new features. In particular, check these out:

✔ Improvements to the browser-based management tools.

✔ Built-in open-source components such as the Apache and Tomcat Web server, the MySQL database manager, and PHP for dynamic Web applications.

✔ A virtual-office feature that enables users to access their e-mail, files, and other network resources from any computer with a browser.

✔ Nterprise Branch Office, a feature that lets you easily integrate a server at a remote branch office with a central office network via the Internet, kind of like a supercharged VPN (Virtual Private Network).

Other Server Operating Systems

Although NetWare and Windows NT/2000 Server are the most popular choices for network operating systems, they're not the only available choices. The following sections briefly describe two other server choices: Linux and the Macintosh OS/X Server.

Linux

Perhaps the most interesting operating system available today is Linux. Linux is a free operating system that is based on Unix, a powerful network operating system often used on large networks. Linux was started by Linus Torvalds, who thought it would be fun to write a version of Unix in his free time — as a hobby. He enlisted help from hundreds of programmers throughout the world who volunteered their time and efforts via the Internet. Today, Linux is a full-featured version of Unix; its users consider it to be as good as or better than Windows. In fact, almost as many people now use Linux as use Macintosh computers.

Linux offers the same networking benefits of Unix and can be an excellent choice as a server operating system.

Apple Mac OS X Server

All the other server operating systems I describe in this chapter run on Intel-based PCs with Pentium or Pentium-compatible processors. But what about Macintosh computers? After all, Macintosh users need networks, too. For Macintosh networks, Apple offers a special network server operating system known as Mac OS X Server. Mac OS X Server has all the features you'd expect in a server operating system: file and printer sharing, Internet features, e-mail, and so on.

Peer-to-Peer Networking with Windows

If you're not up to the complexity of dedicated network operating systems, you may want to opt for a simple *peer-to-peer network* — in which the computers are linked but have no central server or hierarchical relationship — based on a desktop version of Windows.

Advantages of peer-to-peer networks

The main advantage of a peer-to-peer network is that it is easier to set up and use than a network with a dedicated server. Peer-to-peer networks rely on the limited network server features built into Windows, such as the ability to share files and printers. Recent versions of Windows, such as Windows XP, come with networking wizards that automatically configure a basic network for you so you don't have to manually configure any network settings.

Another advantage of peer-to-peer networks is that they can be less expensive than server-based networks. Here are some of the reasons that peer-to-peer networks (when appropriately set up) are inexpensive:

- **Peer-to-peer networks don't require you to use a dedicated server computer.** Any computer on the network can function as both a network server and a user's workstation. (However, you can configure a computer as a dedicated server if you want to. Doing so results in better performance but negates the cost benefit of not having a dedicated server computer.)

- **Peer-to-peer networks are easier to set up and use.** That means you can spend less time figuring out how to make the network work and keep it working. And as Einstein proved, time is money (hence, his famous equation $E=M\$^2$).

- **You don't have to spring for the cost of the server operating system itself.** Both NetWare and Windows Server can cost as much as $200 per user. And the total cost increases as your network grows, although the cost per user drops. For a peer-to-peer Windows server, you pay for Windows once. You don't pay any additional charges based on the number of users on your network.

Drawbacks of peer-to-peer networks

Yes, peer-to-peer networks are easier to install and manage than NetWare or NT, but they do have their drawbacks:

✔ **It's all within Windows.** Because peer-to-peer networks are Windows-based, they're subject to the inherent limitations of Windows. Windows is designed primarily to be an operating system for a single-user, desktop computer rather than function as part of a network, so Windows can't manage a file or printer server as efficiently as a real network operating system.

✔ **Functioning as a server eats up computer resources.** If you don't set up a dedicated network server, someone (hopefully, not you) may have to live with the inconvenience of sharing his or her computer with the network. With NetWare or Windows Server, the server computers are dedicated to network use so that no one has to put up with this inconvenience.

✔ **Savings are relative.** Although a peer-to-peer network may have a lower cost per computer for smaller networks, the cost difference between peer-to-peer networks and NetWare or Windows Server is less significant in larger networks (say, 10 or more clients).

✔ **Larger networks are hard to manage without a dedicated server.** Peer-to-peer networks don't work well when your network starts to grow. Peer-to-peer servers just don't have the security or performance features required for a growing network.

Networking with Windows XP

The current version of Microsoft's desktop operating system, Windows XP, has powerful peer-to-peer networking features built in. Windows XP comes in two flavors: Home Edition and Professional Edition. As its name suggests, the Home Edition is designed for home users. It includes great multimedia features, such as a home movie editor called Windows Movie Maker and built-in support for CD-ROM burners, scanners, video cameras, and many other features. Windows XP Professional Edition is designed for users with more demanding (usually more businesslike) network needs.

Windows XP provides the following networking features:

✔ Built-in file and printer sharing allows you to share files and printers with other network users.

✔ A Network Setup Wizard that automatically sets the most common configuration options. The wizard eliminates the need to work through multiple Properties dialog boxes to configure network settings.

✔ An Internet Connection Sharing feature (ICS) that allows a Windows XP computer to share an Internet connection with other users. The ICS feature includes firewall features that protect your network from unauthorized access via the Internet connection.

✔ Simple user-account management that lets you create multiple users and assign passwords.

✔ Built-in support for wireless networking.

✔ A network *bridge* feature that lets you use a Windows XP computer to link two networks systematically. The computer must have two network adapters, one for each network.

✔ Advanced network diagnostics and troubleshooting tools help you to find and correct networking problems.

Older Windows versions

Previous versions of Windows also offered peer-to-peer networking features. The following list summarizes the networking features of the major Windows releases prior to Windows XP, starting with the most recent and descending into the Dark Ages (just kidding):

✔ **Windows Me:** Short for Windows Millennium Edition, this release was aimed at home users. It provided a Home Networking Wizard to simplify the task of configuring a network. It was the last version of Windows that was based on the old 16-bit MS-DOS code.

✔ **Windows 2000 Professional:** A desktop version of Windows 2000. It has powerful peer-to-peer networking features similar to those found in Windows XP, although they are a bit more difficult to set up. It was the first desktop version of Windows that integrated well with Active Directory.

✔ **Windows 98** and **Windows 98 Second Edition:** These were popular upgrades to Windows 95 that enhanced its basic networking features.

✔ **Windows 95:** This was the first 32-bit version of Windows. However, it still relied internally on 16-bit MS-DOS code, so it wasn't a true 32-bit operating system. It provided basic peer-to-peer network features, with built-in drivers for common network adapters and basic file and printer sharing features.

✔ **Windows for Workgroups** was the first version of Windows to support networking without requiring an add-on product. It simplified the task of creating NetBIOS-based networks for file and printer sharing. However, it had only weak support for TCP/IP, the dominant Internet protocol in use today.

Chapter 9

Oh, What a Tangled Web We Weave: Cables, Adapters, and Other Stuff

Cable is the plumbing of your network. In fact, working with network cable is a lot like working with pipe: You have to use the right kind of pipe (cable), the right valves and connectors (hubs and switches), and the right fixtures (network interface cards).

Network cables have one compelling advantage over pipes: You don't get wet when they leak.

This chapter tells you far more about network cables than you probably need to know. I introduce you to *Ethernet,* the most common system of network cabling for small networks. Then you find out how to work with the cables used to wire an Ethernet network. You also find out how to install a network interface card, which enables you to connect the cables to your computer.

What Is Ethernet?

Ethernet is a standardized way of connecting computers to create a network. You can think of Ethernet as a kind of municipal building code for networks: It specifies what kind of cables to use, how to connect the cables together, how long the cables can be, how computers transmit data to one another using the cables, and more.

Worthless filler about network topology

A networking book wouldn't be complete without the usual textbook description of the three basic *network topologies*. The first type of network topology is called a *bus,* in which network nodes (that is, computers) are strung together in a line, like this:

A *bus* is the simplest type of topology but it has some drawbacks. If the cable breaks somewhere in the middle, the whole network breaks.

The second type of topology is called a *ring:*

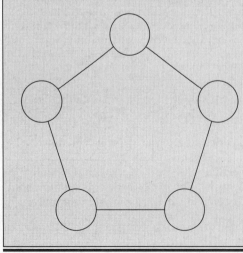

A *ring* is very much like a bus except with no end to the line: The last node on the line is connected to the first node, forming an endless loop.

The third type of topology is called a *star:*

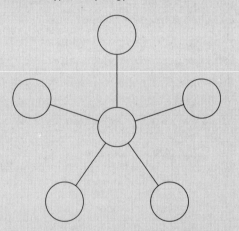

In a star network, all the nodes are connected to a central hub. In effect, each node has an independent connection to the network, so a break in one cable doesn't affect the others.

Ethernet networks are based on a bus design. However, fancy cabling tricks make an Ethernet network appear to be wired like a star when twisted-pair cable is used.

Historical Footnote Warning: Although Ethernet is today the overwhelming choice for networking, that wasn't always the case. In days of old, Ethernet had competition from two other network cabling standards: Token Ring and ARCnet. Token Ring is an IBM standard for networking that is still used in some organizations, especially where older IBM mainframe or midrange systems are included in the network. ARCnet has all but vanished from the office-networking scene but is still commonly used for industrial network applications, such as building automation and factory robot control.

Without regard to the technical merits of Ethernet, Token Ring, or ARCnet, the fact is that the vast majority of business networks use Ethernet. You can purchase inexpensive Ethernet components at just about any computer store, and you can even purchase Ethernet cable and connectors at many hardware warehouse stores. Because Ethernet is inexpensive and readily available, it is really the only choice for new networks — small as well as large.

Here are a few tidbits you're likely to run into at parties (well, okay, *meetings*) where the conversation is about Ethernet standards:

✔ Ethernet is a set of standards for the infrastructure on which a network is built. All the network operating systems that I discuss in this book — including all versions of Windows, NetWare, Linux, and Macintosh OS/X — can operate on an Ethernet network. If you build your network on a solid Ethernet base, you can change network operating systems later.

✔ Ethernet is often referred to by network gurus as 802.3 (pronounced *eight-oh-two-dot-three*), which is the official designation used by the *IEEE* (pronounced *eye-triple-e,* not *aieeee!*), a group of electrical engineers who wear bow ties and have nothing better to do than argue about inductance all day long — and it's a good thing they do. If not for them, you wouldn't be able to mix and match Ethernet components made by different companies.

✔ The original vintage Ethernet transmits data at a rate of 10 million bits per second, or 10 Mbps. (*Mbps* is usually pronounced *megabits per second.*) Because 8 bits are in a byte, that translates into roughly 1.2 million bytes per second. In practice, Ethernet can't actually move information that fast because data must be transmitted in packages of no more than 1,500 bytes, called *packets.* So 150 KB of information has to be split into 100 packets.

Ethernet's transmission speed has nothing to do with how fast electrical signals move on the cable. The electrical signals themselves travel at about 70 percent of the speed of light, or as Captain Picard would say, "Warp factor point-seven-oh."

✔ The newer version of Ethernet, and now the most common, is called *Fast Ethernet* or *100Mbps Ethernet,* moves data ten times as fast as normal Ethernet. Because Fast Ethernet moves data at a whopping 100 Mbps and uses twisted-pair cabling, it's often called *100BaseT* (and sometimes *100BaseT*x).

✔ Most networking components you can buy these days support both 10Mbps and 100Mbps Ethernet. These components are often referred to as *10/100 Mbps components* because they support both speeds.

✔ An even faster version of Ethernet, known as *Gigabit Ethernet,* is also available. Gigabit Ethernet components are expensive, though, so they are usually used to create a high-speed network backbone.

All About Cable

Although you can use wireless technology to create networks without cables, most networks still use cables to physically connect each computer to the network. Over the years, various types of cables have been used with Ethernet networks. Today, almost all networks are built with a type of cable known as *twisted-pair cable*. In this type of cable, pairs of wires are twisted around each other to reduce electrical interference. (You almost need a PhD in physics to understand why twisting the wires helps to reduce interference, so don't feel bad if this doesn't make sense.)

You may encounter other types of cable in an existing network; for example, on older networks, you may encounter two types of *coaxial* cable (also known as *coax,* pronounced *COE-ax*). The first type resembles television cable and is known as RG-58 cable. The second type is a thick yellow cable that used to be the only type of cable used for Ethernet. You may also encounter fiber-optic cables that span long distances at high speeds, or thick twisted-pair bundles that carry multiple sets of twisted-pair cable between wiring closets in a large building. Most networks, however, use simple twisted-pair cable.

Twisted-pair cable is sometimes called *UTP*. (The *U* stands for *Unshielded,* but no one says *unshielded twisted-pair.* Just *twisted-pair* will do.) Figure 9-1 shows a twisted-pair cable.

When you use UTP cable to construct an Ethernet network, you connect the computers in a star arrangement, as Figure 9-2 illustrates. In the center of this star is a device called a *hub.* Depending on the model, Ethernet hubs enable you to connect from 4 to 24 computers using twisted-pair cable.

An advantage of UTP's star arrangement is that if one cable goes bad, only the computer attached to that cable is affected; the rest of the network continues to chug along.

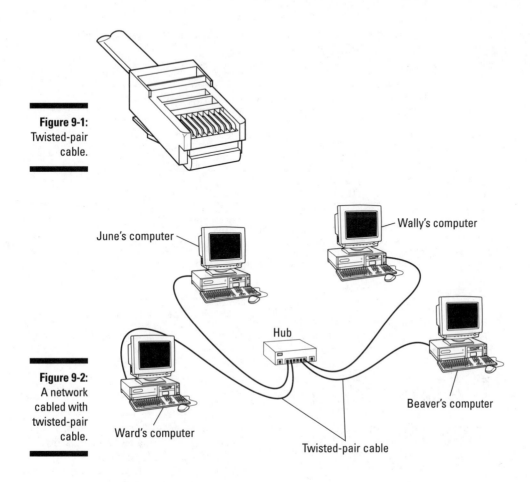

Figure 9-1:
Twisted-pair
cable.

Figure 9-2:
A network
cabled with
twisted-pair
cable.

June's computer

Wally's computer

Hub

Beaver's computer

Ward's computer

Twisted-pair cable

Cable categories

Twisted-pair cable comes in various grades called *Categories*. These Categories are specified by the ANSI/EIA Standard 568. (*ANSI* stands for *American National Standards Institute*; *ESA* stands for *Electronic Industries Association*). The standards indicate the data capacity — also known as the *bandwidth* — of the cable. Table 9-1 lists the various Categories of twisted-pair cable.

Although higher-Category cables are more expensive than lower-Category cables, the real cost of installing Ethernet cabling is the labor required to actually pull the cables through the walls. You should never install anything less than Category 5 cable. And if at all possible, you should invest in Category 5e (the *e* stands for *enhanced*) — or even Category 6 cable — to allow for future upgrades to your network.

If you want to sound like you know what you're talking about, say "Cat 5" instead of saying "Category 5."

Table 9-1	Twisted-pair cable categories	
Category	*Maximum data rate*	*Intended use*
1	1 Mbps	Voice only
2	4 Mbps	4Mbps Token Ring
3	16 Mbps	10BaseT Ethernet
4	20 Mbps	16Mbps Token Ring
5	100 Mbps (2-pair)	100BaseT Ethernet
	1000 Mbps (4-pair)	1000BaseTX
5e	1000 Mbps (2-pair)	1000BaseT
6	1000 Mbps (2-pair)	1000BaseT and faster broadband applications

What's with the pairs?

Most twisted-pair cable has four pairs of wires, for a total of eight wires. Standard 10BaseT or 100BaseT Ethernet actually uses only two of the pairs, so the other two pairs are unused. You may be tempted to save money by purchasing cable with just two pairs of wires, but that's a bad idea. If a network cable develops a problem, you can sometimes fix it by switching over to one of the extra pairs. If you use two-pair cable, though, you won't have any spare pairs to use.

You may also be tempted to use the extra pairs for some other purpose, such as for a voice line. Don't. The electrical noise generated by voice signals in the extra wires can interfere with your network.

To shield or not to shield

Unshielded twisted-pair cable, or *UTP,* is designed for normal office environments. When you use UTP cable, you must be careful not to route cable close to fluorescent light fixtures, air conditioners, or electric motors (such as automatic door motors or elevator motors). UTP is the least expensive type of cable.

In environments that have a lot of electrical interference (such as factories), you may want to use *shielded twisted-pair* cable, also known as *STP*. Because STP can be as much as three times more expensive than regular UTP, you won't want to use STP unless you have to. With a little care, UTP can withstand the amount of electrical interference found in a normal office environment.

Most STP cable is shielded by a layer of aluminum foil. For buildings with unusually high amounts of electrical interference, the more expensive braided-copper shielding offers even more protection.

When to use plenum cable

The outer sheath of both shielded and unshielded twisted-pair cable comes in two varieties: PVC and Plenum. *PVC* cable is the most common and least expensive type. *Plenum cable* is a special type of fire-retardant cable designed for use in the plenum space (definition coming right up) of a building. Plenum cable has a special Teflon coating that not only resists heat, but also gives off fewer toxic fumes if it does burn. Unfortunately, plenum cable costs more than twice as much as ordinary PVC cable.

Most local building codes require that you use plenum cable whenever the wiring is installed within the building's *plenum space* — a compartment that's part of the building's air-distribution system, usually the space above a suspended ceiling or under a raised floor.

Note that the area above a suspended ceiling is *not* a plenum space *if* both the delivery and return lines of the air-conditioning and heating system are ducted. Plenum cable is required only if the air conditioning and heating system are not ducted. When in doubt, it's best to have the local inspector look at your facility before you install cable.

Sometimes solid, sometimes stranded

The actual copper wire that composes the cable comes in two varieties: solid and stranded. Your network will have some of each.

- ✔ In *stranded cable,* each conductor is made from a bunch of very small wires that are twisted together. Stranded cable is more flexible than solid cable, so it doesn't break as easily. However, stranded cable is more expensive than solid cable and isn't very good at transmitting signals over long distances. Stranded cable is best used for *patch cables* (such as patch panels to hubs and switches).

Strictly speaking, the cable that connects your computer to the wall jack is called a *station cable* — not a patch cable — but it's definitely an appropriate use for stranded cable.

✔ In *solid cable*, each conductor is a single, solid strand of wire. Solid cable is less expensive than stranded cable and carries signals farther, but it isn't very flexible. If you bend it too many times, it will break. Normally you find solid cable in use as permanent wiring within the walls and ceilings of a building.

Installation guidelines

The hardest part of installing network cable is the physical task of pulling the cable through ceilings, walls, and floors. This job is just tricky enough that I recommend you don't attempt it yourself except for small offices. For large jobs, hire a professional cable installer. You may even want to hire a professional for small jobs if the ceiling and wall spaces are difficult to access.

Here are some general pointers to keep in mind if you decide to install cable yourself:

✔ You can purchase twisted-pair cable in prefabricated lengths, such as 50 feet, 75 feet, and 100 feet. You can also special-order prefabricated cables in any length you need. However, attaching connectors to bulk cable isn't that difficult. I recommend that you use prefabricated cables only for very small networks and only when you don't need to route the cable through walls or ceilings.

✔ Always use a bit more cable than you need, especially if you're running cable through walls. For example, when you run a cable up a wall, leave a few feet of slack in the ceiling above the wall. That way, you'll have plenty of cable if you need to make a repair later on.

✔ When running cable, avoid sources of interference such as fluorescent lights, big motors, X-ray machines, and so on.

Fluorescent lights are the most common source of interference for cables run behind fake ceiling panels. Be sure to give light fixtures a wide berth as you run your cable. Three feet should do it.

✔ The maximum allowable cable length between the hub and the computer is 100 meters (about 328 feet).

✔ If you must run cable across the floor where people walk, cover the cable so no one trips over it. Inexpensive cable protectors are available at most hardware stores.

✔ When running cables through walls, label each cable at both ends. Most electrical supply stores carry pads of cable labels that are perfect for the job. These pads contain 50 sheets or so of precut labels with letters and numbers. They look much more professional than wrapping a loop of masking tape around the cable and writing on the tape with a marker.

Okay, if you want to scrimp, you can just buy a permanent marker and write directly on the cable.

✔ When several cables come together, tie them with plastic cable ties. Avoid masking tape if you can; the tape doesn't last, but the sticky glue stuff does. It's a mess a year later. Cable ties are available at electrical supply stores.

✔ Cable ties have all sorts of useful purposes. Once, on a backpacking trip, I used a pair of cable ties to attach an unsuspecting buddy's hat to a high tree limb. He wasn't impressed with my innovative use of the cable ties, but my other hiking companions were.

✔ When you run cable above suspended ceiling panels, use cable ties, hooks, or clamps to secure the cable to the actual ceiling or to the metal frame that supports the ceiling tiles. Don't just lay the cable on top of the panels.

Getting the tools that you need

Of course, to do a job right, you must have the right tools.

Start with a basic set of computer tools, which you can get for about $15 from any computer store or large office-supply store. These kits include the right screwdrivers and socket wrenches to open up your computers and insert adapter cards. (If you don't have a computer tool kit, make sure that you have several flat-head and Phillips screwdrivers of various sizes.)

If all your computers are in the same room, and you're going to run the cables along the floor, and you're using prefabricated cables, the computer tool kit should contain everything that you need.

If you're using bulk cable and plan on attaching your own connectors, you need the following tools in addition to the tools that come with the basic computer tool kit:

✔ **Wire cutters:** You need big ones for coax cable; smaller ones are okay for twisted pair cable. If you're using yellow cable, you need the Jaws of Life.

✔ **A crimp tool:** You need the crimp tool to attach the connectors to the cable. Don't use a cheap $25 crimp tool. A good one will cost $100 and will save you many headaches in the long run. Remember this adage: When you crimp, you mustn't scrimp.

✔ **Wire stripper:** You need this only if the crimp tool doesn't include a wire stripper.

If you plan on running cables through walls, you need these additional tools:

✔ **A hammer.**

✔ **A bell.**

✔ **A song to sing.** Just kidding about these last two.

✔ **A keyhole saw.** This is useful if you plan on cutting holes through walls to route your cable.

✔ **A flashlight.**

✔ **A ladder.**

✔ **Someone to hold the ladder.**

✔ **Possibly a fish tape.** A *fish tape* is a coiled-up length of stiff metal tape. To use it, you feed the tape into one wall opening and fish it toward the other opening, where a partner is ready to grab it when the tape arrives. Next, your partner attaches the cable to the fish tape and yells something like "Let 'er rip!" or "Bombs away!" Then you reel in the fish tape and the cable along with it. (You can find fish tape in the electrical section of most well-stocked hardware stores.)

If you plan on routing cable through a concrete subfloor, you need to rent a jackhammer and a backhoe and hire someone to hold a yellow flag while you work. Better yet, find some other route for the cable.

Pinouts for twisted-pair cables

Each pair of wires in a twisted-pair cable is one of four colors: orange, green, blue, or brown. The two wires that make up each pair are complementary: one is white with a colored stripe; the other is colored with a white stripe. For example, the orange pair has an orange wire with a white stripe (called *the orange wire*) and a white wire with an orange stripe (called *the white/ orange wire*). Likewise, the blue pair has a blue wire with a white stripe (*the blue wire*) and a white wire with a blue stripe (*the white/blue wire*).

When you attach a twisted-pair cable to a modular connector or jack, it's crucial to match up the right wires to the right pins. It's harder than it sounds; you can use any of several different standards to wire the connectors. To confuse matters further, you can use one of the two popular standard ways of hooking up the wires. One is known as EIA/TIA 568A; the other is EIA/TIA 568B, also known as AT&T 258A. Both of these wiring schemes are shown in Table 9-2.

It doesn't matter which of these wiring schemes you use, but pick one and stick with it. If you use one wiring standard on one end of a cable and the other standard on the other end, the cable won't work.

Table 9-2	Pin connections for twisted-pair cable		
Pin Number	*Function*	*EIA/TIA 568A*	*EIA/TIA568B AT&T 258A*
Pin 1	Transmit +	White/Green	White/orange wire
Pin 2	Transmit -	Green	Orange wire
Pin 3	Receive +	White/Orange	White/green wire
Pin 4	Unused	Blue	Blue wire
Pin 5	Unused	White/Blue	White/blue wire
Pin 6	Receive -	Orange	Green wire
Pin 7	Unused	White/Brown	White/brown wire
Pin 8	Unused	Brown	Brown wire

10BaseT and 100BaseT actually use only two of the four pairs, connected to Pins 1, 2, 3, and 6. One pair transmits data; the other receives data. The only difference between the two wiring standards is which pair transmits and which receives. In the EIA/TIA 568A standard, the green pair is used for transmit and the orange pair is used for receive. In the EIA/TIA 568B and AT&T 258A standards, the orange pair is used for transmit and the green pair for receive.

If you want, you can get away with connecting only Pins 1, 2, 3, and 6. However, I suggest that you connect all four pairs as indicated in Table 9-2.

Attaching RJ-45 connectors

RJ-45 connectors for twisted-pair cables are not too difficult to attach if you have the right crimping tool. The only trick is making sure that you attach each wire to the correct pin and then pressing the tool hard enough to ensure a good connection.

Here's the procedure for attaching an RJ-45 connector:

1. **Cut the end of the cable to the desired length.**

   Make sure that you make a square cut — not a diagonal cut.

2. **Insert the cable into the stripper portion of the crimp tool so the end of the cable is against the stop.**

   Squeeze the handles and slowly pull the cable out, keeping it square. This strips off the correct length of outer insulation without puncturing the insulation on the inner wires.

3. **Arrange the wires so that they lie flat and line up according to Table 9-2.**

   You'll have to play with the wires a little bit to get them to lay out in the right sequence.

4. **Slide the wires into the pinholes on the connector.**

   Double-check to make sure all the wires slipped into the correct pinholes.

5. **Insert the plug and wire into the crimping portion of the tool and then squeeze the handles to crimp the plug.**

   Squeeze it tight!

6. **Remove the plug from the tool and double-check the connection.**

   You're done!

Here are a few other points to remember when dealing with RJ-45 connectors and twisted-pair cable:

✔ The pins on the RJ-45 connectors are not numbered, but you can tell which is pin 1 by holding the connector so that the metal conductors are facing up, as shown in Figure 9-3. Pin 1 is on the left.

✔ Some people wire 10BaseT cable differently — using the green and white pair for pins 1 and 2, and the orange and white pair for pins 3 and 6. Doing it this way doesn't affect the operation of the network (the network is color-blind), *as long as the connectors on both ends of the cable are wired the same!*

✔ If you're installing cable for a Fast Ethernet system, you should be extra careful to follow the rules of Category-5 cabling. That means, among other things, make sure that you use Category-5 components throughout. The cable and all the connectors must be up to Category-5 specs. When you attach the connectors, don't untwist more than half an inch of cable. And don't try to stretch the cable runs beyond the 100-meter maximum. When in doubt, have cable for a 100Mbps Ethernet system professionally installed.

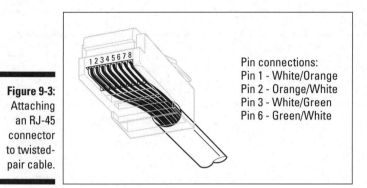

Pin connections:
Pin 1 - White/Orange
Pin 2 - Orange/White
Pin 3 - White/Green
Pin 6 - Green/White

Figure 9-3:
Attaching an RJ-45 connector to twisted-pair cable.

Crossover cables

A *crossover cable* is a cable that can be used to directly connect two devices without a hub or switch. You can use a crossover cable to connect two computers directly to each other, but crossover cables are more often used to daisy-chain hubs and switches to each other.

If you want to create your own crossover cable, you have to reverse the wires on one end of the cable, as shown in Table 9-3. This table shows how you should wire both ends of the cable to create a crossover cable. Connect one of the ends according to the Connector A column and the other according to the Connector B column.

Note that you don't need to use a crossover cable if one of the switches or hubs that you want to connect has a crossover port, usually labeled *uplink* or *daisy-chain*. If the hub or switch has an Uplink port, you can daisy-chain it by using a normal network cable. For more information about daisy-chaining hubs and switches, see the section "Hubs and Switches" later in this chapter.

If you study Table 9-3 long enough, then compare it with Table 9-2, you may notice that a crossover cable is actually a cable that's wired according to the 568A standard on one end and the 568B standard on the other end.

Table 9-3	Creating a crossover cable	
Pin	**Connector A**	**Connector B**
Pin 1	White/Green	White/orange
Pin 2	Green	Orange
Pin 3	White/Orange	White/green

(continued)

Table 9-3 *(continued)*

Pin	Connector A	Connector B
Pin 4	Blue	Blue
Pin 5	White/Blue	White/blue
Pin 6	Orange	Green
Pin 7	White/Brown	White/brown
Pin 8	Brown	Brown

Wall jacks and patch panels

If you want, you can run a single length of cable from a network hub or switch in a wiring closet through a hole in the wall, up the wall to the space above the ceiling, through the ceiling space to the wall in an office, down the wall, through a hole, and all the way to a desktop computer. That's not a good idea, however, for a variety of reasons. For one, every time someone moves the computer or even cleans behind it, the cable will get moved a little bit. Eventually, the connection will fail and the RJ-45 plug will have to be replaced. Then the cables in the wiring closet will quickly become a tangled mess.

The alternative is to put a *wall jack* in the wall at the user's end of the cable, and connect the other end of the cable to a *patch* panel. Then, the cable itself is completely contained within the walls and ceiling spaces. To connect a computer to the network, you plug one end of a patch cable (properly called a *station cable*) into the wall jack and plug the other end into the computer's network interface. In the wiring closet, you use a patch cable to connect the wall jack to the network hubs or switches. Figure 9-4 shows how this arrangement works.

Connecting a twisted-pair cable to a wall jack or a patch panel is similar to connecting it to an RJ-45 plug. However, you don't usually need any special tools. Instead, the back of the jack has a set of slots that you lay each wire across. You then snap a removable cap over the top of the slots and press it down. This forces the wires into the slots, where little metal blades pierce the insulation and establish the electrical contact.

When you connect the wire to a jack or patch panel, be sure to untwist as little of the wire as possible. If you untwist too much of the wire, the signals that pass through the wire may become unreliable.

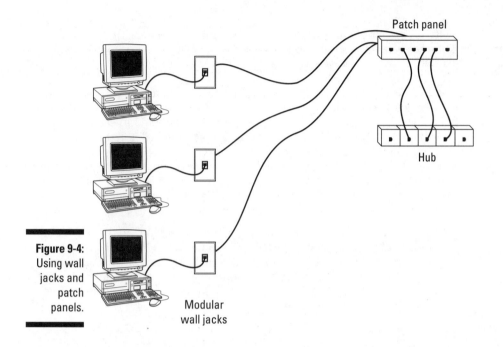

Figure 9-4:
Using wall
jacks and
patch
panels.

Patch panel

Hub

Modular
wall jacks

Hubs and Switches

When you use twisted-pair cable to wire a network, you don't plug the computers into each other. Instead, each computer plugs into a separate device called a *hub*. Years ago, hubs were expensive devices — expensive enough that most do-it-yourself networkers who were building *small* networks opted for coax cable instead of twisted-pair, because networks wired with coax cable don't require hubs.

Nowadays, the cost of hubs has dropped so much that the advantages of using twisted-pair cabling outweigh the hassle and cost of using hubs. With twisted-pair cabling, you can more easily add new computers to the network, move computers, find and correct cable problems, and service the computers that you need to remove from the network temporarily.

Hubs or switches?

A *switch* is simply a more sophisticated type of hub. Because the cost of switches has come down dramatically in the past few years, new networks are built with switches rather than hubs. If you have an older network that uses hubs and seems to run slowly, you may be able to improve the network's speed by replacing the older hubs with newer switches.

Switches are more efficient than hubs, but not just because they are faster. If you really want to know, here's the actual difference between a hub and a switch:

✔ In a hub, every packet that arrives at the hub on any of its ports is automatically sent out on every other port. The hub has to do this because it doesn't keep track of which computer is connected to each port. For example, suppose Wally's computer is connected to port 1 on an 8-port hub, and Ward's computer is connected to port 5. If Ward's computer sends a packet of information to Wally's computer, the hub receives the packet on port 1 and then sends it out on ports 2-8. All the computers connected to the hub get to see the packet so they can determine whether or not the packet was intended for them.

✔ A switch does keep track of which computer is connected to each port. So if Wally's computer on port 1 sends a packet to Ward's computer on port 5, the switch receives the packed on port 1 and then sends the packet out only on port 5. This is not only faster, but also improves the security of the system because other computers aren't shown packets that aren't meant for them.

Working with hubs and switches

You only need to know a few details when working with hubs and switches. Here they are, in no particular order:

✔ Installing a hub or switch is usually very simple. Just plug in the power cord and then plug in patch cables to connect the network.

✔ Each port on the hub or switch has an RJ-45 jack and a single LED indicator labeled *Link* that lights up when a connection has been established on the port. If you plug one end of a cable into the port and the other end into a computer or other network device, the Link light should come on. If it doesn't, something is wrong with the cable, the hub or switch port, or the device on the other end of the cable.

✔ Each port may also have an LED indicator that flashes to indicate network activity. If you stare at a hub or switch for a while, you can find out who uses the network most by noting which activity indicators flash the most.

✔ The ports may also have a Collision indicator that flashes whenever a packet collision occurs on the port. It's perfectly acceptable for this light to flash now and then, but if it flashes a lot, you may have a problem with the network. Usually this just means that the network is overloaded and should be segmented with a switch to improve performance. But in some cases, a flashing Collision indicator may be caused by a faulty network node that clogs up the network with bad packets.

Daisy-chaining hubs or switches

If a single hub or switch doesn't have enough ports for your entire network, you can connect hubs or switches together by *daisy-chaining* them, as shown in Figure 9-5. If one of the hubs or switches has an uplink port, you can use a normal patch cable to connect the uplink port to one of the regular ports on the other hub or switch. If neither device has an uplink port, use a crossover cable to connect them. (For instructions on making a crossover cable, see the section "Crossover cables," earlier in this chapter.)

On some hubs and switches, a button is used to switch one of the ports between a normal port and an uplink port. This button is often labeled MDI/MDIX. To use the port as a normal port, switch the button to the MDI position. To use the port as an uplink port, switch the button to MDIX.

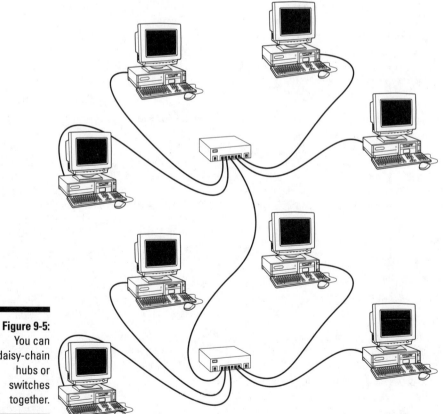

Figure 9-5:
You can
daisy-chain
hubs or
switches
together.

Some hubs and switches have a separate jack for the uplink port, but it turns out that the uplink port shares one of the normal ports internally. If that's the case, plugging a cable into the uplink port disables one of the normal ports. You shouldn't plug cables into both of these jacks. If you do, the hub or switch won't work properly.

Keep in mind these two simple rules when daisy-chaining hubs:

- The number of hubs that you can chain together is limited. For 10BaseT networks, you shouldn't connect more than three hubs to each other. For 100BaseT, you can chain only two hubs together.

- The cable you use to daisy-chain a 100BaseT hub can't be longer than 5 meters.

You can get around the first rule by using *stackable hubs.* Stackable hubs have a special type of cable connector that connects two or more hubs so they function as a single hub. Stackable hubs are a must for large networks.

If your building is pre-wired and has a network jack near each desk, you can use a small hub or switch to connect two or more computers to the network via a single jack. Just use one cable to plug the daisy-chain port of the hub into the wall jack, then plug each computer into one of the hub's ports.

Ten Base what?

The IEEE, in its infinite wisdom, has decreed that the following names shall be used to designate the various types of cable used with 802.3 networks (in other words, with Ethernet):

- 10Base5 is old-fashioned thick coaxial cable (the yellow stuff).

- 10Base2 is thin coaxial cable (Thinnet).

- 10BaseT is unshielded twisted-pair cable (UTP).

In each moniker, the number *10* means that the cable operates at 10 Mbps, and *Base* means that the cable is used for baseband networks as opposed to broadband networks (don't ask). The number *5* in 10Base5 is the maximum length of a yellow cable segment: 500 meters. The number *2* in 10Base2 stands for 200 meters, which is about the 185-meter maximum segment length for Thinnet cable. (For engineers, the IEEE is an odd bunch; I didn't know that the word *about* could be part of an engineer's vocabulary.) And the letter *T* in 10BaseT stands for *twisted.*

Of these three official monikers, 10BaseT is the only one used frequently; 10Base5 and 10Base2 are usually just called *thick* and *thin*, respectively.

Also, Fast Ethernet running over 10BaseT cabling uses the designation 100BaseT.

Network Interface Cards

Every computer that connects to your network must have a network interface. Most new computers come with a built-in network interface. But you may need to add a separate network interface card to older computers that don't have built-in interfaces. The following sections show you what you need to know to purchase and install a network interface card.

Picking a network interface card

You can buy inexpensive network interface cards at any computer supply store, and most large office supply stores also carry them. The following pointers should help you pick the right card for your system:

- ✔ The network interface cards that you use must have a connector that matches the type of cable that you use. If you plan on wiring your network with Thinnet cable, make sure that the network cards have a BNC connector. For twisted-pair wiring, make sure that the cards have an RJ-45 connector.

- ✔ Some network cards provide two or three connectors. I see them in every combination: BNC and AUI, RJ-45 and AUI, BNC and RJ-45, and all three. AUI connectors are pretty much obsolete. As for BNC connectors, get them only if your network has existing coax wiring. If it doesn't, cards that have just RJ-45 connectors will be adequate.

- ✔ Most newer network cards are designated as 10/100Mbps cards, which means they work on older 10Mbps networks as well as the 100Mbps variety. These cards automatically detect the network speed and switch accordingly. Ah, progress.

- ✔ When you purchase a network card, make sure that you get one that's compatible with your computer. Many older computers can accommodate cards designed for the standard 16-bit ISA bus. Newer computers can accommodate cards with that use the PCI bus. If your computer supports PCI, you should purchase a PCI card. Not only are PCI cards faster than ISA cards, they are also easier to configure. So you should use ISA cards only for older computers that can't accommodate PCI cards.

- ✔ Network cards can be a bit tricky to set up. Each different card has its own nuances. You can simplify your life a bit if you use the same card for every computer in your network. Try not to mix and match network cards.

- ✔ Some computers come with network interfaces built in. In that case, you don't have to worry about adding a network card.

Installing a network card

Installing a network interface card is a manageable task, but you have to be willing to roll up your sleeves. If you've installed one adapter card, you've installed them all. In other words, installing a network interface card is just like installing a modem, a new video-controller card, a sound card, or any other type of card. If you've ever installed one of these cards, you can probably install a network interface card blindfolded.

Here's a step-by-step procedure for installing a network interface card:

1. **Shut down Windows and then turn off the computer and unplug it.**

   Never work in your computer's insides with the power on or the power cord plugged in!

2. **Remove the cover from your computer.**

   Figure 9-6 shows the screws that you must typically remove in order to open the cover. Put the screws someplace where they won't wander off.

Remove these screws

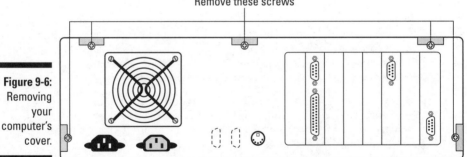

Figure 9-6:
Removing
your
computer's
cover.

3. **Find an unused expansion slot inside the computer.**

   The expansion slots are lined up in a neat row near the back of the computer; you can't miss 'em. Most newer computers have at least two or three slots known as *PCI slots.*

   Many older computers also have several slots known as *ISA slots.* You can distinguish ISA slots from PCI slots by noting the size of the slots. PCI slots are smaller than ISA slots, so you can't accidentally insert a PCI card in an ISA slot or vice versa.

   Some computers also have other types of slots — mainly VESA and EISA slots. Standard ISA or PCI networking cards won't fit into these types of slots, so don't try to force them.

4. **When you find the right type of slot that doesn't have a card in it, remove the metal slot protector from the back of the computer's chassis.**

   If a small retaining screw holds the slot protector in place, remove the screw and keep it in a safe place. Then, pull the slot protector out, and put the slot protector in a box with all your other old slot protectors. (After a while, you collect a whole bunch of slot protectors. Keep them as souvenirs or use them as Christmas-tree ornaments.)

5. **Insert the network interface card into the slot.**

   Line up the connectors on the bottom of the card with the connectors in the expansion slot, and then press the card straight down. Sometimes you have to press uncomfortably hard to get the card to slide into the slot.

6. **Secure the network interface card with the screw that you removed in Step 4.**

7. **Put the computer's case back together.**

   Watch out for the loose cables inside the computer; you don't want to pinch them with the case as you slide it back on. Secure the case with the screws that you removed in Step 2.

8. **Turn the computer back on.**

   If you're using a Plug and Play card with Windows, the card is automatically configured after you start the computer again. If you're working with an older computer or an older network interface card, you may need to run an additional software installation program. See the installation instructions that come with the network interface card for details.

Network starter kits

Often, the easiest way to buy the equipment that you need to build a network is to purchase a network starter kit. A typical network starter kit includes everything that you need to network two computers. To add additional computers, you purchase add-on kits that include everything that you need to add one computer to the network.

For example, suppose you want to network three computers in a small office. You could start with a two-computer network starter kit, which would include the following items:

✔ Two 10/100 Mbps auto-switching PCI Ethernet cards

✔ One 4-port Ethernet 100 Mbps switch

✔ Two 25-foot-long 10BaseT twisted-pair cables

✔ Software for the cards

✔ Instructions

This kit, which should set you back about $100, connects two of the three computers. To connect the third computer, purchase an add-on kit that includes a 10/100 auto-switching PCI Ethernet card, another 25-foot-long twisted-pair cable, software, and instructions — all for about $40.

Other Network Devices

In addition to network interface cards, cables, and hubs or switches, some networks may require one or more of the devices described in the following sections.

Repeaters

A *repeater* is a gizmo that gives your network signals a boost so that the signals can travel farther. It's kind of like the Gatorade stations in a marathon. As the signals travel past the repeater, they pick up a cup of Gatorade, take a sip, splash the rest of it on their heads, toss the cup, and hop in a cab when they're sure that no one is looking.

You need a repeater when the total length of a single span of network cable is larger than the maximum allowed for your cable type:

Cable	*Maximum Length*
10Base2 (coaxial)	185 meters or 606 feet
10/100BaseT (twisted-pair)	100 meters or 328 feet

For coaxial cable, the cable lengths given here apply to cable segments — not individual lengths of cable. A *segment* is the entire run of cable from one terminator to another and may include more than one computer. In other words, if you have ten computers and you connect them all with 25-foot lengths of thin coaxial cable, the total length of the segment is 225 feet. (Made you look! Only nine cables are required to connect ten computers — that's why it's not 250 feet.)

For 10BaseT or 100BaseT cable, the 100-meter length limit applies to the cable that connects a computer to the hub or the cable that connects hubs to each other when hubs are daisy-chained with twisted-pair cable. In other words, you can connect each computer to the hub with no more than 100 meters of cable, and you can connect hubs to each other with no more than 100 meters of cable.

Figure 9-7 shows how you can use a repeater to connect two groups of computers that are too far apart to be strung on a single segment. When you use a repeater like this, the repeater divides the cable into two segments. The cable length limit still applies to the cable on each side of the repeater.

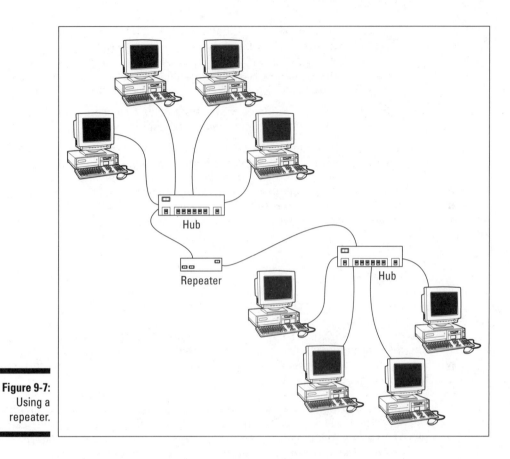

Figure 9-7:
Using a
repeater.

Here are some points to ponder when you lie awake tonight wondering about repeaters (who doesn't?):

✔ Repeaters are used only with Ethernet networks wired with coaxial cable; 10/100BaseT networks don't use repeaters.

Actually, that's not quite true: 10/100BaseT *does* use repeaters. It's just that the repeater isn't a separate device. In a 10/100BaseT network, the hub is actually a multiport repeater. That's why the cable used to attach each computer to the hub is considered a separate segment.

✔ Some 10/100BaseT hubs have a BNC connector on the back. This BNC connector is a Thinnet repeater that enables you to attach a full 185-meter Thinnet segment. The segment can attach other computers, 10BaseT hubs, or a combination of both.

✔ A basic rule of Ethernet life is that a signal can't pass through more than three repeaters on its way from one node to another. That doesn't mean you can't have more than three repeaters or hubs, but if you do, you have to carefully plan the network cabling so that the three-repeater rule isn't violated.

✔ A two-port 10Base2 repeater costs about $200. (Sheesh! I guess that's one of the reasons few people use coaxial cable anymore.)

✔ Repeaters are legitimate components of a by-the-book Ethernet network. They don't extend the maximum length of a single segment; they just enable you to tie two segments together. Beware of the little black boxes that claim to extend the segment limit beyond the standard 185-meter limit for Thinnet or the 100-meter limit for 10/100BaseT cable. These products usually work, but playing by the rules is better.

Bridges

A *bridge* is a device that connects two networks. Bridges are used to partition one large network into two smaller networks for performance reasons. You can think of a bridge as a kind of smart repeater. Repeaters listen to signals coming down one network cable, amplify them, and send them down the other cable. They do this blindly, paying no attention to the content of the messages that they repeat.

In contrast, a bridge is a little smarter about the messages that come down the pike. For starters, most bridges have the capability to listen to the network and automatically figure out the address of each computer on both sides of the bridge. Then the bridge can inspect each message that comes from one side of the bridge and broadcast it on the other side of the bridge, but only if the message is intended for a computer that's on the other side.

This key feature enables bridges to partition a large network into two smaller, more efficient networks. Bridges work best in networks that are highly segregated. For example, suppose your network consists of two distinct groups of users: the Marketing Department and the Accounting Department, each with their own servers.

A bridge would let you partition this network so that the Marketing side of the network isn't bogged down by Accounting, and vice-versa. The bridge automatically learns which computers are on each side of the bridge and forwards messages from the one side to the other only when necessary. The overall performance of both networks improves, although the performance of any network operation that has to travel over the bridge slows down a bit.

Here are a few additional things to consider about bridges:

- As I mentioned, some bridges also have the capability to translate the messages from one format to another. For example, if the Marketing folks build their network with Ethernet and the accountants use Token Ring, a bridge can tie the two together.

- You can get a basic bridge to partition two Ethernet networks for about $500 from mail-order suppliers. More sophisticated bridges can cost as much as $5,000 or more.

Routers

A *router* is like a bridge, but with a key difference. Bridges use actual hardware addresses (known as MAC addresses) to tell which network node each message is sent to so it can forward the message to the appropriate segment. However, a bridge doesn't have the ability to actually look inside the message to see what type of information is being sent. A router can. As a result, routers work at a higher level than bridges. Thus, routers can perform additional tasks such as filtering packets based on their content. (Note that many routers also have built-in bridging functions, so routers are often used as bridges.)

You can configure a network with several routers that can work cooperatively together. For example, some routers are able to monitor the network to determine the most efficient path for sending a message to its ultimate destination. If a part of the network is extremely busy, a router can automatically route messages along a less-busy route. In this respect, the router is kind of like a traffic reporter up in a helicopter. The router knows that the 101 is bumper-to-bumper all the way through Sunnyvale, so it sends the message on the 280 instead.

Here is some additional information about routers:

- Routers used to be expensive and used only on large networks. However, the price of small routers has dropped substantially in recent years, so they're now becoming common even on small networks.

- The functional distinctions between bridges and routers — and switches and hubs, for that matter — get blurrier all the time. *Multifunction routers*, which combine the functions of routers, bridges, hubs, and switches are often used to handle some of the chores that used to require separate devices.

- Some routers are nothing more than computers with delusions of grandeur — along with several network interface cards and special software to perform the router functions.

> ✔ Routers can also connect networks that are geographically distant from each other via a phone line (using modems) or ISDN.

> ✔ One of the main reasons for using routers is to connect a LAN to the Internet. Figure 9-8 shows a router used for this purpose.

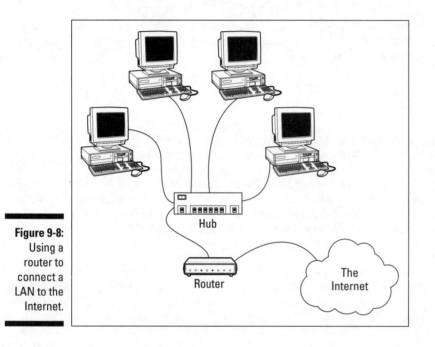

Figure 9-8:
Using a router to connect a LAN to the Internet.

Chapter 10

Setting Up a Wireless Network

. . . .

In This Chapter

▶ Looking at wireless network standards

▶ Reviewing some basic radio terms

▶ Considering infrastructure and ad-hoc networks

▶ Working with a wireless access point

▶ Worrying about wireless security

. . . .

Since the beginning of Ethernet networking, cable has been getting smaller and easier to work with. The original Ethernet cable was about as thick as your thumb, weighed a ton, and was difficult to bend around tight corners. Then came Thinnet cable, which was lighter and easier to work with. Thinnet cable was supplanted by unshielded twisted-pair (UTP) cable, which is lighter yet. UTP cable is still *cable,* though — which means you have to drill holes and pull cable through walls and ceilings in order to wire your entire home or office.

That's why *wireless networking* has become so popular. With wireless networking, you don't need cables to connect your computers. Instead, wireless networks use radio waves to send and receive network signals. As a result, a computer can connect to a wireless network at any location in your home or office.

Wireless networks are especially useful for notebook computers. After all, the main benefit of a notebook computer is that you can carry it around with you wherever you go. At work, you can use your notebook computer at your desk, in the conference room, in the break room, or even out in the parking lot. At home, you can use it in the bedroom, kitchen, den, game room, or out by the pool. With wireless networking, your notebook computer can be connected to the network, no matter where you take it.

This chapter introduces you to the ins and outs of setting up a wireless network. I tell you what you need to know about wireless networking standards, how to plan a wireless network, how to install and configure wireless network components, and how to create a network that mixes both wireless and cabled components.

Diving into Wireless Networking

A *wireless network* is a network that uses radio signals rather than direct cable connections to exchange information. A computer with a wireless network connection is like a cell phone. Just as you don't have to be connected to a phone line to use a cell phone, you don't have to be connected to a network cable to use a wireless networked computer.

The following paragraphs summarize some of the key concepts and terms that you need to understand in order to set up and use a basic wireless network:

✔ The most common type of wireless technology is called *Wi-Fi*. Technically, Wi-Fi refers to wireless Ethernet implemented according to a standard called 802.11b. Wi-Fi networking is now becoming so commonplace that you can buy wireless devices at home improvement stores like Home Depot. For more information about wireless standards including Wi-Fi, see the section "Eight-Oh-Two-Dot-Eleventy Something? (Or, Understanding Wireless Standards)," later in this chapter, for more information.

✔ A wireless network is also sometimes referred to as a *WLAN,* for *wireless local-area network.* Some people prefer to switch the acronym around to *local-area wireless network,* or *LAWN.*

✔ A wireless network has a name, known as a SSID. *SSID* stands for *service set identifier* — wouldn't that make a great *Jeopardy!* question? (I'll take obscure four-letter acronyms for $400, please!) All computers that belong to a single wireless network must have the same SSID.

✔ Wireless networks can transmit over any of several channels. In order for computers to talk to each other, they must be configured to transmit on the same channel.

✔ The simplest type of wireless network consists of two or more computers with wireless network adapters. This type of network is called an *ad-hoc mode network.*

✔ A more complex type of network is an *infrastructure mode network.* All this really means is that a group of wireless computers can be connected not only to each other, but also to an existing cabled network via a device called a *wireless access point,* or WAP. (I tell you more about ad-hoc and infrastructure networks later in this chapter.)

A Little High-School Electronics

I was a real nerd in high school: I took three years of electronics. The electronics class at my school was right next door to the auto shop. Of course, all the cool kids took auto shop and only nerds like me took electronics. We hung in there, though, and learned all about capacitors and diodes while the cool kids were learning how to raise their cars and install 2-Gigawatt stereo systems.

It turns out that a little of that high-school electronics information proves useful when it comes to wireless networking. Not much, mind you. But you'll understand wireless networking much better if you know the meanings of some basic radio terms.

Waves and frequencies

For starters, *radio* consists of electromagnetic waves that are sent through the atmosphere. You can't see or hear them, but radio receivers can pick them up and convert them into sounds, images, or — in the case of wireless networks — data.

Radio waves are actually cyclical waves of electromagnetic energy that repeat at a particular rate, called the *frequency.* Figure 10-1 shows two frequencies of radio waves: the first is one cycle per second; the second is two cycles per second. (Real radio doesn't operate at that low of a frequency, but I figured one and two cycles per second would be easier to draw than 680,000 cycles per second or 2.4 million cycles per second.)

The measure of a frequency is *cycles per second,* which indicates how many complete cycles the wave makes in one second (duh). In honor of Heinrich Hertz, the first person to successfully send and receive radio waves (it happened in the 1880s), *cycles per second* is usually referred to as *Hertz,* abbreviated *Hz.* Thus, 1 Hz is one cycle per second. Incidentally, when the prefix *K* (for *Kilo,* or 1,000), *M* (for *Mega,* 1 million), or *G* (for *Giga,* 1 billion) is added to the front of Hz, the *H* is still capitalized. Thus, 2.4GHz is correct (not 2.4Ghz).

The beauty of radio frequencies is that transmitters can be tuned to broadcast radio waves at a precise frequency. Likewise, receivers can be tuned to receive radio waves at a precise frequency, ignoring waves at other frequencies. That's why you can tune the radio in your car to listen to dozens of different radio stations: Each station broadcasts at its own frequency.

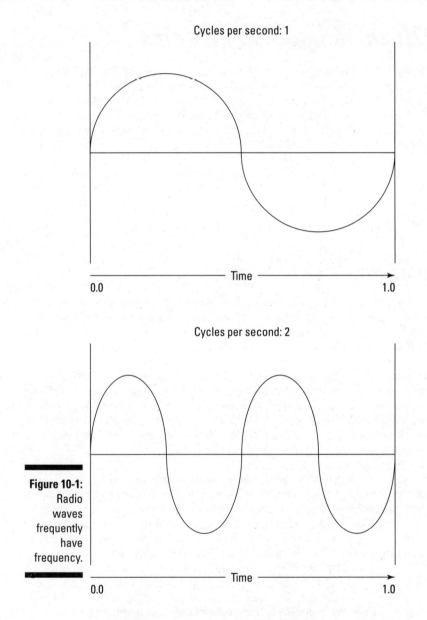

Cycles per second: 1

0.0 ——————— Time ———————→ 1.0

Figure 10-1:
Radio
waves
frequently
have
frequency.

Cycles per second: 2

0.0 ——————— Time ———————→ 1.0

Wavelength and antennas

A term related to frequency is *wavelength*. Radio waves travel at the speed of light. The term *wavelength* refers to how far the radio signal travels with each cycle. For example, since the speed of light is roughly 300,000,000 meters per second, the wavelength of a 1Hz radio wave is about 300,000,000 meters. The wavelength of a 2Hz signal is about 150,000,000 meters.

As you can see, the wavelength decreases as the frequency increases. The wavelength of a typical AM radio station broadcasting at 580KHz is about 500 meters. For a TV station broadcasting at 100MHz, it's about 3 meters. For a wireless network broadcasting at 2.4GHz, the wavelength is about a 12 centimeters.

It turns out that the shorter the wavelength, the smaller the antenna needs to be in order to adequately receive the signal. As a result, higher-frequency transmissions need smaller antennas. You may have noticed that AM radio stations usually have huge antennas mounted on top of tall towers, but cell-phone transmitters are much smaller and their towers aren't nearly as tall. That's because cell phones operate on a higher frequency than do AM radio stations. So who decides what type of radio gets to use specific frequencies? That's where spectra and the FCC come in.

Getting a spectrum via the FCC

The term *spectrum* (plural: *spectra*) refers to a continuous range of frequencies on which radio can operate. In the United States, the Federal Communications Commission (FCC) regulates how various portions of the radio spectrum can be used. Essentially, the FCC has divided the radio spectrum into dozens of small ranges called *bands* and restricted certain uses to certain bands. For example, AM radio operates in the band from 535KHz to 1,700KHz.

Table 10-1 lists some of the most popular bands. Note that some of these bands are wide — for example, UHF television begins at 470MHz and ends at 806MHz, but other bands are restricted to a specific frequency. The difference between the lowest and highest frequency within a band is called the *bandwidth*.

Table 10-1	Popular bands of the radio spectrum
Band	*Use*
535KHz – 1,700KHz	AM radio
5.9MHz – 26.1MHz	Short wave radio
26.96MHz – 27.41MHz	Citizens Band (CB) radio
54MHz – 88MHz	Television (VHF channels 2 through 6)
88MHz – 108MHz	FM radio
174MHz – 220MHz	Television (VHF channels 7 through 13)
470MHz – 806MHz	Television (UHF channels)
806MHz – 890MHz	Cellular networks
900MHz	Cordless phones

(continued)

Table 10-1 (continued)	
Band	**Use**
1850MHz – 1990MHz	PCS Cellular
2.4GHz - 2.4835GHz	Cordless phones and wireless networks (802.11b and 802.11g)
4GHz – 5GHz	Large dish satellite TV
5GHz	Wireless networks (802.11a)
11.7GHz – 12.7GHz	Small dish satellite TV

Two of the bands in the spectrum are allocated for use by wireless networks: 2.4 GHz and 5 GHz. Note that these bands aren't devoted exclusively to wireless networks. In particular, the 2.4GHz band shares its space with cordless phones and other devices like wireless speakers, wireless cable TV extenders, and who knows what else. As a result, cordless phones can sometimes interfere with wireless networks.

Eight-Oh-Two-Dot-Eleventy Something? (Or, Understanding Wireless Standards)

The most popular standards for wireless networks are the IEEE 802.11 standards. These standards are essential wireless Ethernet standards and use many of the same networking techniques that the cabled Ethernet standards (in other words, 802.3) use. Most notably, 802.11 networks use the same basic transmission technique to recover from data collisions (called CSMA/CD) as cabled Ethernet.

The original 802.11 standard was adopted in 1997. Two additions to the standard, 802.11a and 802.11b, were adopted in 1999, and the latest standard — 802.11g — was adopted in 2003.

Table 10-2 summarizes the basic characteristics of the three variants of 802.11.

Table 10-2		802.11 Variations	
Standard	**Speeds**	**Frequency**	**Typical Range (Indoors)**
802.11a	Up to 54 Mbps	5 GHz	150 feet
802.11b	Up to 11 Mbps	2.4 GHz	300 feet
802.11g	Up to 54 Mbps	2.4 GHz	300 feet

Currently, most wireless networks are based on the 802.11b standard. Although 802.11a is faster than 802.11b, it is considerably more expensive and has less range. In addition, 802.11a and 802.11b aren't compatible with each other because 802.11a transmits at 5 GHz and 802.11b transmits at 2.4 GHz. As a result, 802.11a and 802.11b devices can't receive each other's signals.

The new standard, 802.11g, solves this problem by enabling high-speed connections at 2.4 GHz. As a result, 802.11g devices are compatible with existing 802.11b networks.

802.11b networks operate on the same radio frequency as many cordless phones: 2.4 GMHz. If you set up an 802.11b network in your home and you also have a 2.4GHz cordless phone, you may find that the network and phone occasionally interfere with each other. The only way to completely avoid the interference is to switch to a 900MHz phone or use more expensive 802.11a network components, which transmit at 5 GHz rather than 2.4 GHz.

Home on the Range

The maximum range of an 802.11b wireless device indoors is about 300 feet. This can have an interesting effect when you get a bunch of wireless computers together — such that some of them are in range of each other, but others are not. For example, suppose that Wally, Ward, and the Beaver all have wireless notebooks. Wally's computer is 200 feet away from Ward's computer, and Ward's computer is 200 feet away from Beaver's in the opposite direction (see Figure 10-2). In this case, Ward can access both Wally's computer and Beaver's computer, but Wally can access only Ward's computer, and Beaver can access only Ward's computer. In other words, Wally and Beaver won't be able to access each other's computers, because they're not within range of each other. (This is starting to sound suspiciously like an algebra problem. Now suppose that Wally starts walking towards Ward at 2 miles per hour, and Beaver starts running towards Ward at 4 miles per hour . . .)

Although the normal range for 802.11b is 300 feet, the range may be less in actual practice. Obstacles such as solid walls, bad weather, cordless phones, microwave ovens, backyard nuclear reactors, and so on can all conspire together to reduce the effective range of a wireless adapter. If you're having trouble connecting to the network, sometimes just adjusting the antenna helps.

Also, wireless networks tend to slow down when the distance increases. 802.11b network devices claim to operate at 11Mbps, but they usually achieve that speed only at ranges of 100 feet or less. At 300 feet, they often slow down to 1Mbps. You should also realize that when you're at the edge of the wireless device's range, you're more likely to suddenly lose your connection due to bad weather.

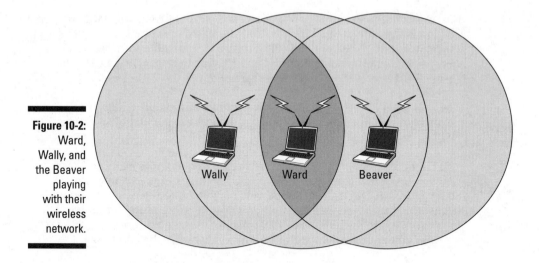

Figure 10-2:
Ward,
Wally, and
the Beaver
playing
with their
wireless
network.

Wireless Network Adapters

Each computer that you plan to connect to your wireless network needs a *wireless network adapter*. The wireless network adapter is similar to the network interface card (NIC) used for a standard Ethernet connection. However, instead of having a cable connector on the back, a wireless network adapter has an antenna. Makes sense.

You can get several basic types of wireless network adapters, depending on your needs and the type of computer you will use it with:

✔ **Wireless PCI card:** This card is a wireless network adapter that you install into an available slot inside a desktop computer. To install this type of card, you have to take your computer apart. So use this type of card only if you have the expertise and the nerves to dig into your computer's guts.

✔ **Wireless USB adapter:** This is a separate box that plugs into a USB port on your computer. Because the USB adapter is a separate device, it takes up extra desk space. However, you can install it without taking your computer apart.

✔ **Wireless PC card:** This card — designed to slide into the PC card slot found in most notebook computers — is what to get if you want to network your notebook.

You can purchase an 802.11b wireless PCI adapter for about $40. USB 802.11b adapters cost about $50, as do PC card 802.11 adapters for notebooks. You can expect to pay about $25 more for an equivalent 802.11g adapter.

At first, you may think that wireless network adapters are prohibitively expensive. After all, you can buy a regular Ethernet adapter for as little as $20. However, when you consider that you don't have to purchase and install all that cable to use a wireless adapter, the price of wireless networking becomes more palatable.

Figure 10-3 shows a typical wireless network adapter. This one is a Linksys WUSB11, which sells for about $60. To install this device, you simply connect it to one of your computer's USB ports with the included USB connector. You then install the driver software that comes on the CD, and you're ready to network. The device is relatively small. You'll find a little strip of Velcro on the back, which you can use to mount it on the side of your computer or desk if you want. The adapter gets its power from the USB port itself, so there's no separate power cord to plug in.

Figure 10-3:
A Linksys
WUSB11
USB 802.11b
Wireless
networking
adapter.

Wireless Access Points

Unlike cabled networks, wireless networks don't need a hub or switch. If all you want to do is network a group of wireless computers, you just purchase a wireless adapter for each computer, put them all within 300 feet of each other, and *voilà!* — instant network.

But what if you already have an existing cabled network? For example, suppose you work at an office with 15 computers all cabled up nicely, and you just want to add a couple of wireless notebook computers to the network. Or suppose you have two computers in your den connected to each other with network cable, but you want to link up a computer in your bedroom without pulling cable through the attic.

That's where a *wireless access point,* also known as a *WAP* comes in. It's a box that has an antenna (or pair of antennae) and an RJ-45 Ethernet port. You just plug it into a network cable, and then plug the other end of the cable into a hub or switch, and your wireless network should be able to connect to your cabled network. A WAP actually performs two functions.

- ✔ It acts as a central connection point for all of your computers that have wireless network adapters. In effect, the WAP performs the same function that a hub or switch performs for a wired network.

- ✔ It links your wireless network to your existing wired network so your wired computer and your wireless computers get along like one big happy family.

Wireless access points are sometimes just called *access points,* or *APs.*

Figure 10-4 shows how an access point acts as a central connection point for wireless computers — and how it bridges (that is, connects) your wireless network to your wired network.

Infrastructure mode

When you set up a wireless network with an access point, you are creating an *infrastructure mode* network. It's called *infrastructure mode* because the access point provides a permanent infrastructure for the network. The access points are installed at fixed physical locations, so the network has relatively stable boundaries. Whenever a mobile computer wanders into the range of one of the access points, it has come into the sphere of the network and can connect.

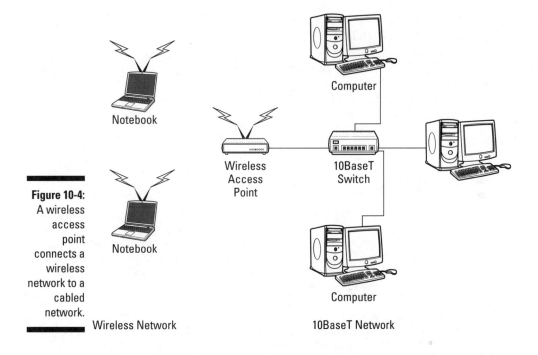

Figure 10-4:
A wireless access point connects a wireless network to a cabled network.

Notebook

Notebook

Wireless Access Point

Computer

10BaseT Switch

Computer

Wireless Network

10BaseT Network

An access point and all of the wireless computers that are connected to it are referred to as a *Basic Service Set,* or *BSS.* Each BSS is identified by a *Service Set Identifier,* or *SSID.* When you configure an access point, you specify the SSID that you want to use. The SSID is often a generic name such as *wireless,* or it can be a name that you create. Some access points use the MAC address of the WAP as the SSID.

Multifunction WAPs

Wireless access points often include other built-in features. For example, some access points double as Ethernet hubs or switches; some include broadband cable or DSL firewall routers that enable you to connect to the Internet. I have a Linksys BEFW11S4 wireless access point router in my home. This inexpensive (about $80) device includes the following features:

✔ An 802.11b wireless access point that lets me connect a notebook computer and a computer located on the other side of the house because I didn't want to run cable through the attic.

✔ A four-port 10/100MHz switch that I can connect up to four computers to via twisted-pair cable.

✔ A DSL/cable router that I connect to my cable modem. This enables all the computers on the network (cabled and wireless) to access the Internet.

A multifunction access point will have more than one RJ-45 port. If it's designed to serve as an Internet gateway for home networks, it's sometimes called a *residential gateway.*

Roaming

You can use two or more wireless access points to create a large wireless network in which computer users can roam from area to area and still be connected to the same wireless network. As the user moves out of range of one access point, another access point automatically picks up the user and takes over without interrupting the user's network service. (This is similar to the way cell phone "roaming" works.)

To set up two or more access points for roaming, you must carefully place the WAPs so that all areas of the office or building that are being networked are in range of at least one of the WAPs. Then, just make sure that all of the computers and access points use the same SSID and channel.

Two or more access points joined for the purposes of roaming, along with all of the wireless computers connected to any of the access points, form what's called an *Extended Service Set,* or *ESS.* The access points in the ESS are usually connected to a wired network.

One of the current limitations of roaming is that each access point in an ESS must be on the same TCP/IP subnet. That way, a computer that roams from one access point to another within the ESS retains the same IP address. If the access points had a different subnet, a roaming computer would have to change IP addresses when it moved from one access point to another.

Wireless bridging

Another use for wireless access points is to bridge separate subnets that can't easily be connected by cable. For example, suppose that you have two office buildings that are only about 50 feet apart. To run cable from one building to the other, you'd have to bury conduit — a potentially expensive job. Because the buildings are so close, though, you can probably connect them with a pair of wireless access points that function as a *wireless bridge* between the two networks. Connect one of the access points to the first network and the other access point to the second network. Then configure both access points to use the same SSID and channel.

Ad-hoc Networks

A wireless access point is not necessary to set up a wireless network. Any time two or more wireless devices come within range of each other, they can link up to form an *ad-hoc network*. For example, if you and a few of your friends all have notebook computers with 802.11b wireless network adapters, you can meet anywhere and form an ad-hoc network.

All of the computers within range of each other in an ad-hoc network are called an *Independent Basic Service Set,* or *IBSS.*

Configuring a Wireless Access Point

The physical setup for a wireless access point is pretty simple: You take it out of the box, put it on a shelf or on top of a bookcase near a network jack and a power outlet, plug in the power cable, and plug in the network cable.

The software configuration for an access point is a little more involved, but still not very complicated. It's usually done via a Web interface. To get to the configuration page for the access point, you need to know the access point's IP address. Then, you just type that address into the address bar of a browser from any computer on the network. For example, Figure 10-5 shows the main configuration page for a Linksys wireless access point set up for use as a router.

This configuration page offers the following configuration options that are related to the wireless access point functions of the device. Although the options given here are specific to this particular device, most access points have configuration options similar to these:

- **Enable/Disable:** Enables or disables the device's wireless-access-point functions.

- **SSID:** The Service Set Identifier used to identify the network. Most access points have well-known defaults. You can talk yourself into thinking that your network is more secure by changing the SSID from the default to something more obscure, but in reality, that protects you only from first-grade hackers. By the time most hackers get into the second grade, they learn that even the most obscure SSID is easy to get around. So I recommend that you leave the SSID at the default and apply better security measures, as described in the next section.

- **Allow broadcast SSID to associate?** Disables the access point's periodic broadcast of the SSID. Normally, the access point regularly broadcasts its SSID so that wireless devices that come within range can detect the network and join in. For a more secure network, you can disable this function. Then, a wireless client must already know the network's SSID in order to join the network.

✔ **Channel:** Lets you select one of 11 channels on which to broadcast. All of the access points and computers in the wireless network should use the same channel. If you find that your network is frequently losing connections, try switching to another channel. You may be experiencing interference from a cordless phone or other wireless device operating on the same channel.

Switching channels is also a friendly way for neighbors with wireless networks to stay out of each other's way. For example, if you share a building with another tenant who also has a wireless network, you can agree to use separate channels so your wireless networks don't interfere with each other. Keep in mind that this doesn't give you any real measure of security because your neighbor could secretly switch *back* to your channel and listen in on your network. So you still need to secure your network as described in the next chapter.

✔ **WEP — Mandatory or Disable:** Lets you use a security protocol called *wired-equivalent privacy*. I have more to say about this later in this chapter, in next section.

Figure 10-5:
The main configuration page for a Linksys wireless access point that functions as a router.

Securing a Wireless Network

Before you dive headfirst into the deep end of the wireless networking pool, you should first consider the security risks that are inherent in setting up a wireless network. With a cabled network, the best security tool you have is the lock on the front door of your office. Unless someone can physically get to one of the computers on your network, he or she can't get into your network. (Well, we're sort of ignoring your wide-open broadband Internet connection for the sake of argument.)

If you go wireless, an intruder doesn't have to get into your office to hack into your network. He or she can do it from the office next door. Or the lobby. Or the parking garage beneath your office. Or the sidewalk outside. In short, when you introduce wireless devices into your network, you usher in a whole new set of security issues to deal with.

The following sections explore some of the basic security issues that come with the territory when you go wireless.

Understanding wireless security threats

Wireless networks have the same basic security considerations as wired networks. As a network administrator, you need to balance the need of legitimate users to access network resources against the risk of illegitimate users breaking into your network. That's the basic dilemma of network security. Whether the network uses cables, wireless devices, kite strings and tin cans, or smoke signals, the basic issues are the same.

The following paragraphs describe the most likely types of security threats that wireless networks encounter. You should take each of these kinds of threats into consideration when you plan your network's security.

- **Intruders:** With a wired network, an intruder must usually gain access to your facility to physically connect to your network. Not so with a wireless network. With wireless, anyone with a notebook that has wireless-network capability can gain access to your network if they can place themselves physically within range of your network's radio signals. There are all sorts of possibilities: nearby offices, the floor immediately above or below you, the lobby outside of your office building, the parking lot, or even the building next door.

- **Freeloaders:** *Freeloaders* are intruders who want to piggyback on your wireless network to get free access to the Internet. If they manage to gain access to your wireless network, they probably won't do anything malicious: They'll just fire up their Web browsers and surf the Internet.

These are folks who are too cheap to spend $45 per month on their own broadband connection at home; they'd rather drive into your parking lot and steal yours.

✔ **Eavesdroppers:** *Eavesdroppers* just like to listen to your network traffic. They don't actually try to gain access via your wireless network — at least, not at first. They just listen. Unfortunately, wireless networks give them plenty to listen to, including user names, passwords, files, and perhaps personal information such as credit-card numbers.

✔ **Jammers:** A *jammer* is a hacker who gets kicks from jamming networks so they become unusable. This is usually done by flooding the network with meaningless traffic so that legitimate traffic gets lost in the flow. They might also try to place viruses or worm programs on your network via an unsecured wireless connection.

✔ **Rogue access points:** A *rogue access point* is an access point that suddenly appears out of nowhere on your network. What usually happens is that an employee decides he or she would like to connect a notebook computer to the network via a wireless computer. So the user stops at Computers-R-Us on the way home from work one day, buys a simple wireless access port for $75, and plugs it into the network — without asking permission. Now, in spite of all the elaborate security precautions you've taken to fence in your network, this well-meaning user has opened the barn door. It's *very* unlikely that the user will enable the security features of the wireless access point; in fact, he or she probably isn't even *aware* of the security implications. (Gee — you mean setting up an unprotected access point is *risky* for company data? Ya think?)

✔ **War drivers:** *War driving* refers to the practice of driving around town with notebook computers just looking for open access to wireless networks just to see what networks are out there. Some war drivers even make maps and put them on the Internet.

Securing your wireless network

With any luck (and a little reflection), you're probably convinced that wireless networks do indeed pose many security risks. Don't despair. Here's a quick list of steps you can take to help secure your wireless network:

✔ **Changing the password:** Probably the first thing you should do when you install a wireless access point is change its administrative password. Most access points have a built-in Web-based setup page you can access from any Web browser to configure the access point's configuration settings. The setup page is protected by a user name and password. However, the user name and password are initially set to default values that are easy to guess. You should change them so users won't be able to access your configuration page by using the default passwords.

✔ **Securing the SSID:** The next step is to secure the SSID that identifies the network. A client must know the access point's SSID in order to join the wireless network. If you can prevent unauthorized clients from discovering the SSID, you can prevent them from accessing your network.

There are three things you can do to secure your SSID:

- Change the SSID from the default value (yeah, I know I said doing that won't keep hackers out by itself, but it's worth doing as *part* of a security plan).

- Disable the automatic broadcast of the SSID so client computers have to know the SSID before they can connect.

- Disable guest mode, which allows computers to join the network without knowing the SSID.

✔ **Enabling WEP:** WEP stands for *wired-equivalent privacy,* a data-encryption feature designed to make wireless transmission as secure as transmission over a network cable by scrambling data before transmission. You should make sure this feature is enabled.

✔ **Using MAC address filtering:** MAC address filtering allows you to specify a list of hardware MAC addresses for the computers that are allowed to access the network. If a computer with a different address tries to join the network via the access point, the access point will deny access. MAC address filtering is a great idea for wireless networks with a fixed number of clients. For example, if you set up a wireless network at your office so a few workers can connect their notebook computers, you can specify the MAC addresses of those computers in the *MAC filtering table.* Then no other computers can access the network via the access point.

✔ **Placing your access points outside the firewall:** The most effective security technique for wireless networking is to place all of your wireless access points *outside* your network's firewall. That way, all network traffic from wireless users will have to travel through the firewall to access the network. For more information about firewalls, refer to Chapter 13.

Chapter 11

Configuring Client Computers

*B*efore your network setup is complete, you must configure the network's client computers. In particular, you have to configure each client's network interface card so it works properly, and you have to install the right protocols so the clients can communicate with other computers on the network.

Fortunately, the task of configuring client computers for the network is child's play with Windows. For starters, Windows automatically recognizes your network interface card when you start up your computer. All that remains is to make sure that Windows properly installed the network protocols and client software.

With each version of Windows, Microsoft has simplified the process of configuring client network support. In this chapter, I describe the steps for configuring networking for Windows XP. (Configuration for other versions of Windows is similar.)

Configuring Network Connections

Windows automatically detects the presence of a network adapter; normally you don't have to install device drivers manually for the adapter. When Windows detects a network adapter, it automatically creates a network connection and configures it to support basic networking protocols. However, you may need to change the configuration of a network connection manually. The following steps show how to configure your network connection:

1. **Click Start⇨Control Panel to open the Control Panel.**

   The Control Panel appears.

2. **Double-click the Network Connections icon.**

   The Network Connections folder appears, as shown in Figure 11-1.

Figure 11-1:
The
Network
Connections
folder.

3. **Right-click the connection that you want to configure, and then choose Properties from the menu that appears.**

   You can also select the network connection and click Change Settings of This Connection from the task pane. Either way, the Properties dialog box for the network connection appears, as shown in Figure 11-2.

4. **To configure the network adapter card settings, click Configure.**

   This action summons the Properties dialog box for the network adapter, as shown in Figure 11-3. This dialog box has five tabs that let you configure the NIC:

   • **General:** This tab shows basic information about the NIC, such as the device type and status. For example, the device shown in Figure 11-3 is a D-Link DFE-530TX+ PCI Adapter (it's installed in slot 3 of the computer's PCI bus). If you are having trouble with the adapter, you can click the Troubleshoot button to call up the Windows XP Hardware Troubleshooter. You can also disable the device if it is preventing other components of the computer from working properly.

- **Advanced:** This tab lets you set a variety of device-specific parameters that affect the operation of the NIC. For example, some cards allow you to set the speed parameter (typically at 10Mbps or 100Mbps) or the number of buffers the card should use.

Consult the manual that came with the card before you play around with any of those settings.

- **Driver:** This tab displays information about the device driver that is bound to the NIC and lets you update the driver to a newer version, roll back the driver to a previously working version, or uninstall the driver.

- **Resources:** With this tab, you can use manual settings to limit the system resources used by the card — including the memory range, I/O range, IRQ, and DMA channels. In the old days, before Plug and Play cards, you had to configure these settings whenever you installed a card, and it was easy to create resource conflicts. Windows configures these settings automatically so you should rarely need to fiddle with them.

- **Power Management:** This tab lets you set power-management options. You can specify that the network card be shut down when the computer goes into sleep mode — and that the computer wake up periodically to refresh its network state.

When you click OK to dismiss the network adapter's Properties dialog box, the network connection's Properties dialog box closes. You'll need to click Change Settings for This Connection again to continue the procedure.

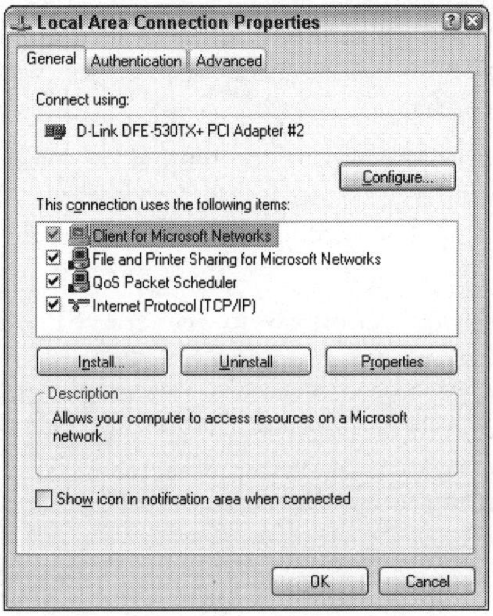

Figure 11-2:
The Properties dialog box for a network connection.

Figure 11-3:
The
Properties
dialog box
for a
network
adapter.

5. **Make sure that the network items that your client requires are listed in the network connection Properties dialog box.**

The following paragraphs describe the items you'll commonly see listed here. Note that not all networks need all of these items.

- **Client for Microsoft Networks:** This item is required if you want to access a Microsoft Windows network. It should always be present.

- **File and Printer Sharing for Microsoft Networks:** This item allows your computer to share its files or printers with other computers on the network. This option is usually used with peer-to-peer networks, but you can use it even if your network has dedicated servers. However, if you don't plan to share files or printers on the client computer, you should disable this item.

- **Internet Protocol (TCP/IP):** This item enables the client computer to communicate via the TCP/IP protocol. If all servers on the network support TCP/IP, this should be the only protocol installed on the client.

- **NWLink IPX/SPX/NetBIOS Compatible Transport Protocol:** This protocol is required only if your network needs to connect to an older NetWare network that uses the IPX/SPX protocol. In most modern networks, you should enable TCP/IP only and leave this item disabled.

6. **If a protocol that you need isn't listed, click the Install button to add the needed protocol.**

   A dialog box appears, asking whether you want to add a network client, protocol, or service. Click Protocol and then click Add. A list of available protocols appears. Select the one you want to add; then click OK. (You may be asked to insert a disk or the Windows CD-ROM.)

7. **Make sure that the network client that you want to use appears in the list of network resources.**

   For a Windows-based network, make sure that Client for Microsoft Networks is listed. For a NetWare network, make sure that Client Service for NetWare appears. If your network uses both types of servers, you can choose both clients.

   If you have NetWare servers, use the NetWare client software that comes with NetWare rather than the client supplied by Microsoft with Windows.

8. **If the client that you need isn't listed, click the Install button to add the client that you need, click Client, and then click Add. Then choose the client that you want to add and click OK.**

   The client you selected is added to the network connection's Properties dialog box.

9. **To remove a network item that you don't need (such as File and Printer Sharing for Microsoft Networks), select the item and click the Uninstall button.**

   For security reasons, you should make it a point to remove any clients, protocols, or services that you don't need.

10. **To configure TCP/IP settings, click Internet Protocol (TCP/IP) and click Properties to display the TCP/IP Properties dialog box. Adjust the settings, and then click OK.**

    The TCP/IP Properties dialog box, shown in Figure 11-4, lets you choose from the following options:

    - **Obtain an IP address automatically:** Choose this option if your network has a DHCP server that assigns IP addresses automatically. Choosing this option drastically simplifies the administering TCP/IP on your network. (See Chapter 25 for more information about DHCP.)

    - **Use the following IP address:** If your computer must have a specific IP address, choose this option, and then type in the computer's IP address, subnet mask, and default gateway address. (For more information about these settings, see Chapter 24.)

- **Obtain DNS server address automatically:** The DHCP server can also provide the address of the Domain Name System (DNS) server that the computer should use. Choose this option if your network has a DHCP server. (See Chapter 25 for more information about DNS.)

- **Use the following DNS server addresses:** Choose this option if a DNS server is not available. Then type the IP address of the primary and secondary DNS servers.

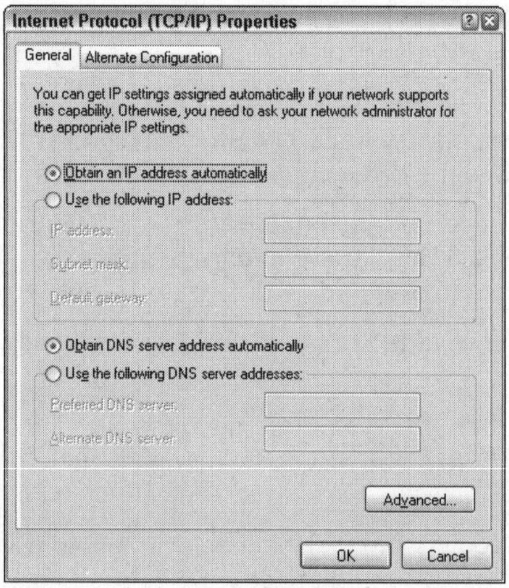

Figure 11-4:
Configuring
TCP/IP.

Configuring Client Computer Identification

Every client computer must identify itself in order to participate in the network. The computer identification consists of the computer's name, an optional description, and the name of either the workgroup or the domain to which the computer belongs.

The computer name must follow the rules for NetBIOS names; it may be 1 to 15 characters long and may contain letters, numbers, or hyphens, but no spaces or periods. For small networks, it's common to make the computer name the same as the user name. For larger networks, you may want to develop a naming scheme that identifies the computer's location. For example, a name such as C-305-1 may be assigned to the first computer in Room 305 of Building C. Or MKTG010 may be a computer in the marketing department.

If the computer will join a domain, you will need to have access to an Administrator account on the domain unless the administrator has already created a computer account on the domain. Note that only Windows 2000, Windows XP, and Windows server (NT, 2000, and 2003) computers can join a domain. (Windows 98 or 95 users can still access the domain's resources by logging on to the domain as users, but domain computer accounts for Windows 9*x* clients are not required.)

When you install Windows on the client system, the Setup program asks for the computer name and workstation or domain information. You can change this information later if you want. To change the computer identification, follow these steps:

1. **Open the Control Panel and double-click the System icon to bring up the System Properties dialog box.**

2. **Click the Computer Name tab.**

   The computer identification information is displayed.

3. **Click the Change button.**

   This displays the Computer Name Changes dialog box, as shown in Figure 11-5.

Figure 11-5: The Computer Name Changes dialog box (Windows XP).

4. **Type the new computer name, and then specify the workgroup or domain information.**

   To join a domain, select the Domain radio button and type the domain name into the appropriate text box. To join a workgroup, select the

Workgroup radio button, and type the workgroup name in the corresponding text box.

5. **Click OK.**

6. **If prompted, enter the user name and password for an Administrator account.**

   You'll be asked to provide this information only if a computer account has not already been created for the client computer.

7. **When a dialog box appears, informing you that you need to restart the computer, click OK. Then restart the computer.**

   You're done!

Configuring Network Logon

Every user who wants to access a domain-based network must log on to the domain by using a valid user account. The user account is created on the domain controller — not on the client computer.

Network logon isn't required to access workgroup resources. Instead, work-group resources can be password-protected to restrict access.

When you start a Windows computer that has been configured to join a domain, as described in the section "Configuring Client Computer Identifica-tion" earlier in this chapter, the Log On to Windows dialog box is displayed. The user can use this dialog box to log on to a domain by entering a domain user name and password, and then selecting the domain that he or she wants to log on to (from the Log On To drop-down list).

You can create local user accounts in Windows that allow users to access resources on the local computer. To log on to the local computer, the user selects This Computer from the Log On To drop-down list and enters the user name and password for a local user account. When a user logs on by using a local account, he or she is not connected to a network domain. To log on to a domain, the user must select the domain from the Log On To drop-down list.

If the computer is not part of a domain, Windows can display a friendly logon screen that displays an icon for each of the computer's local users. The user can log on simply by clicking the appropriate icon and entering a password. (This feature is not available for computers that have joined a domain.)

Note that if the user logs on by using a local computer account rather than a domain account, he or she can still access domain resources. A Connect To dialog box appears whenever the user attempts to access a domain resource. Then the user can enter a domain user name and password to connect to the domain.

Configuring Wireless Networking

If you're using a wireless network, Windows client configuration is a bit different from what's required for a wired network. The first step in configuring Windows XP for wireless networking is to install the appropriate device driver for your wireless network adapter. To do that, you'll need the installation CD disk that came with the adapter. Follow the instructions that came with the adapter to install the drivers.

Windows XP has some nice built-in features for working with Wireless networks. You can configure these features by opening the Network Connections folder (choose Start⇨Control Panel, then double-click the Network Connections icon). Right-click the wireless network connection, and then choose Properties to bring up the Properties dialog box. Then, click the Wireless Networks tab to display the wireless networking options shown in Figure 11-6.

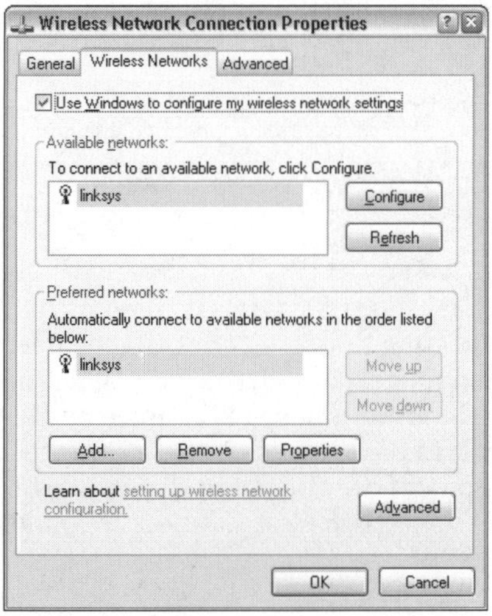

Figure 11-6:
Configuring
wireless
networking.

Each time you connect to a wireless network, Windows adds that network to this dialog box. Then, if you find yourself within range of two or more networks at the same time, you can juggle the order of the networks in the Preferred Networks section to indicate which network you'd prefer to join. You can use the Move Up and Move Down buttons next to the Preferred Networks list to change your preferences.

To add a network that you haven't yet actually joined, click the Add button. This brings up the dialog box shown in Figure 11-7. Here, you can type the SSID value for the network you want to add. You can also specify other information, such as whether to use data encryption, how to authenticate yourself, and whether the network is an ad-hoc rather than an infrastructure network.

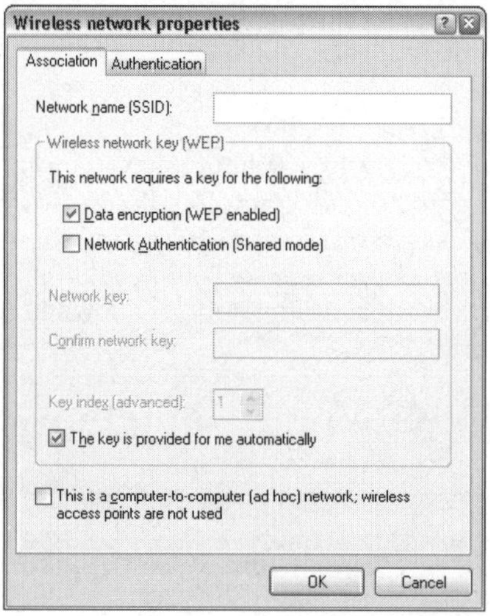

Figure 11-7:
Configuring
wireless
networking
in Windows
XP.

When the computer comes within range of a wireless network, a pop-up balloon appears in the taskbar, indicating that a network is available. If one of your Preferred Networks is within range, clicking the balloon will automatically connect you to that network. If Windows doesn't recognize any of the networks, clicking the balloon displays the Wireless Network Connection dialog box. With this dialog box, you can choose the network you want to join (if more than one network is listed), and then click Connect to join the selected network.

After you've joined a wireless network, a network-status icon appears in the notification area of the taskbar. You can quickly see network status by hovering the mouse pointer over this icon; a balloon will appear, indicating the state of the connection. For more detailed information, you can click the status icon to display the Wireless Network Connection Status dialog box, shown in Figure 11-8.

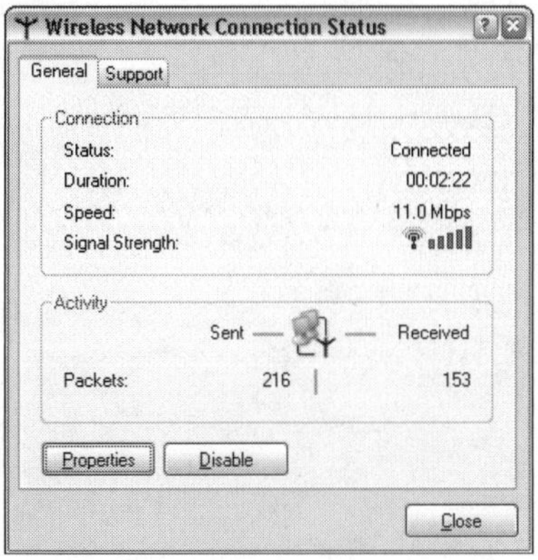

Figure 11-8:
The
Wireless
Network
Connection
Status
dialog box.

Wireless Network Connection Status

General | Support

Connection
Status: Connected
Duration: 00:02:22
Speed: 11.0 Mbps
Signal Strength:

Activity
Sent — Received
Packets: 216 | 153

Properties | Disable

Close

This dialog box provides the following items of information:

- **Status:** Indicates whether you are connected or not.

- **Duration:** Indicates how long you've been connected.

- **Speed:** Indicates the current network speed. Ideally, this should say 11Mbps for an 802.11b network, or 54Mbps for an 802.11a or 802.11g network. However, if the network connection is not of the highest quality, the speed may drop to a lower value.

- **Signal Strength:** Displays a graphic representation of the quality of the signal.

- **Packets Sent and Received:** Indicates how many packets of data you've sent and received over the network.

You can click the Properties button to bring up the Connection Properties dialog box.

Part III

Network Management For Dummies

The 5th Wave   By Rich Tennant

"We take network security very seriously here."

In this part . . .

You discover that there's more to networking than installing the hardware and software. After you get the network up and running, you have to keep it up and running. That's called *network management*.

The chapters in this part show you how to set up your network's security system, how to improve its performance, and how to protect your network from disaster. At times things may get a bit technical, but no one said life was easy.

Chapter 12

Help Wanted: Job Description for a Network Administrator

*H*elp wanted. Network administrator to help small business get control of a network run amok. Must have sound organizational and management skills. Only moderate computer experience required. Part-time only.

Does this sound like an ad that your company should run? Every network needs a network administrator, whether the network has 2 computers or 200. Of course, managing a 200-computer network is a full-time job, whereas managing a 2-computer network isn't. At least, it shouldn't be.

This chapter introduces you to the boring job of network administration. Oops . . . you're probably reading this chapter because you've been elected to be the network manager, so I'd better rephrase that: This chapter introduces you to the wonderful, exciting world of network management! Oh boy! This is going to be fun!

What Network Administrators Do

Simply put, network administrators "administer" networks. This means they take care of the tasks of installing, configuring, expanding, protecting, upgrading, tuning, and repairing the network. Network administrators take care of the network hardware (such as cables, hubs, switches, routers, servers, and clients), as well as network software (such as network operating systems, e-mail servers, backup software, database servers, and application software). Most importantly, network administrators take care of network users by answering their questions, listening to their troubles, and solving their problems.

On a big network, these responsibilities constitute a full-time job. Large networks tend to be volatile: Users come and go, equipment fails, cables break, and life in general seems to be one crisis after another.

Smaller networks are much more stable. After you get your network up and running, you probably won't have to spend much time managing its hardware and software. An occasional problem may pop up, but with only a few computers on the network, problems should be few and far between.

Regardless of the network's size, all network administrators must attend to several common chores:

- The network administrator should be involved in every decision to purchase new computers, printers, or other equipment.

- The network administrator must put on the pocket protector whenever a new computer is added to the network. The network administrator's job includes considering what changes to make to the cabling configuration, what computer name to assign to the new computer, how to integrate the new user into the security system, what rights to grant the user, and so on.

- Every once in a while, your trusty operating-system vendor (in other words, Microsoft or Novell) releases a new version of your network operating system. The network administrator must read about the new version and decide whether its new features are beneficial enough to warrant an upgrade. In most cases, the hardest part of upgrading to a new version of your network operating system is determining the *migration path* — that is, how to upgrade your entire network to the new version while disrupting the network or its users as little as possible. Upgrading to a new version of the network operating system is a major chore, so you need to carefully consider the advantages that the new version can bring.

- Between upgrades, Microsoft and Novell have a nasty habit of releasing patches and service packs that fix minor problems with their server operating systems. For more information, see the section "Patching Things Up" later in this chapter.

- Network administrators perform routine chores, such as backing up the servers, archiving old data, freeing up server disk space, and so on. Much of network administration is making sure that things keep working, finding and correcting problems before any users notice that something is wrong. In this sense, network administration can be a thankless job.

✔ Network administrators are also responsible for gathering, organizing, and tracking the entire network's software inventory. You never know when something is going to go haywire on Joe in Marketing's ancient Windows 95 computer and you're going to have to reinstall that old copy of Lotus Approach. Do you have any idea where the installation disks are?

The Part-Time Administrator

The larger the network, the more technical support it needs. Small networks — with just one or two dozen computers — can get by with a part-time network administrator. Ideally, this person should be a closet computer geek: someone who has a secret interest in computers but doesn't like to admit it. Someone who will take books home with him or her and read them over the weekend. Someone who enjoys solving computer problems just for the sake of solving them.

The job of managing a network requires some computer skills, but it isn't entirely a technical job. Much of the work that the network administrator does is routine housework. Basically, the network administrator does the electronic equivalent of dusting, vacuuming, and mopping the network periodically to keep it from becoming a mess.

Here are some additional ideas that go into picking a part-time network administrator:

✔ **The network administrator needs to be an organized person.** Conduct a surprise office inspection and place the person with the neatest desk in charge of the network. (Don't warn them in advance, or everyone may mess up their desks intentionally the night before the inspection.)

✔ **Allow enough time for network administration.** For a small network (say, no more than 20 or so computers), an hour or two each week is enough. More time is needed upfront as the network administrator settles into the job and discovers the ins and outs of the network. After an initial settling-in period, though, network administration for a small office network doesn't take more than an hour or two per week. (Of course, larger networks take more time to manage.)

✔ **Give the position some teeth.** Make sure that everyone knows who the network administrator is and that the network administrator has the authority to make decisions about the network, such as what access rights each user has, what files can and can't be stored on the server, how often backups are done, and so on.

✔ **Pick someone who is assertive and willing to irritate people to get the job done.** A good network administrator should make sure that backups are working *before* a disk fails and make sure that everyone is following good antivirus practices *before* a virus wipes out the entire network. This will irritate people, but it's for their own good.

✔ **Pick someone who knows how to install the software.** In most cases, the person who installs the network is also the network administrator. This is appropriate because no one understands the network better than the person who designs and installs it.

✔ **Provide backup.** The network administrator needs an understudy — someone who knows almost as much about the network, is eager to make a mark, and smiles when the worst network jobs are "delegated."

✔ **A title and a job description are also good.** The network manager has some sort of official title, such as Network Boss, Network Czar, Vice President in Charge of Network Operations, or Dr. Net. A badge, a personalized pocket protector, or a set of Spock ears helps, too.

Documenting the Network

One of the network administrator's main jobs is to keep the network documentation up-to-date. I suggest that you keep all the important information about your network in a three-ring binder. Give this binder a clever name, such as *The Network Binder*. Here are some things that it should include:

✔ **An up-to-date diagram of the network.** This diagram can be a detailed floor plan, showing the actual location of each computer, or something more abstract and Picasso-like. Any time you change the network layout, update the diagram. Also include a detailed description of the change, the date that the change was made, and the reason for the change.

Microsoft sells a program called *Visio* that is specially designed for creating network diagrams. I highly recommend it.

✔ **A detailed inventory of your computer equipment.** Table 12-1 provides a sample checklist you can use to keep track of your computer equipment:

Table 12-1	Computer Equipment Checklist
Computer location:	
User:	
Manufacturer:	
Model number:	

Serial number:

Date purchased:

CPU type and speed:

Memory:

Hard drive size:

Video type:

Printer type:

Other equipment:

Operating system version:

Application software and version:

Network card type:

MAC address:

✔ A System Information printout from System Information for each computer. (Start⇨All Programs⇨Accessories⇨System Tools⇨System Information.)

✔ A detailed list of network resources and drive assignments.

✔ Any other information that you think may be useful, such as details about how you must configure a particular application program to work with the network, and copies of every network component's original invoice — just in case something breaks and you need to seek warranty service.

✔ Backup schedules.

✔ Don't put passwords in the binder!

You may want to keep track of the information in your network binder by using a spreadsheet or a database program. However, make sure that you keep a printed copy of the information on hand.

If your network is large, you may want to invest in a *network-discovery* program such as NetRAT Software's NetRAT (www.netrat.com) or NetworkView Software's NetworkView (www.networkview.com). These programs can gather the network documentation automatically. This software scans the network carefully, looking for every computer, printer, router, and other device it can find, and builds a database of information. It then automatically draws a pretty diagram and chugs out helpful reports.

Routine Chores

Much of the network manager's job is routine stuff — the equivalent of vacuuming, dusting, and mopping. Or, if you prefer, changing the oil and rotating the tires every 3,000 miles. Yes, it's boring, but it has to be done:

✔ **Backups:** The network manager needs to make sure that the network is properly backed up. If something goes wrong and the network isn't backed up, guess who gets the blame? On the other hand, if disaster strikes, yet you're able to recover everything from yesterday's backup with only a small amount of work lost, guess who gets the pat on the back, the fat bonus, and the vacation in the Bahamas? Chapter 15 describes the options for network backups. You'd better read it soon.

✔ **Security:** Another major task for network administrators is sheltering your network from the evils of the outside world. These evils come in many forms, including hackers trying to break into your network and virus programs arriving through e-mail. Chapter 16 describes this task in more detail.

✔ **Cleanup:** Users think that the network server is like the attic: They want to throw files up there and leave them forever. No matter how much disk storage your network has, your users will fill it up sooner than you think. So the network manager gets the fun job of cleaning up the attic once in a while. The best advice I can offer is to constantly complain about how messy it is up there and warn your users that Spring Cleaning Is Coming Up.

Managing Network Users

Managing network technology is the easiest part of network management. Computer technology can be confusing at first, but computers are not nearly as confusing as people. The real challenge of managing a network is managing the network's users.

The difference between managing technology and managing users is obvious: You can figure out computers, but who can ever really figure out people? The people who use the network are much less predictable than the network itself. Here are some tips for dealing with users:

✔ Training is a key part of the network manager's job. Make sure that everyone who uses the network understands it and knows how to use it. If the network users don't understand the network, they may unintentionally do all kinds of weird things to it.

✔ Never treat your network users as if they were idiots. If they don't understand the network, it's not their fault. Explain it to them. Offer a class. Buy them each a copy of this book and tell them to read it during lunch hour. Hold their hands. But don't treat them like idiots.

✔ Make up a network cheat sheet that contains everything that the users need to know about using the network — on one page. Make sure that everyone gets a copy.

✔ Be as responsive as possible when a network user complains of a network problem. If you don't fix the problem soon, the user may try to fix it. You probably don't want that.

✔ The better you understand the psychology of network users, the more prepared you'll be for the strangeness they often serve up. Toward that end, I recommend that you read the *Diagnostic and Statistical Manual of Mental Disorders* (also known as *DSM-IV*) cover to cover.

Patching Things Up

One of the annoyances that every network manager faces is applying software patches to keep the operating system and other software up to date. A software *patch* is a minor update that fixes the small glitches that crop up from time to time, such as minor security or performance issues. These glitches are not significant enough to merit a new version of the software, but they are important enough to require fixing. Most of the patches correct security flaws that computer hackers have uncovered in their relentless attempts to prove that they are smarter than the security programmers at Microsoft or Novell.

Periodically, all the recently released patches are combined into a *service pack*. Although the most diligent network administrators apply all patches as they are released, many administrators just wait for the service packs.

For all versions of Windows, you can use the Windows Update Web site to apply patches to keep your operating system and other Microsoft software up-to-date. You can find Windows Update in the Start menu. If all else fails, just fire up Internet Explorer and go to `windowsupdate.microsoft.com`. Windows Update automatically scans your computer's software and creates a list of software patches and other components that you can download and install. You can also configure Windows Update to automatically notify you of updates so you don't have to remember to check for new patches.

Novell periodically posts patches and updates to NetWare on its product-support Web site (`support.novell.com`). You can subscribe to an e-mail notification service that automatically sends you e-mail to let you know of new patches and updates.

Software Tools for Network Administrators

Network managers need certain tools to get their jobs done. Managers of big, complicated, expensive networks need big, complicated, expensive tools. Managers of small networks need small tools.

Some of the tools that the manager needs are hardware tools, such as screw-drivers, cable crimpers, and hammers. The tools that I'm talking about here, however, are software tools. I've already mentioned a couple: Visio (to help you draw network diagrams) and a network-discovery tool to help you map your network. Here are a few others:

> ✔ **Built-in TCP/IP commands:** Many of the software tools that you need to manage a network come with the network itself. As the network manager, you should read through the manuals that come with your network soft-ware to see what management tools are available. For example, Windows includes a `net diag` command that you can use to make sure that all the computers on a network can communicate with each other. (You can run `net diag` from an MS-DOS prompt.) For TCP/IP networks, you can use the TCP/IP diagnostic commands that are summarized in Table 12-2.

Table 12-2	TCP/IP Diagnostic Commands
Command	*What it does*
`arp`	Displays address resolution information used by the Address Resolution Protocol (ARP).
`hostname`	Displays your computer's host name.
`ipconfig`	Displays current TCP/IP settings.
`nbtstat`	Displays the status of NetBIOS over TCP/IP connections.
`netstat`	Displays statistics for TCP/IP.
`nslookup`	Displays DNS information.
`ping`	Verifies that a specified computer can be reached.
`route`	Displays the PC's routing tables.
`tracert`	Displays the route from your computer to a specified host.

- ✔ **System Information:** This program that comes with Windows is a useful utility for network managers.

- ✔ **Hotfix Checker:** This handy tool from Microsoft scans your computers to see what patches need to be applied. You can download the Hotfix Checker free of charge from Microsoft's Web site. Just go to `www.microsoft.com` and search for `hfnetchk.exe`.

- ✔ **Baseline Security Analyzer:** If you prefer GUI-based tools, check out this program that you can download from the Microsoft Web site free of charge. To find it, go to `www.microsoft.com` and search `for Microsoft Baseline Security Analyzer`.

- ✔ **Third-party utilities:** I suggest that you get one of those 100-in-1 utility programs, such as Symantec's Norton Utilities. Norton Utilities includes invaluable utilities for repairing damaged hard drives, rearranging the directory structure of your hard drive, gathering information about your computer and its equipment, and so on.

Never use a hard drive repair program that was not designed to work with the operating system or version that your computer uses or the file system you've installed. Any time that you upgrade to a newer version of your operating system, you should also upgrade your hard drive repair programs to a version that supports the new operating system version.

- ✔ **Protocol analyzers:** A *protocol analyzer* is a program that's designed to monitor and log the individual packets that travel along your network. (Protocol analyzers are also called *packet sniffers.*) You can configure the protocol analyzer to filter specific types of packets, watch for specific types of problems, and provide statistical analysis of the captured packets. Most network administrators agree that *Sniffer,* by Sniffer Technologies (`www.snifer.com`) is the best protocol analyzer available. However, it's also one of the most expensive. If you prefer a free alternative, check out *Ethereal,* which you can download free from `www.ethereal.com`.

- ✔ **Network Monitor:** Windows 2000 and XP — as well as Windows 2000 Server and Windows Server 2003 — include this program; it provides basic protocol analysis and can often help solve pesky network problems.

Building a Library

One of Scotty's best lines in the original *Star Trek* series was when he refused to take shore leave so he could get caught up on his technical journals. "Don't you ever relax?" asked Kirk. "I am relaxing!" Scotty replied.

To be a good network administrator, you'll need to read computer books. Lots of them. And you'll need to enjoy doing it. If you're the type who takes computer books with you to the beach, you'll make a great network administrator.

You need books on a variety of topics. I'm not going to recommend specific titles, but I do recommend that you get a good, comprehensive book on each of the following topics:

- Network cabling and hardware
- Ethernet
- Windows NT 4.0
- Windows 2000 Server
- Windows Server 2003
- NetWare 6
- Linux
- TCP/IP
- DNS and BIND
- SendMail
- Exchange Server
- Security and hacking
- Wireless networking

In addition to books, you may also want to subscribe to some magazines to keep up with what's happening in the networking industry. Here are a few you should probably consider, along with their Web addresses:

- *InformationWeek,* www.informationweek.com
- *InfoWorld,* www.infoworld.com
- *Network Computing,* www.networkcomputing.com
- *Network Magazine,* www.networkmagazine.com
- *Windows & .NET Magazine,* www.winntmag.com
- *2600 Magazine,* www.2600.com (a great magazine on computer hacking and security)

The Internet is one of the best sources of technical information for network administrators. You'll want to stock your browser's Favorites menu with plenty of Web sites that contain useful networking information. In addition, many of the Web sites I listed here have online newsletters you can subscribe to so you'll get fresh information on a regular basis via e-mail.

Certification

Remember the scene near the end of *The Wizard of Oz*, when the Wizard grants the Scarecrow a diploma, the Cowardly Lion a medal, and the Tin Man a testimonial?

Network certifications are kind of like that. I can picture the scene now:

The Wizard: "And as for you, my network-burdened friend, any geek with thick glasses can administer a network. Back where I come from, there are people who do nothing but configure Cisco routers all day long. And they don't have any more brains than you do. But they do have one thing you don't have: certification. And so, by the authority vested in me by the Universita Committee-atum E Pluribus Unum, I hereby confer upon you the coveted certification of CND."

You: "CND?"

The Wizard: "Yes, that's, uh, *Certified Network Dummy.*"

You: "The Seven Layers of the OSI Reference Model are equal to the Sum of the Layers on the Opposite Side. Oh rapture! I feel like a network administrator already!"

My point is that certification in and of itself doesn't guarantee that you really know how to administer a network. That ability comes from real-world experience — not exam crams.

Nevertheless, certification is becoming increasingly important in today's competitive job market. So you may want to pursue certification — not just to improve your skills, but also to improve your résumé. Certification is an expensive proposition. The tests can cost several hundred dollars each, and depending on your technical skills, you may need to buy books to study or enroll in training courses before you take the tests.

You can pursue two basic types of certification: vendor-specific certification and vendor-neutral certification. The major networking vendors such as Microsoft, Novell, and Cisco provide certification programs for their own equipment and software. CompTIA, a nonprofit industry trade association, provides the best-known vendor-neutral certification.

Chapter 13

Big Brother's Guide to Network Security

In This Chapter

▶ Assessing the risk for security

▶ Determining your basic security philosophy

▶ Physically securing your network equipment

▶ Implementing user account security

▶ Exploring other network security techniques

*B*efore you had a network, computer security was easy. You simply locked your door when you left work for the day. You could rest easy, secure in the knowledge that the bad guys would have to break down the door to get to your computer.

The network changes all that. Now, anyone with access to any computer on the network can break into the network and steal *your* files. Not only do you have to lock your door, but you also have to make sure that other people lock their doors, too.

Fortunately, network operating systems have built-in provisions for network security. This situation makes it difficult for someone to steal your files, even if they do break down the door. All modern network operating systems have security features that are more than adequate for all but the most paranoid users.

When I say *more* than adequate, I mean it. Most networks have security features that would make even Maxwell Smart happy. Using all these security features is kind of like Smart insisting that the Chief lower the "Cone of Silence." The Cone of Silence worked so well that Max and the Chief couldn't hear each other! Don't make your system so secure that even the good guys can't get their work done.

If any of the computers on your network are connected to the Internet, you have to contend with a whole new world of security issues. For more information about Internet security, refer to Chapter 23 of this book. Also, if your network supports wireless devices, you have to contend with wireless security issues. For more information about security for wireless networks, see Chapter 10.

Do You Need Security?

Most small networks are in small businesses or departments where everyone knows and trusts everyone else. Folks don't lock up their desks when they take a coffee break, and although everyone knows where the petty-cash box is, money never disappears.

Network security isn't necessary in an idyllic setting like this one, is it? You bet it is. Here's why any network should be set up with at least some minimal concern for security:

✔ Even in the friendliest office environment, some information is — and should be — confidential. If this information is stored on the network, you want to store it in a directory that's available only to authorized users.

✔ Not all security breaches are malicious. A network user may be routinely scanning through his or her files and come across a filename that isn't familiar. The user may then call up the file, only to discover that it contains confidential personnel information, juicy office gossip, or your résumé. Curiosity, rather than malice, is often the source of security breaches.

✔ Sure, everyone at the office is trustworthy now. However, what if someone becomes disgruntled, a screw pops loose, and he or she decides to trash the network files before jumping out the window? What if someone decides to print a few $1,000 checks before packing off to Tahiti?

✔ Sometimes the mere opportunity for fraud or theft can be too much for some people to resist. Give people free access to the payroll files, and they may decide to vote themselves a raise when no one is looking.

✔ If you think your network doesn't contain any data that would be worth stealing, think again. For example, your personnel records probably contain more than enough information for an identity thief: names, addresses, phone numbers, Social Security numbers, and so on. Also, your customer files may contain your customers' credit-card numbers.

✔ Hackers who break into your network may not be interested in stealing your data. Instead, they may be looking to plant a *Trojan horse* program on your server, which enables them to use your server for their own purposes. For example, someone may use your server to send thousands of unsolicited spam e-mail messages. The spam won't be traced back to the hackers; it will be traced back to you.

✔ Finally, remember that not everyone on the network knows enough about the inner workings of Windows and the network to be trusted with full access to your network's data and systems. One careless mouse click can wipe out an entire directory of network files. One of the best reasons for activating your network's security features is to protect the network from mistakes made by users who (no offense) don't know what they're doing.

Two Approaches to Security

When you're planning how to implement security on your network, you should first consider which of two basic approaches to security you will take:

✔ An *open-door* type of security, in which you grant everyone access to everything by default, and then place restrictions just on those resources to which you want to limit access.

✔ A *closed-door* type of security, in which you begin by denying access to everything, and then grant specific users access to the specific resources that they need.

In most cases, the open-door policy is easier to implement. Typically, only a small portion of the data on a network really needs security, such as confidential employee records or secrets such as the Coke recipe. The rest of the information on a network can be safely made available to everyone who can access the network.

If you choose the closed-door approach, you set up each user so that he or she has access to nothing. Then, one begrudging step at a time, you grant each user access only to those specific files or folders that he or she needs.

The closed-door approach results in tighter security, but can lead to the Cone of Silence Syndrome: Like Max and the Chief, who can't hear each other talk while they're under the Cone of Silence, your network users will constantly complain that they can't access the information that they need. As a result, you'll find yourself frequently adjusting users' access rights. Choose the closed-door approach only if your network contains a lot of information that is very sensitive, and only if you are willing to invest a lot of time in administrating your network's security policy.

You can think of the open-door approach as an *entitlement model,* in which the basic assumption is that users are entitled to network access. In contrast, the closed-door policy is a *permissions model,* in which the basic assumption is that users are not entitled to anything but must get permissions for every network resource that they access.

Physical Security: Locking Your Doors

The first level of security in any computer network is physical security. I'm amazed when I walk into the reception area of an accounting firm and see an unattended computer sitting on the receptionist's desk. As often as not, the receptionist has logged on to the system and then walked away from the desk, leaving the computer unattended.

Physical security is important for workstations — but *vital* for servers. Any hacker worth his or her salt can quickly defeat all but the most paranoid security measures after gaining physical access to a server. To protect the server, follow these guidelines:

- ✔ Lock the computer room.
- ✔ Give the key only to people you trust.
- ✔ Keep track of who has the keys.
- ✔ Mount the servers on cases or racks that have locks.
- ✔ Disable the floppy drive on the server. (A common hacking technique is to boot the server from a floppy, thus bypassing the carefully crafted security features of the network operating system.)
- ✔ Keep a trained guard dog in the computer room and feed it only enough to keep it hungry and mad. (Just kidding.)

There's a big difference between a *locked door* and a *door with a lock*. Locks are worthless if you don't use them.

Client computers should be physically secure as well. You should instruct users to not leave their computers unattended while they are logged on. In high-traffic areas (such as the receptionist's desk), users should secure their computers with the keylock. Additionally, users should lock their office doors when they leave.

Here are some other potential threats to physical security that you may not have considered:

- ✔ The nightly cleaning crew probably has complete access to your facility. How do you know that the person who vacuums your office every night doesn't really work for your chief competitor or doesn't consider computer hacking to be a sideline hobby? You don't, so you'd better consider the cleaning crew to be a threat.
- ✔ What about your trash? Paper shredders aren't just for Enron accountants. Your trash can contain all sorts of useful information: sales reports, security logs, printed copies of the company's security policy, even handwritten passwords. For the best security, every piece of paper that leaves your building via the trash bin should first go through a shredder.

✔ Where do you store your backup tapes? Don't just stack them up next to the server. Not only does that make them easy to steal, it also defeats one of the main purposes of backing up your data in the first place: securing your server from physical threats, such as fires. If a fire burns down your computer room and the backup tapes are sitting unprotected next to the server, your company may go out of business and you'll certainly be out of a job. Store the backup tapes securely in a fireproof safe, and keep a copy off-site, too.

✔ I've seen some networks in which the servers are in a locked computer room, but the hubs or switches are in an unsecured closet. Remember that every unused port on a hub or a switch represents an open door to your network. The hubs and switches should be secured just like the servers.

Securing User Accounts

Next to physical security, the careful use of user accounts is the most important type of security for your network. Properly configured user accounts can prevent unauthorized users from accessing the network, even if they gain physical access to the network. The following sections describe some steps you can take to strengthen your network's use of user accounts.

Obfuscating your usernames

Huh? When it comes to security, *obfuscation* simply means picking obscure usernames. For example, most network administrators assign usernames based on some combination of the user's first and last name, such as `BarnyM` or `baMiller`. However, a hacker can easily guess such a user ID if he or she knows the name of at least one employee. After the hacker knows a username, he or she can focus on breaking the password.

You can slow down a hacker by using names that are more obscure. Here are some suggestions on how to do that:

✔ Add a random three-digit number to the end of the name. For example: `BarnyM320` or `baMiller977`.

✔ Throw a number or two into the middle of the name. For example: `Bar6nyM` or `ba9Miller2`.

✔ Make sure that usernames are different from e-mail addresses. For example, if a user's e-mail address is `baMiller@Mydomain.com`, do *not* use `baMiller` as the user's account name. Use a more obscure name.

Do *not* rely on obfuscation to keep people out of your network! Security by obfuscation doesn't work. A resourceful hacker can discover even the most obscure names. The purpose of obfuscation is to slow intruders down — not to stop them. If you slow an intruder down, you're more likely to discover that he or she is trying to crack your network before he or she successfully gets in.

Using passwords wisely

One of the most important aspects of network security is the use of passwords. Usernames are not usually considered secret. Even if you use obscure names, even casual hackers will eventually figure them out.

Passwords, on the other hand, are top secret. Your network password is the one thing that keeps an impostor from logging on to the network by using your username and therefore receiving the same access rights that you ordinarily have. *Guard your password with your life.*

Here are some tips for creating good passwords:

- Don't use obvious passwords, such as your last name, your kid's name, or your dog's name.

- Avoid profanities or other sophomoric phrases. Most hackers can swear like sailors, so there aren't any profanities they don't know and won't try.

- Don't pick passwords based on your hobbies, either. A friend of mine is into boating, and his password is the name of his boat. Anyone who knows him can guess his password after a few tries. Five lashes for naming your password after your boat.

- Store your password in your head — not on paper. Especially bad: Writing your password down on a sticky note and sticking it on your computer's monitor. Ten lashes for that. (If you must write your password down, write it on digestible paper that you can swallow after you've memorized the password.)

- Most network operating systems enable you to set an expiration time for passwords. For example, you can specify that passwords expire after 30 days. When a user's password expires, the user must change it. Your users may consider this process a hassle, but it helps to limit the risk of someone swiping a password and then trying to break into your computer system later.

- You can also configure user accounts so that when they change passwords, they can't specify a password that they've used recently. For example, you can specify that the new password can't be identical to any of the user's past three passwords.

✔ You can also configure security policies so that passwords must include a mixture of uppercase letters, lowercase letters, numerals, and special symbols. Thus, passwords like DIMWIT or DUFUS are out. Passwords like 87dIM@wit or duF39&US are in.

✔ Some administrators of small networks opt against passwords altogether because they feel that security is not an issue on their network. Or short of that, they choose obvious passwords, assign every user the same password, or print the passwords on giant posters and hang them throughout the building. In my opinion, ignoring basic password security is rarely a good idea, even in small networks. You should consider not using passwords only if your network is very small (say, two or three computers), if you don't keep sensitive data on a file server, or if the main reason for the network is to share access to a printer rather than sharing files. (Even if you don't use passwords, imposing basic security precautions — such as limiting access that certain users have to certain network directories — is still possible. Just remember that if passwords aren't used, nothing prevents a user from signing on by using someone else's username.)

Generating Passwords For Dummies

How do you come up with passwords that no one can guess but that you can remember? Most security experts say that the best passwords don't correspond to any words in the English language but consist of a random sequence of letters, numbers, and special characters. Yet, how in the heck are you supposed to memorize a password like Dks4%DJ2? Especially when you have to change it three weeks later to something like 3pQ&X(d8?

Here's a compromise solution that enables you to create passwords that consist of two four-letter words back to back. Take your favorite book (if it's this one, you need to get a life) and turn to any page at random. Find the first four- or five-letter words on the page. Suppose that word is When. Then repeat the process to find another four- or five-letter word; say you pick the word Most the second time. Now combine the words to make your password: WhenMost. I think you agree that WhenMost is easier to remember than 3PQ&X(D8 and is probably just about as hard to guess. I probably wouldn't want the folks at the Los Alamos Nuclear Laboratory using this scheme, but it's good enough for most of us.

Here are some additional thoughts on concocting passwords from your favorite book:

✔ If the words end up being the same, pick another word. And pick different words if the combination seems too commonplace, such as WestWind or FootBall.

✔ For an interesting variation, insert a couple of numerals or special characters between the words. You end up with passwords like into#cat, ball3%and, or tree47wing. If you want, use the page number of the second word as separator. For example, if the words are *know* and *click* and the second word comes from page 435, use know435click.

✔ To further confuse your friends and enemies, use medieval passwords by picking words from Chaucer's *Canterbury Tales*. Chaucer is a great source for passwords because he lived before the days of word processors with spell-checkers. He wrote *seyd* instead of *said, gret* instead of *great, welk* instead of *walked, litel* instead of *little*. And he used lots of seven-letter and eight-letter words suitable for passwords, such as *glotenye* (gluttony), *benygne* (benign), and *opynyoun* (opinion). And he got As in English.

✔ If you use any of these password schemes and someone breaks into your network, don't blame me. You're the one who's too lazy to memorize D#Sc$h4@bb3xaz5.

✔ If you do decide to go with passwords such as KdI22UR3xdkL, you can find random password generators on the Internet. Just go to a search engine, such as Google (www.google.com), and search for Password Generator. You'll find Web pages that generate random passwords based on criteria that you specify, such as how long the password should be, whether it should include letters, numbers, punctuation, uppercase and lowercase letters, and so on.

Securing the Administrator account

It stands to reason that at least one network user must have the authority to use the network without any of the restrictions imposed on other users. This user is called the *administrator*. The administrator is responsible for setting up the network's security system. To do that, the administrator must be exempt from all security restrictions.

Many networks automatically create an administrator user account when you install the network software. The username and password for this initial administrator are published in the network's documentation and are the same for all networks that use the same network operating system. One of the first things that you must do after getting your network up and running is *to change the password for this standard administrator account.* Otherwise your elaborate security precautions will be a complete waste of time. Anyone who knows the default administrator username and password can access your system with full administrator rights and privileges, thus bypassing the security restrictions that you so carefully set up.

Don't forget the password for the administrator account! If a network user forgets his or her password, you can log in as the supervisor and change that user's password. If you forget the administrator's password, though, you're stuck.

Managing User Security

User accounts are the backbone of network security administration. Through the use of user accounts, you can determine who can access your network as well as what network resources each user can and cannot access. You can restrict access to the network to just specific computers or to certain hours of the day. In addition, you can lock out users who no longer need to access your network. The following sections describe the basics of setting up user security for your network.

User accounts

Every user who accesses a network must have a *user account*. User accounts allow the network administrator to determine who can access the network and what network resources each user can access. In addition, the user account can be customized to provide many convenience features for users, such as a personalized Start menu or a display of recently used documents.

Every user account is associated with a *username* (sometimes called a *user ID*), which the user must enter when logging in to the network. Each account also has other information associated with it — in particular, these items:

✔ **The user's password:** This also includes the password policy, such as how often the user has to change his or her password, how complicated the password must be, and so on.

✔ **The user's contact information:** This includes full name, phone number, e-mail address, mailing address, and other related information.

✔ **Account restrictions:** This includes restrictions that allow the user to log on only during certain times of the day. This feature enables you to restrict your users to normal working hours, so that they can't sneak in at 2 a.m. to do unauthorized work. This feature also discourages your users from working overtime (because they can't access the network after hours), so use it judiciously. You can also specify that the user can log on only at certain computers.

✔ **Account status:** You can temporarily disable a user account so the user can't log on.

- ✔ **Home directory:** This specifies a shared network folder where the user can store documents.

- ✔ **Dial-in permissions:** These authorize the user to access the network remotely via a dialup connection.

- ✔ **Group memberships:** These grant the user certain rights based on groups to which they belong. For more information, see the section "Group therapy" later in this chapter.

Built-in accounts

Most network operating systems come preconfigured with two built-in accounts, named "Administrator" and "Guest." In addition, some server services, such as Web or database servers, create their own user accounts under which to run. The following sections describe the characteristics of these accounts:

- ✔ **The Administrator account:** The Administrator account is the King of the Network. This user account is not subject to any of the account restrictions to which other, mere mortal accounts must succumb. If you log in as the Administrator, you can do anything. For this reason, you should avoid using the Administrator account for routine tasks. Log in as the Administrator only when you really need to.

  Because the Administrator account has unlimited access to your network, it is imperative that you secure it immediately after you install the server. When the NOS Setup program asks for a password for the Administrator account, start off with a good random mix of uppercase and lowercase letters, numbers, and symbols. Don't pick some easy-to-remember password to get started, thinking you'll change it to something more cryptic later. You'll forget, and in the meantime, someone will break in and reformat the server's C: drive or steal your customers' credit-card numbers.

- ✔ **The Guest account:** Another commonly created default account is called the *Guest account*. This account is set up with a blank password and — if any — access rights. The Guest account is designed to allow anyone to step up to a computer and log on, but after they do, it then prevents them from doing anything. Sounds like a waste of time to me. I suggest you disable the Guest account. I don't know why it's there in the first place.

- ✔ **Service accounts:** Some network users aren't actual people. I don't mean that some of your users are subhuman. Rather, some users are actually software processes that require access to secure resources, and therefore, require user accounts. These user accounts are usually created automatically for you when you install or configure server software.

For example, when you install Microsoft's Web server (IIS), an Internet user account called `IUSR` is created. The complete name for this account is `IUSR_<servername>`. So if the server is named `WEB1`, the account is named `IUSR_WEB1`. IIS uses this account to allow anonymous Internet users to access the files of your Web site.

As a general rule, you shouldn't mess with these accounts unless you know exactly what you're doing. For example, if you delete or rename the IUSR account, you must reconfigure IIS to use the changed account. If you don't, IIS will deny access to anyone trying to reach your site. (Assuming that you *do* know what you're doing, renaming these accounts can increase your network's security. However, don't start playing with these accounts until you've researched the ramifications.)

User rights

User accounts and passwords are only the front line of defense in the game of network security. After a user gains access to the network by typing a valid user ID and password, the second line of security defense — rights — comes into play.

In the harsh realities of network life, all users are created equal, but some users are more equal than others. The Preamble to the Declaration of Network Independence contains the statement, "We hold these truths to be self-evident, that *some* users are endowed by the network administrator with certain inalienable rights. . ."

The specific rights that you can assign to network users depend on which network operating system you use. Here is a partial list of the user rights that are possible with Windows servers:

✔ **Log on locally:** The user can log on to the server computer directly from the server's keyboard.

✔ **Change system time:** The user can change the time and date registered by the server.

✔ **Shut down the system:** The user can perform an orderly shutdown of the server.

✔ **Back up files and directories:** The user can perform a backup of files and directories on the server.

✔ **Restore files and directories:** The user can restore backed-up files.

✔ **Take ownership of files and other objects:** The user can take over files and other network resources that belong to other users.

NetWare has a similar set of user rights.

Network rights we'd like to see

The network rights allowed by most network operating systems are pretty boring. Here are a few rights I wish would be allowed:

✔ **Cheat:** Provides a special option that enables you to see what cards the other players are holding when you're playing Hearts.

✔ **Spy:** Eavesdrops on other user's Internet sessions so you can find out what Web sites they're viewing.

✔ **Complain:** Automatically sends e-mail messages to other users that explain how busy, tired, or upset you are.

✔ **Set pay:** Grants you special access to the payroll system so that you can give yourself a pay raise.

✔ **Sue:** In America, everyone has the right to sue. So this right should be automatically granted to all users.

Permissions (who gets what)

User rights control what a user can do on a network-wide basis. *Permissions* enable you to fine-tune your network security by controlling access to specific network resources, such as files or printers, for individual users or groups. For example, you can set up permissions to allow users into the accounting department to access files in the server's \ACCTG directory. Permissions can also enable some users to read certain files but not modify or delete them.

Each network operating system manages permissions in a different way. Whatever the details, the effect is that you can give permission to each user to access certain files, folders, or drives in certain ways. For example, you might grant a user full access to some files but grant read-only access to other files.

Any permissions that you specify for a folder apply automatically to any of that folder's subfolders, unless you explicitly specify a different set of permissions for the subfolder.

You can use Windows permissions only for files or folders that are created on drives formatted as NTFS volumes. If you insist on using FAT or FAT32 for your Windows shared drives, you can't protect individual files or folders on the drives. This is one of the main reasons for using NTFS for your Windows servers.

Group therapy

A *group account* is an account that doesn't represent an individual user. Instead, it represents a group of users who use the network in a similar way. Instead of granting access rights to each of these users individually, you can grant the rights to the group, and then assign individual users to the group. When you assign a user to a group, that user inherits the rights specified for the group.

For example, suppose that you create a group named "Accounting" for the accounting staff, and then allow members of the Accounting group access to the network's accounting files and applications. Then, instead of granting each accounting user access to those files and applications, you simply make each accounting user a member of the Accounting group.

Here are a few additional details about groups:

✔ Groups are one of the keys to network management nirvana. As much as possible, you should avoid managing network users individually. Instead, clump them into groups and manage the groups. When all 50 users in the accounting department need access to a new file share, would you rather update 50 user accounts or just one group account?

✔ A user can belong to more than one group. Then, the user inherits the rights of each group. For example, suppose that you have groups set up for Accounting, Sales, Marketing, and Finance. A user who needs to access both Accounting and Finance information can be made a member of both the Accounting and Finance groups. Likewise, a user who needs access to both Sales and Marketing information can be made a member of both the Sales and Marketing groups.

✔ You can grant or revoke specific rights to individual users to override the group settings. For example, you may grant a few extra permissions for the manager of the accounting department. You may also impose a few extra restrictions on certain users.

User profiles

User profiles are a Windows feature that keeps track of an individual user's preferences for his or her Windows configuration. For a non-networked computer, profiles enable two or more users to use the same computer, each with his or her own desktop settings, such as wallpaper, colors, Start menu options, and so on.

The real benefit of user profiles becomes apparent when profiles are used on a network. A user's profile can be stored on a server computer and accessed whenever that user logs on to the network from any Windows computer on the network.

The following are some elements of Windows that are governed by settings in the user profile:

- ✔ Desktop settings from the Display Properties dialog box, including wallpaper, screen savers, and color schemes.
- ✔ Start menu programs and Windows toolbar options.
- ✔ Favorites, which provide easy access to the files and folders that the user accesses frequently.
- ✔ Network settings, including drive mappings, network printers, and recently visited network locations.
- ✔ Application settings, such as option settings for Microsoft Word.
- ✔ The My Documents folder.

Logon scripts

A *logon script* is a batch file that runs automatically whenever a user logs on. Logon scripts can perform several important logon tasks for you, such as mapping network drives, starting applications, synchronizing the client computer's time-of-day clock, and so on. Login scripts reside on the server. Each user account can specify whether to use a login script, and which script to use.

Here's a sample logon script that maps a few network drives and synchronizes the time:

```
net use m: \\MYSERVER\Acct
net use n: \\MYSERVER\Admin
net use o: \\MYSERVER\Dev
net time \\MYSERVER /set /yes
```

Logon scripts are a little out of vogue because most of what a logon script does can be done via user profiles. Still, many administrators prefer the simplicity of logon scripts, so they're still used even on Windows Server 2003 systems.

Hardening Your Network

In addition to taking care of physical security and user account security, you should also take steps to protect your network from intruders by configuring the other security features of the network's servers and routers. The following sections describe the basics of hardening your network.

Using a firewall

A *firewall* is a security-conscious router that sits between your network and the outside world and prevents Internet users from wandering into your LAN and messing around. Firewalls are the first line of defense for any network that's connected to the Internet. You should *never* connect a network to the Internet without installing a carefully configured firewall. For more information about firewalls, refer to Chapter 23.

Disabling unnecessary services

A typical network operating system can support dozens of different types of network services: file and printer sharing, Web server, mail server, and many others. In many cases, these features are installed on servers that don't need or use them. When a server runs a network service that it doesn't really need, the service not only robs CPU cycles from other services that are needed, but also poses an unnecessary security threat.

When you first install a network operating system on a server, you should enable only those network services that you know the server will require. You can always enable services later if the needs of the server change.

Patching your servers

Hackers regularly find security holes in network operating systems. After those holes are discovered, the operating system vendors figure out how to plug the hole and release a software patch for the security fix. The trouble is that most network administrators don't stay up-to-date with these software patches. As a result, many networks are vulnerable because they have well-known holes in their security armor that should have been fixed but weren't.

Even though patches are a bit of a nuisance, they are well worth the effort for the protection that they afford. Fortunately, newer versions of the popular network operating systems have features that automatically check for updates and let you know when a patch should be applied.

Securing Your Users

Security techniques, such as physical security, user account security, server security, and locking down your servers are child's play compared to the most difficult job of network security: securing your network's users. All the best-laid security plans will go for naught if your users write their passwords down on sticky notes and post them on their computers.

The key to securing your network users is to create a written network security policy and to stick to it. Have a meeting with everyone to go over the security policy to make sure that everyone understands the rules. Also, make sure to have consequences when violations occur.

Here are some suggestions for some basic security rules that can be incorporated into your security policy:

- Never write down your password or give it to someone else.

- Accounts should not be shared. Never use someone else's account to access a resource that you can't access under your own account. If you need access to some network resource that isn't available to you, you should formally request access under your own account.

- Likewise, never give your account information to a coworker so that he or she can access a needed resource. Your coworker should instead formally request access under his or her own account.

- Do not install any software or hardware on your computer without first obtaining permission. This especially includes wireless access devices or modems.

- Do not enable file- and printer-sharing capabilities on workstations without first getting permission.

- Never attempt to disable or bypass the network's security features.

Chapter 14

If I Could Save Time in a Bottleneck: Optimizing Your Network's Performance

*T*he term *network performance* refers to how efficiently the network responds to users' needs. It goes without saying that any access to resources that involves the network will be slower than similar access that doesn't involve the network. For example, it takes longer to open a Word document that resides on a network file server than it takes to open a similar document that resides on the user's local hard drive. However, it shouldn't take *much* longer. If it does, you have a network performance problem.

This chapter is a general introduction to the practice of tuning your network so it performs as well as possible. Keep in mind that many specific bits of network tuning advice are scattered throughout this book. In this chapter, you can find some specific techniques for analyzing your network's performance, taking corrective action when a performance problem develops, and charting your progress.

Why Administrators Hate Performance Problems

Network performance problems are among the most difficult network problems to track down and solve. If a user simply can't access the network, it usually doesn't take long to figure out why: the cable is broken, a network card or hub is malfunctioning, the user doesn't have permission to access the resource, and so on. After a little investigation, the problem usually reveals itself — you fix it, and move on to the next problem.

Unfortunately, performance problems are messier. Here are just a few of the reasons that network administrators hate performance problems:

- **Performance problems are difficult to quantify.** Exactly how much slower is the network now than it was a week ago, a month ago, or even a year ago? Sometimes the network just *feels* slow, but you can't quite define exactly how slow it really is.

- **Performance problems usually develop gradually.** Sometimes a network slows down suddenly and drastically. More often, though, the network gradually gets slower, a little bit at a time, until one day the users notice that the network is slow.

- **Performance problems often go unreported.** They gripe about the problem to each other around the water cooler, but they don't formally contact you to let you know that their network seems 20 percent slower than usual. As long as they can still access the network, they just assume that the problem is temporary, or that it's just their imaginations.

- **Many performance problems are intermittent.** Sometimes a user calls you and complains that a certain network operation has become slower than molasses, and by the time you get to the user's desk, the operation performs like a snap. Sometimes you can find a pattern to the intermittent behavior — say, it's slower in the morning than in the afternoon, or it's slow only while backups are running or while the printer is working. Other times, you can't find a pattern. Sometimes, the operation is slow; sometimes, it isn't.

- **Performance tuning is not an exact science.** Improving performance sometimes involves educated guesswork. Will segmenting the network improve performance? Maybe. Will adding another 512 MB of RAM to the server improve performance? Well, hope springs eternal.

- **The solution to performance problems is sometimes a hard sell.** If a user is unable to access the network due to a malfunctioning component, there's usually not much question that the purchase of a replacement is justified. However, if the network is slow and you think you can fix it by offloading your server's contents onto a separate server, you may have trouble selling management on the new purchase.

What Exactly Is a Bottleneck?

The term *bottleneck* does not in any way refer to the physique of your typical computer geek. (Well, I guess it *could,* in some cases.) Rather, computer geeks coined the phrase when they discovered that the tapered shape of a bottle of Jolt Cola limited the rate at which they could consume the beverage. "Hey," a computer geek said one day, "the gently tapered narrowness of this bottle's neck imposes a distinct limiting effect upon the rate at which I can consume the tasty caffeine-laden beverage contained within. This draws to mind a hitherto-undiscovered (yet obvious) analogy to the limiting effect that a single slow component can have upon the performance of an entire computer system as a whole."

"Fascinating," replied all the other computer geeks, who were fortunate enough to be present at that historic moment.

The phrase stuck — and is used to this day to draw attention to the simple fact that a computer system is only as fast as its slowest component. It's the computer equivalent of the old truism that a chain is only as strong as its weakest link.

For a simple demonstration of this concept, consider what happens when you print a word processing document on a slow printer. Your word processing program reads the data from disk and sends it to the printer. Then you sit and wait while the printer prints the document.

Would buying a faster CPU or adding more memory make the document print faster? No. The CPU is already much faster than the printer, and your computer already has more than enough memory to print the document. The printer itself is the bottleneck, so the only way to print the document faster is to replace the slow printer with a faster one.

Here are some other random thoughts about bottlenecks:

- ✔ **A computer system always has a bottleneck.** For example, suppose you've decided that the bottleneck on your file server is a slow IDE hard drive, so you replace it with the fastest SCSI drive money can buy. Now, the hard drive is no longer the bottleneck — but (oops) now the drive can process information faster than the controller card to which it's connected. You haven't really eliminated the bottleneck; you've just moved it from the hard drive to the disk controller. No matter what you do, the computer will always have some component that limits the overall performance of the system.

- ✔ **One way to limit the effect of a bottleneck is to avoid waiting for the bottleneck.** For example, print spooling lets you avoid waiting for a slow printer. Spooling doesn't speed up the printer, but it does free you up to do other work while the printer chugs along. Similarly, disk caching lets you avoid waiting for a slow hard drive.

- ✔ **One of the reasons computer geeks are switching from Jolt Cola to Snapple is that Snapple bottles have wider necks.**

The Five Most Common Network Bottlenecks

Here are the five most common network bottlenecks, in no particular order.

The hardware inside your servers

Your servers should be powerful computers capable of handling all the work your network will throw at them. Don't cut corners by using a bottom-of-the-line computer that you bought at a discount computer store.

The following are the four most important components of your server hardware:

- ✔ **Processor:** Your server should have a powerful processor. As a general rule, any processor that is available in an $800 computer from Best Buy is not a processor that you want to see in your file server. In other words, avoid processors that are designed for consumer-grade home computers.

- ✔ **Memory:** You can't have too much memory. Memory is cheap, so don't skimp. Don't even think about running a server with less than 512 MB of RAM.

  One rule of thumb for determining if you have enough memory in your server is that the lights should dim when you turn it on. (Just kidding, but you get the idea: More is better.)

- ✔ **Disk:** Don't mess around with inexpensive IDE hard drives. To get respectable performance, you should have nothing but SCSI drives.

- ✔ **Network card:** Cheap $14.95 network cards are fine for home networks, but don't use one in a file server that supports 200 users and expect to be happy with the server's performance. Remember: The server computer uses the network a lot more than any of the clients. So equip your servers with good network cards. In fact, for best performance, consider installing more than one network card in the server.

The server's configuration options

All network operating systems have options that you can configure. Some of these options can make the difference between a pokey network and a zippy network. Unfortunately, no hard-and-fast rules exist for setting these options. Otherwise, you wouldn't have options.

The following are some of the more important tuning options available for most servers:

- **Virtual-memory options:** *Virtual memory* refers to disk-paging files (temporary hard-disk locations) that the server uses when it doesn't have enough real memory to do its work. Few servers ever have enough real memory, so virtual memory is always an important server feature. You can specify the size and location of the virtual memory paging files. For best performance, you should provide at least 1.5 times the amount of real memory. For example, if you have 1 GB of real memory, allocate at least 1.5 GB of virtual memory. If necessary, you can increase this size later.

- **Disk striping:** Use the disk defragmenter to optimize the data storage on your server's disks. If the server has more than one hard drive, you can increase performance by creating *striped volumes,* which allow disk I/O operations to run concurrently on each of the drives in the stripe set.

- **Network protocols:** Make sure that your network protocols are configured correctly, and remove any protocols that aren't necessary.

- **Free disk space on the server:** Servers like to have plenty of breathing room on their disks. If the amount of free disk space on your server drops precipitously low, the server chokes up and slows to a crawl. Make sure that your server has plenty of space — a few GBs of unused disk space provides a healthy buffer.

Servers that do too much

One common source of network performance problems is that servers can easily become overloaded with too many duties. Just because modern network operating systems come equipped with dozens of different types of services doesn't mean that you should enable and use them all on a single server. If a single server is bogged down because of too much work, add a second server to relieve the first server of some of its chores. Remember the old saying: "Many hands make light work."

For example, if your network needs more disk space, consider adding a second file server, rather than adding another drive to a server that already has four drives that are nearly full. Or, better yet, purchase a file-server appliance that is dedicated to only the task of serving files.

As a side benefit, your network will be easier to administer and more reliable if you place separate functions on separate servers. For example, if you have a single server that doubles as a file server and a mail server, you'll lose both services if you have to take the server down to perform an upgrade or repair a failed component. However, if you have separate file and mail server computers, only one of the services will be interrupted if you have to take down one of the servers.

There's no reason to run fancy 3D screen savers on your servers. They eat up a lot of CPU resources that could be better used servicing network tasks. I suggest the basic black screen saver, or perhaps a marquee with the server's name. (Or, no screen saver at all. Today's monitors don't have the same problems with image burn-in that older monitors did.)

Malfunctioning components

Sometimes a malfunctioning network card or other component slows down the network. For example, a switch may malfunction intermittently, occasionally letting packets through but dropping enough of them to slow down the network. After you've identified the faulty component, replacing it will restore the network to its original speed.

The network infrastructure

The infrastructure consists of the cables and any switches, hubs, routers, and other components that sit between your clients and your servers. The following network infrastructure items can slow down your network:

 ✔ **Hubs:** Because switches are so inexpensive now, you can affordably solve a lot of performance problems by replacing old, outdated hubs with switches. Using switches instead of hubs reduces the overall load on your network.

 ✔ **Segment sizes:** Keep the number of computers and other devices on each network segment to a reasonable number. About 20 devices is usually the right number. (Note that if you replace your hubs with switches, you instantly cut the size of each segment because each port on a switch constitutes a separate segment.)

 ✔ **The network's speed:** If you have an older network, you'll probably discover that many — if not all — of your users are still working at 10 Mbps. Upgrading to 100Mbps will speed up the network dramatically. Also, make sure that all of the devices on the network have speeds of at least

100 Mbps. All it takes is one old 10Mbps component to slow down a whole segment of your network.

✔ **The backbone speed:** If your network uses a backbone to connect segments, consider upgrading the backbone to 1 Gbps.

The hardest part of improving the performance of a network is determining what the bottlenecks are. With sophisticated test equipment and years of experience, network gurus can make pretty good educated guesses. Without the equipment and experience, you can *still* make pretty good (if uneducated) guesses. In the remaining section of this chapter, I give you some pointers on what to do after you've zeroed in on the bottlenecks — that is, tune the network to improve performance.

Tuning Your Network the Compulsive Way

You have two ways to tune your network. The first is to think about it a bit, take a guess at what may improve performance, try it, and see whether the network seems to run faster. This approach is the way most people go about tuning the network.

Then you have the compulsive way, which is suitable for people who organize their sock drawers by color and their food cupboards alphabetically by food groups. The compulsive approach to tuning a network goes something like this:

1. **Establish a method for objectively testing the performance of some aspect of the network.**

   This method is called a *benchmark,* and the result of your benchmark is called a *baseline*. (For information about how to test performance, see the section "Monitoring Network Performance" later in this chapter.)

2. **Change one variable of your network configuration and rerun the test.**

   For example, suppose you think that increasing the size of the disk cache can improve performance. Change the cache size, restart the server, and run the benchmark test. Note whether the performance improves, stays the same, or becomes worse.

3. **Repeat Step 2 for each variable that you want to test.**

Here are some salient points to keep in mind if you decide to tune your network the compulsive way:

✔ If possible, test each variable separately — in other words, reverse the changes you've made to other network variables before proceeding.

✔ Write down the results of each test so that you have an accurate record of the impact that each change has made on your network's performance.

✔ Be sure to change only one aspect of the network each time you run the benchmark. If you make several changes, you won't know which one caused the change. One change may improve performance, but the other change may worsen performance so the changes cancel each other out — kind of like offsetting penalties in a football game.

✔ If possible, conduct the baseline test during normal working hours, when the network is undergoing its normal workload.

✔ To establish your baseline performance, run your benchmark test two or three times to make sure that the results are repeatable.

Monitoring Network Performance

One way to monitor network performance is to use a stopwatch to see how long it actually takes to complete common network tasks, such as opening documents or printing reports. (If you choose to monitor your network with a stopwatch, you'll want to get a clipboard, baseball cap, and gray sweatsuit to complete the ensemble.)

A more high-tech approach to monitoring network performance is to use a monitor program that automatically gathers network statistics for you. After you've set up the monitor, it plugs away, silently spying on your network and recording what it sees in performance logs. You can then review the performance logs to see how your network is doing.

For large networks, you can purchase sophisticated monitoring programs that run on their own dedicated servers. For small- and medium-size networks, you can probably get by with the built-in monitoring facilities that come with the network operating system. For example, Figure 14-1 shows the Performance Monitor tool that comes with Windows Server 2003. Other operating systems come with similar tools.

The Windows Performance Monitor lets you keep track of several different aspects of system performance at once. You track each performance aspect by setting up a *counter*. You can choose from dozens of different counters. Table 14-1 describes some of the most commonly used counters. Note that each counter refers to a server object such as a physical disk, memory, or processor.

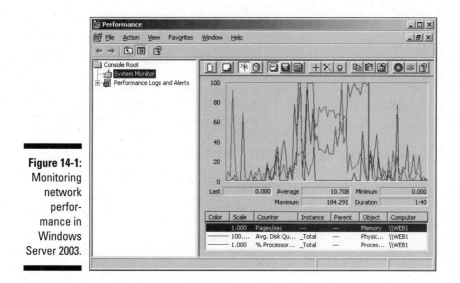

Figure 14-1:
Monitoring
network
perfor-
mance in
Windows
Server 2003.

Table 14-1		Commonly Used Performance Counters
Object	**Counter**	**Description**
Physical Disk	% Free Space	The percentage of free space on the server's physical disks. Should be at least 15 percent.
Physical Disk	Average Queue Length	Indicates how many disk operations are waiting while the disk is busy servicing other disk operations. Should be 2 or less.
Memory	Pages/second	The number of pages retrieved from the virtual memory page files per second. A typical threshold is about 2,500 pages per second.
Processor	% Processor Time	Indicates the percentage of the processor's time that it is busy doing work rather than sitting idle. Should be 85 percent or less.

Here are a few more things to consider about performance monitoring:

✔ The Performance Monitor enables you to view real-time data or to view data that you've saved in a log file. Real-time data gives you an idea about what's happening with the network at a particular moment, but the more useful information comes from the logs.

✔ You can schedule logging to occur at certain times of the day, and for certain intervals. For example, you may schedule the log to gather data every 15 seconds from 9:00 to 9:30 every morning, and then again from 3:00 to 3:30 every afternoon.

✔ Even if you don't have a performance problem now, you should set up performance logging and let it run for a few weeks to gather some baseline data. If you develop a problem later on, the baseline data will prove invaluable as you research the problem.

✔ The act of gathering performance data slows down your server. Have mercy: Don't leave performance logging on all the time. Use it only occasionally to gather baseline data or when you're experiencing a performance problem.

More Performance Tips

Here are a few last-minute performance tips that barely made it in:

✔ You can often find the source of a slow network by staring at the network hubs or switches for a few minutes. These devices have colorful arrays of green and red lights. The green lights flash whenever data is transmitted; the red lights flash when a collision occurs. An occasional red flash is normal, but if one or more of the red lights is flashing repeatedly, the computer connected to that port may have a faulty network card.

✔ Check for scheduled tasks, such as backups, batched database updates, or report jobs. If at all possible, schedule these tasks to run after normal business hours (for example, at night when no one is in the office). These jobs tend to slow down the network by hogging the server's hard drives.

✔ Sometimes faulty application programs can degrade performance. For example, some programs develop what is known as a *memory leak*: They use memory, but forget to release the memory after they finish. Programs with memory leaks can slowly eat up all the memory on a server, until the server runs out and grinds to a halt. If you think a program may have a memory leak, contact the manufacturer of the program to see whether a fix is available.

✔ A relatively new source of performance trouble is so-called *spyware* — software that installs itself into your computer, monitors what you do, and periodically reports your activities to another computer on the Internet. Spyware is often associated with advertising programs installed by music-sharing software. If your users have been downloading music, they are probably infected by spyware. To find out more, use Google or another search engine to search for information about "spyware." (You'll also find more about spyware in Chapter 16.)

Chapter 15

How to Sleep Well at Night (Or, Backing Up Your Network Data)

In This Chapter

▶ Understanding the need for backups

▶ Exploring tape drives and other backup media

▶ Comparing different types of backups

▶ Rotating backup tapes and other details

*I*f you're the hapless network manager, the safety of the data on your network is your responsibility. You get paid to lie awake at night worrying about your data. Will it be there tomorrow? If it's not, will *you* be able to get it back? And — most importantly — if you can't get it back, will *you* be there tomorrow?

This chapter covers the ins and outs of being a good, responsible, trustworthy network manager. They don't give out merit badges for this stuff, but they should.

Planning for Disaster

On April Fool's Day almost 20 years ago, my colleagues and I discovered that some loser had broken into the office the night before and pounded our computer equipment to death with a crowbar. (I'm not making this up.)

Sitting on a shelf right next to the mangled piles of what used to be a Wang minicomputer system was an undisturbed disk pack that contained the only complete backup of all the information that was on the destroyed computer.

The vandal didn't realize that one more swing of the crowbar would have esca-
lated this major inconvenience into a complete catastrophe. Sure, we were
up a creek until we could get the computer replaced. And in those days, you
couldn't just walk into your local Computer Depot and buy a new computer off
the shelf — this was a Wang minicomputer system that had to be specially
ordered. But after we had the new computer, a simple restore operation from
the backup disk brought us right back to where we were on March 31. Without
that backup, getting back on track would have taken months.

I've been paranoid about disaster planning ever since. Before then, I thought
that disaster planning simply meant doing good backups. That's a part of it,
but I can never forget the day we came within one crowbar-swing of losing
everything. Vandals are probably much smarter now: They know to smash
the backup disks as well as the computers themselves. There's more to being
prepared for disasters than doing regular backups.

Don't think it can happen to you? A few years ago, wildfires in New Mexico
came close to destroying the Los Alamos labs. How many computers do
you think were lost to Hurricane Andrew? Not to mention the floods along
the Mississippi in 1993 or the San Francisco earthquake in 1989? (I doubt
that many computers were lost in the 1906 earthquake.) And I assume you
saw *Armageddon* — if all else fails, nature can throw big rocks at us from
outer space.

Most disasters are of the less spectacular variety. Make at least a rudimen-
tary plan for how you can get your computer network back up and running
should a major or minor disaster strike.

Here are a few additional things you can lie awake at night worrying about
when it comes to disaster planning:

> ✔ The cornerstone of any disaster-recovery plan is a program of regular
> backups. I devote much of this chapter to helping you get a backup pro-
> gram started. Keep in mind, though, that your backups are only one swing
> of the crowbar from being useless. Don't leave your backup disks or tapes
> sitting on the shelf next to your computer: Store them in a fireproof box
> or safe — and store at least one set at a whole other location.

> ✔ Your network binder is an irreplaceable source of information about your
> network. You should have more than one copy. I suggest that you take a
> copy home so that if the entire office burns to the ground, you still have
> a copy of your network documentation. Then you can decide quickly
> what equipment you need to purchase, and how you need to configure it
> to get your network back up and running again.

> ✔ After your computers are completely destroyed by fire, vandalism, or
> theft, how can you prove to your insurance adjuster that you really *had*
> all that equipment? A frequently overlooked part of planning for disaster

is keeping a detailed record of what computer equipment you own. Keep copies of all invoices for computer equipment and software in a safe place. And consider making a videotape or photographic record of your equipment, too.

✔ Another aspect of disaster planning that's often overlooked is expertise. In many businesses, the one person who takes charge of all the computers is the only one who knows anything more than how to start Word and print a letter. What if that person becomes ill, decides to go work for the competition, or wins the lottery and retires to the Bahamas? Don't let any one person at the office form a computer dynasty that only he or she can run. As much as possible, spread the computer expertise around.

Backing Up Your Data

An effective backup plan, faithfully followed, is the cornerstone of any disaster-recovery plan. Without backups, a simple hard-drive failure can set your company back days or even weeks as it tries to reconstruct lost data. In fact, without backups, your company's very existence is in jeopardy.

The main goal of backups is simple: Keep a spare copy of your network's critical data so that, no matter what happens, you never lose more than one day's work. The stock market may crash, hanging chads may factor into another presidential election, and Jar-Jar Binks may be in yet another *Star Wars* movie. However, you never lose more than one day's work if you stay on top of your backups.

The way to do this, naturally, is to make sure that data is backed up on a daily basis. In many networks, it's feasible to back up all network hard drives every night. However, even if full nightly backups are not possible, you can still use techniques that can ensure every file on the network a backup copy that's no more than one day old.

All About Tapes and Tape Drives

If you plan on backing up the data on your network server's hard drives, you need something to back up the data to. You *could* copy the data onto diskettes — how twentieth-century! — but a 40GB hard drive would need about 28,000 diskettes to do a full backup. That's a few more diskettes than most of us want to keep in the closet. It's understandable that the usual medium for backing up network data is tape. Depending on the make and model of the tape drive, you can copy as much as 80 GB of data onto a single tape.

Alternatives to Tape Backup?

Okay, tape may seem a little archaic to compulsive modernists (you know who you are). And yes, some alternatives to tape drives do exist:

✔ Removable hard drives: These are housed in cartridges that you can insert or remove like giant floppy disks. The best-known removable hard drives — the Iomega Zip drives — sell for about $175 and can back up 750 MB of data on each cartridge.

✔ Rewritable CD drives: These, also known as *CD-RW* drives, use special compact discs that can be reused. A CD-RW drive can write about 600 MB of data to each CD.

✔ DVD-R recorders: These can write up to 4.7GB of data on a single DVD disc.

Pretty cool, huh? But let's get real: Frankly, a 750MB Zip drive or a 600MB CD-RW drive doesn't have enough capacity to do backups properly. If your network fills up a 100GB hard drive, you'd need more than 130 Zip cartridges or 150 CDs to back it all up. For all practical purposes, Zip drives and CD-RW drives are a viable backup option only for small networks.

One benefit of tape backup is that you can run it unattended. In fact, you can schedule tape backup to run automatically during off hours, when no one is using the network. In order for unattended backups to work, you must ensure that you have enough tape capacity to back up your entire network server's hard drive without having to manually switch tapes. If your network server has only 20 GB of data, you can easily back it up onto a single tape. However, if you have 200 GB of data, you should invest in several tape drives that have a combined capacity of at least 200 GB. That way you'll be able to run your backups unattended.

Here are some additional thoughts concerning tape backups:

✔ The most popular style of tape backup for smallish networks is called *Travan drives*. Travan drives come in a variety of models with tape capacities ranging from 8GB to 20GB. You can purchase an 8GB drive for under $200 and a 20GB unit for about $300. (Travan drives used to be known as *QIC drives*.)

✔ For larger networks, you can get tape-backup units that offer higher capacity and faster backup speed than Travan drives (for more money, of course). DAT (digital audio tape) units can back up as much as 40GB on a single tape, and DLT (digital linear tape) drives can store up to 80 GB on one tape. DAT and DLT drives can cost $1,000 or more, depending on the capacity.

✔ If you're really up the backup creek with hundreds of gigabytes to back up, you can get robotic tape-backup units that automatically fetch and load tape cartridges from a library, so you can do complete backups without having to load tapes manually. Naturally, these units aren't cheap: The small ones, which have a library of eight tapes and a total backup capacity of over 300 GB, start at about $5,000.

Backup Software

All versions of Windows come with a built-in backup program. In addition, most tape drives come with backup programs that are often faster or more flexible than the standard Windows backup. You can also purchase sophisticated backup programs that are specially designed for large networks, which have multiple servers with data that must be backed up.

For a basic Windows file server, you can use the backup program that comes with Windows Server. Server versions of Windows come with a decent backup program that can run scheduled, unattended tape backups.

Backup programs do more than just copy data from your hard drive to tape. Backup programs use special compression techniques to squeeze your data so that you can cram more data onto fewer tapes. Compression factors of 2:1 are common, so you can usually squeeze 20GB of data onto a tape that would hold only 10GB of data without compression. (Tape drive manufacturers tend to state the capacity of their drives by using compressed data, assuming a 2:1 compression ratio. So a 20GB tape has an uncompressed capacity of 10GB.)

Backup programs also help you to keep track of which data has been backed up and which hasn't, and they offer options such as incremental or differential backups that can streamline the backup process, as described in the next section.

Types of Backups

You can perform five different types of backups. Many backup schemes rely on full backups daily, but for some networks, it's more practical to use a scheme that relies on two or more of these backup types.

The differences among the five types of backups involve a little technical detail known as the *archive bit.* The archive bit indicates whether a file has been modified since the last time it was backed up. The archive bit is a little flag that's stored along with the file's name, creation date, and other directory information. Any time that a program modifies a file, the archive bit is set to the On position. That way, backup programs know that the file has been modified and needs to be backed up.

The differences among the various types of backup center around whether they use the archive bit to determine which files to back up, and whether they flip the archive bit to the Off position after they back up a file. These differences are summarized in Table 15-1 and explained in the following sections.

Backup programs allow you to select any combination of drives and folders to back up. As a result, you can customize the file selection for a backup operation to suit your needs. For example, you can set up one backup plan that backs up all a server's shared folders and drives *plus* its mail-server stores, leaving out folders that rarely change (such as operating-system folders or installed program folders, which you can back up less frequently). The drives and folders that you select for a backup operation are collectively called the *backup selection*.

Table 15-1	How Backup Types Use the Archive Bit	
Backup type	*Selects files by archive bit?*	*Resets archive bit after backing up?*
Normal	No	Yes
Copy	No	No
Daily	No *	No
Incremental	Yes	Yes
Differential	Yes	No

* Selects files based on the Last Modified date.

Normal backups

A *normal backup*, also called a *full backup*, is the most basic type of backup. In a normal backup, all files in the backup selection are backed up — regardless of whether the archive bit has been set. In other words, the files are backed up even if they haven't been modified since the last time they were backed up. As each file is backed up, its archive bit is reset; any backups that select files according to the archive-bit setting won't back up those files.

When a normal backup finishes its work, none of the files in the backup selection will have their archive bits set. As a result, if you immediately follow a normal backup with an incremental backup or a differential backup, no files will be selected for backup by the incremental or differential backup — because no files will have their archive bits set.

The easiest backup scheme is to simply schedule a normal backup every night. That way, all your data is backed up on a daily basis. So if the need arises, you can restore files from a single tape or set of tapes. Restoring files is more complicated when other types of backups are involved.

As a result, I recommend that you do normal backups nightly if you have the tape capacity to do them unattended — that is, without having to swap tapes. If you can't do an unattended normal backup because the amount of data to be backed up is greater than the capacity of your tape drive or drives, you may prefer to use other types of backups in combination with normal backups.

If you can't get a normal backup on a single tape and you can't afford a second tape drive, take a hard look at the data that's being included in the backup selection. I recently worked on a network that was having trouble backing up onto a single tape. When I examined the data that was being backed up, I discovered about 5 GB of static data that was essentially an online archive of old projects. This data was necessary because network users needed it for research purposes, but the data was read-only. Even though the data never changed, it was being backed up to tape every night, and the backups required two tapes. After we removed this data from the cycle of nightly backups, the backups could squeeze onto a single tape again.

If you do remove static data from the nightly backup, make sure that you have a secure backup of the static data — on tape, CD-RW, or some other medium.

Copy backups

A *copy backup* is similar to a normal backup, except the archive bit is not reset as each file is copied. As a result, copy backups don't disrupt the cycle of normal, incremental, or differential backups.

Copy backups are usually not incorporated into regular, scheduled backups. Instead, you use a copy backup when you want to do an occasional one-shot backup. For example, if you're about to perform an operating-system upgrade, you should back up the server before proceeding. If you do a full backup, the archive bits will be reset and your regular backups will be disrupted. However, if you do a copy backup, the archive bits of any modified files will remain unchanged. As a result, your regular normal, incremental, or differential backups will be unaffected.

Note that if you don't incorporate incremental or differential backups into your backup routine, the difference between a copy backup and a normal backup is moot.

Daily backups

A *daily backup* backs up just those files that have been changed the same day that the backup is performed. A daily backup examines the modification date stored with each file's directory entry to determine whether a file should be backed up.

Daily backups don't reset the archive bit.

I'm not a big fan of this option because of the small possibility that some files may slip through the cracks. Someone may be working late one night and modify a file after the evening's backups have completed, but before midnight. Those files won't be included in the following night's backups. Incremental or differential backups, which rely on the archive bit rather than on the modification date, are more reliable.

Incremental backups

An *incremental backup* backs up only those files that you've modified since the last time you did a backup. Incremental backups are a lot faster than full backups because your network users probably modify only a small portion of the files on the server in any given day. As a result, if a full backup takes three tapes, you can probably fit an entire week's worth of incremental backups onto a single tape.

As an incremental backup copies each file, it resets the file's archive bit. That way, the file is backed up before your next normal backup only if a user modifies the file again.

Here are some thoughts about using incremental backups:

✔ The easiest way to use incremental backups is to do a normal backup every Monday and then do an incremental backup on Tuesday, Wednesday, Thursday, and Friday. (This assumes, of course, that you can do a full backup overnight on Monday. If your full backup takes more than 12 hours, you may want to do it on Friday instead so it can run over the weekend.)

✔ When you use incremental backups, the *complete* backup consists of the full backup tapes and all the incremental backup tapes you've made since you did the full backup. If the hard drive crashes and you have to restore the data onto a new drive, you first restore Monday's normal backup, and then you restore each of the subsequent incremental backups.

✔ Incremental backups complicate the task of restoring individual files because the most recent copy of the file may be on the full backup tape or on any of the incremental backups. Fortunately, backup programs keep track of the location of the most recent version of each file, which simplifies the process.

✔ When you use incremental backups, you can choose whether you want to store each incremental backup on its own tape, or append each backup to the end of an existing tape. In many cases, you can use a single tape for an entire week's worth of incremental backups.

Differential backups

A *differential backup* is similar to an incremental backup, except that it doesn't reset the archive bit as files are backed up. As a result, each differential backup represents the difference between the last normal backup and the current state of the hard drive. To do a full restore from a differential backup, you first restore the last normal backup, and then you restore the most recent differential backup.

For example, suppose you do a normal backup on Monday, differential backups on Tuesday, Wednesday, and Thursday, and your hard drive crashes Friday morning. Friday afternoon you install a new hard drive. Then, to restore the data, you first restore the normal backup from Monday. Then, you restore the differential backup from Thursday. The Tuesday and Wednesday differential backups aren't needed.

The main difference between incremental and differential backups is that incremental backups result in smaller and faster backups, but differential backups are easier to restore. If your users frequently ask you to restore individual files, you may want to consider differential backups.

Local versus Network Backups

When you back up network data, you have two basic approaches to running the backup software: You can perform a *local backup,* in which the backup software runs on the file server itself and backs up data to a tape drive that's installed in the server, or you can perform a *network backup,* in which you use one network computer to back up data from another network computer. In a network backup, the data has to travel over the network to get to the computer that's running the backup.

If you run the backups from the file server, you tie up the server while the backup is running. Your users will complain that their access to the server has slowed to a snail's pace. On the other hand, if you run the backup over the network from a client computer or a dedicated backup server, you'll flood the network with gigabytes of data being backed up. Your users will then complain that the entire network has slowed to a snail's pace.

Network performance is one of the main reasons you should try to run your backups during off hours, when other users are not accessing the network. Another reason to do this is so you can perform a more thorough backup. If you run your backup while other users are accessing files, the backup program is likely to skip any files being accessed by users at the time the backup runs — and it won't include those files. Ironically, the files most likely to get left out of the backup are often the files that most need backing up — the ones being used and modified.

Here are some extra thoughts on client and server backups:

✔ You may think that backing up directly from the server would be more efficient than backing up from a client because data doesn't have to travel over the network. Actually, this assumption doesn't always hold, because the network may well be faster than the tape drive. The network probably won't slow down backups unless you back up during the busiest time of the day, when hordes of network users are storming the network gates.

✔ Any files that happen to be open while the backups are run won't get backed up. That's usually not a problem, because backups are run at off hours when people have gone home for the day. However, if someone leaves his or her computer on with a Word document open, that Word document won't be backed up.

✔ Some backup programs have special features that enable them to back up open files. For example, the Windows Server 2003 backup does this by creating a snapshot of the volume when it begins, thus making temporary copies of any files that are modified during the backup. The backup backs up the temporary copies rather than the versions being modified. When the backup finishes, the temporary copies are deleted.

How Many Sets of Backups Should You Keep?

Don't try to cut costs by purchasing one backup tape and reusing it every day. What happens if you accidentally delete an important file on Tuesday and don't discover your mistake until Thursday? Because the file didn't exist on Wednesday, it won't be on Wednesday's backup tape. If you have only one tape that's reused every day, you're outta luck.

The safest scheme is to use a new backup tape every day and keep all your old tapes in a vault. Pretty soon, though, your tape vault can start to look like the warehouse where they stored the Ark of the Covenant at the end of *Raiders of the Lost Ark.*

As a compromise between these two extremes, most users purchase several tapes and rotate them. That way, you always have several backup tapes to fall back on, just in case the file you need isn't on the most recent backup tape. This technique is called *tape rotation,* and several variations are commonly used:

✔ The simplest approach is to purchase three tapes and label them A, B, and C. You use the tapes on a daily basis in sequence: A the first day, B the second day, C the third day; then A the fourth day, B the fifth day, C the sixth day, and so on. On any given day, you have three *generations* of backups: today's, yesterday's, and the day-before-yesterday's. Computer geeks like to call these the *grandfather, father,* and *son* tapes.

✔ Another simple approach is to purchase five tapes and use one each day of the week.

✔ A variation of this scheme is to buy eight tapes. Take four of them and write *Monday* on one label, *Tuesday* on the second, *Wednesday* on the third, and *Thursday* on the fourth label. On the other four tapes, write *Friday 1, Friday 2, Friday 3,* and *Friday 4.* Now, tack a calendar up on the wall near the computer and number all the Fridays in the year: 1, 2, 3, 4, 1, 2, 3, 4, and so on.

On Monday through Thursday, you use the appropriate daily backup tape. When you do backups on Friday, you consult the calendar to decide which Friday tape to use. With this scheme, you always have four weeks' worth of Friday backup tapes, plus individual backup tapes for the past five days.

✔ If bookkeeping data lives on the network, it's a good idea to make a backup copy of all your files (or at least all your accounting files) immediately before closing the books each month; then retain those backups for each month of the year. Does that mean you should purchase 12 additional tapes? Not necessarily. If you back up just your accounting files, you can probably fit all 12 months on a single tape. Just make sure that you back up with the "append to tape" option rather than the "erase tape" option so the previous contents of the tape aren't destroyed. Also, treat this accounting backup as completely separate from your normal daily backup routine.

You should also keep at least one recent full backup at another location. That way, if your office should fall victim to an errant Scud missile or a rogue asteroid, you can re-create your data from the backup copy you stored offsite.

A Word About Tape Reliability

From experience, I've found that although tape drives are very reliable, they do run amok once in a while. Problem is, they don't always tell you they're not working. A tape drive — especially the less expensive Travan drives — can spin along for hours, pretending to back up your data, when in reality, your data isn't being written reliably to the tape. In other words, a tape drive can trick you into thinking that your backups are working just fine, but when disaster strikes and you need your backup tapes, you may just discover that the tapes are worthless.

Don't panic! You have a simple way to reassure yourself that your tape drive is working. Just activate the Compare After Backup feature of your backup software. Then, as soon as your backup program finishes backing up your data, it rewinds the tape, reads each backed-up file, and compares it with the original version on the hard drive. If all files compare, you know your backups are trustworthy.

Here are some additional thoughts about the reliability of tapes:

- ✔ The Compare After Backup feature doubles the time required to do a backup, but that doesn't matter if your entire backup fits on one tape. You can just run the backup after hours. Whether the backup and repair operation takes one hour or ten doesn't matter, as long as it's finished by the time you arrive at work the next morning.

- ✔ If your backups require more than one tape, you may not want to run the Compare After Backup feature every day. However, be sure to run it periodically to check that your tape drive is working as it should.

- ✔ If your backup program reports errors, throw away the tape and use a new tape — after you clean the tape heads.

- ✔ Actually, you should ignore that last comment about waiting for your backup program to report errors. You should discard tapes *before* your backup program reports errors. Most experts recommend that you should use a tape only about 20 times before discarding it. If you use the same tape every day, replace it monthly. If you have tapes for each day of the week, replace them twice a year. If you have more tapes than that, figure out a cycle that replaces tapes after about 20 uses. And don't forget to clean the heads.

About Cleaning the Heads

Yep, there's a theme here. An important aspect of backup reliability is proper maintenance of your tape drives. Every time you back up to tape, little bits and specs of the tape rub off onto the read and write heads inside the tape drive. Eventually, the heads become too dirty to reliably read or write data.

To counteract this problem, you should clean the tape heads regularly. The easiest way to do this is to use a special tape-cleaning cartridge. To clean the heads with a tape-cleaning cartridge, you just insert the cartridge into the tape drive. The drive automatically recognizes that you've inserted a cleaning cartridge, and performs a special routine that wipes the special cleaning tape back and forth over the heads to clean them. When the cleaning routine is done, the tape is ejected. The whole thing takes about 30 seconds.

Because the maintenance requirements of each drive differ, you should check the drive's user's manual to find out how and how often to clean the drive. As a rule of thumb, clean the drives once a week.

The most annoying aspect of tape-drive cleaning is that the cleaning cartridges have a limited lifespan. Unfortunately, if you insert a used-up cleaning cartridge, the drive accepts it and pretends to clean the drive. For this reason, you should keep track of the number of times you've used the cleaning cartridge and replace it when you've exceeded the number of uses recommended by the manufacturer.

Backup Security

Backups create an often-overlooked security exposure for your network. No matter how carefully you set up user accounts and enforce password policies, if any user (including a guest) can perform a backup of the system, that user can also make an unauthorized backup. In addition, your backup tapes or removable drives are vulnerable to theft. As a result, you should make sure that your backup policies and procedures are secure by taking the following measures:

✔ Set up a user account for the user who does backups. Because this user account will have backup permission for the entire server, guard its password carefully. Anyone who knows the username and password of the backup account can log in and bypass any security restrictions you've placed on that user's normal user ID.

✔ You can counter potential security problems by restricting the backup user ID to a certain client and a certain time of the day. If you're really clever (and paranoid), you can probably set up the backup user's account so the only program it can run is (yep) the backup program.

✔ Use encryption to protect the contents of your backup tapes.

✔ Secure the backup tapes in a safe location, such as, um, a safe.

Chapter 16

Major Annoyances

*T*his chapter covers some of the most common annoyances that modern network administrators must deal with. In particular, you'll learn techniques for dealing with virus threats and fixing e-mail problems.

Contending with Virus Threats

Viruses are one of the most misunderstood computer phenomena around these days. What is a virus? How does it work? How does it spread from computer to computer? I'm glad you asked.

What is a virus?

Make no mistake — viruses are real and they're here to stay. Now that most of us are connected to the Internet, viruses have really taken off. Every computer user is susceptible to attacks by computer viruses, and using a network — especially one that's connected to the Internet — increases your vulnerability because it exposes all network users to the risk of being infected by a virus that lands on any one network user's computer.

Viruses don't just spontaneously appear out of nowhere. Viruses are computer programs that are created by malicious programmers who've lost a few screws and should be locked up.

What makes a virus a virus is its capability to make copies of itself that can be spread to other computers. These copies, in turn, make still more copies that spread to still more computers, and so on, ad nauseam.

Then, the virus patiently waits until something triggers it — perhaps when you type a particular command or press a certain key, when a certain date arrives, or when the virus creator sends the virus a message. What the virus does when it strikes also depends on what the virus creator wants the virus to do. Some viruses harmlessly display a "gotcha" message. Some send e-mail to everyone it finds in your address book. Some wipe out all the data on your hard drive. Ouch.

A few years back, viruses moved from one computer to another by latching themselves onto floppy disks. Whenever you borrowed a floppy disk from a buddy, you ran the risk of infecting your own computer with a virus that may have stowed away on the disk.

Nowadays, virus programmers have discovered that e-mail is a much more efficient method to spread their viruses. Typically, a virus masquerades as a useful or interesting e-mail attachment, such as instructions on how to make $1,000,000 in your spare time, pictures of naked celebrities, or a Valentine's Day greeting from your long-lost sweetheart. When a curious but unsuspecting user double-clicks the attachment, the virus springs to life, copying itself onto the user's computer and, in some cases, sending out copies of itself to all the names in the user's address book.

After the virus has worked its way onto a networked computer, the virus can then figure out how to spread itself to other computers on the network.

Here are some more tidbits about protecting your network from virus attacks:

- The term *virus* is often used to refer not only to true virus programs (which are able to replicate themselves) but also to any other type of program that's designed to harm your computer. These programs include so-called *Trojan horse* programs that usually look like games but are, in reality, hard drive formatters.

- A *worm* is similar to a virus, but it doesn't actually infect other files. Instead, it just copies itself onto other computers on a network. After a worm has copied itself onto your computer, there's no telling what it may do there. For example, a worm may scan your hard drive for interesting information, such as passwords or credit card numbers, and then e-mail them to the worm's author.

- Computer virus experts have identified several thousand "strains" of viruses. Many of them have colorful names, such as the I Love You virus, the Stoned virus, and the Michelangelo virus.

✔ Antivirus programs can recognize known viruses and remove them from your system, and they can spot the telltale signs of unknown viruses. Unfortunately, the idiots who write viruses aren't idiots (in the intellectual sense), so they're constantly developing new techniques to evade detection by antivirus programs. New viruses are frequently discovered, and the antivirus programs are periodically updated to detect and remove them.

✔ A *virus hoax* can be just as dangerous as an actual virus. A virus hoax is an e-mail that warns you that you may have a virus, and that you should check to see whether a particular file exists on your computer to see. If you find the file, you're then instructed to delete it or to perform some other action to remove the virus. Trouble is, the file you're told to look for is actually a file that is present on all Windows systems, and the file or files you're told to delete turn out to be files that are essential to Windows' operation. You should educate your users to *never* trust virus alerts that arrive via e-mail.

✔ *Spyware* and *adware,* though not technically viruses because they don't self-replicate, are a troublesome type of software that can sneak onto users' computers as they visit various Web sites. These programs monitor how you use your computer and are often responsible for those annoying pop-up ads that seem to appear out of nowhere. In some cases, these programs can completely take over your browser, making your computer virtually unusable. For information about programs that can help deal with spyware and adware, search the Web for *spyware* or *adware.*

Antivirus programs

The best way to protect your network from virus infection is to use an antivirus program. These programs have a catalog of several thousand known viruses that they can detect and remove. In addition, they can spot the types of changes that viruses typically make to your computer's files, thus decreasing the likelihood that some previously unknown virus will go undetected.

It would be nice if Windows came with built-in antivirus software, but alas, it does not. So you have to purchase a program on your own. The two best-known antivirus programs for Windows are Norton Antivirus by Symantec and McAfee's VirusScan.

The people who make antivirus programs have their finger on the pulse of the virus world and frequently release updates to their software to combat the latest viruses. Because virus writers are constantly developing new viruses, your antivirus software is next to worthless unless you keep it up-to-date by downloading the latest updates.

The following are several approaches to deploying antivirus protection on your network:

- ✔ You can install antivirus software on each network user's computer. This technique would be the most effective if you could count on all your users to keep their virus software up-to-date. Because that's an unlikely proposition, you may want to adopt a more reliable approach to virus protection.

- ✔ Managed antivirus services place antivirus client software on each client computer in your network. Then, an antivirus server automatically updates the clients on a regular basis to make sure that they are kept up-to-date.

- ✔ Server-based antivirus software protects your network servers from viruses. For example, you can install antivirus software on your mail server to scan all incoming mail for viruses and remove them before your network users ever see them.

- ✔ Some firewall appliances include antivirus enforcement checks that don't allow your users to access the Internet unless their antivirus software is up-to-date. This type of firewall provides the best antivirus protection available.

Safe computing

Besides using an antivirus program, you can take a few additional precautions to ensure virus-free computing. If you haven't talked to your kids about these safe-computing practices, you had better do so soon.

- ✔ Regularly back up your data. If a virus hits you and your anti-virus software can't repair the damage, you may need the backup to recover your data. Make sure that you restore from a backup that was created before you were infected by the virus!

- ✔ Use your antivirus software to scan your disk for virus infection after your computer has been to a repair shop or worked on by a consultant. These guys don't intend harm, but they occasionally spread viruses accidentally, simply because they work on so many strange computers.

- ✔ Don't open e-mail attachments from people you don't know or attachments you weren't expecting. And configure Outlook and Exchange so they block dangerous attachments, such as executable files.

- ✔ Use your antivirus software to scan any floppy disk or CD-ROM that doesn't belong to you before you access any of its files.

Dealing with Dysfunctional E-mail

E-mail is a vital function of most computer networks. Unfortunately, e-mail is also one of the most troublesome aspects of networking. Why? Because the very nature of e-mail requires your network to communicate with other networks in order to send and receive messages. Opportunities for this communication to go wrong are endless.

That most mail gets through to its intended recipient is a testament to the quality of the Internet's e-mail system, which is based on standards that have endured for more than 20 years. Once in awhile, though, something goes wrong and an outgoing e-mail message gets returned with an error message. When that happens, the user who sent the mail often picks up the phone and calls the network administrator. Then it's time for you to go to work.

In this chapter, you learn how to diagnose and correct the most common problems that lead to undeliverable e-mail. Unfortunately, delivery problems are often a result of errors on the recipient's end of the communication, so you can't do a whole lot besides contacting the recipient so they can correct the problem. Of course, that's not always easy to do because you can't just e-mail them to tell them that their e-mail isn't working.

The dreaded nondelivery report

The software that routes e-mail through the Internet is almost as diligent as the real post office in the efforts that it makes to deliver mail. However, the e-mail system isn't perfect, and sometimes the mail just doesn't get through.

When an e-mail can't be delivered, the person who originally sent the undeliverable mail receives a report in his or her inbox called a *nondelivery report,* also known as an *NDR.* Figure 16-1 shows a typical nondelivery report.

The nondelivery report should give you a clue as to why the mail could not be delivered. The most common causes of undeliverable mail are:

✔ **The e-mail address is incorrect.** This results in one of two types of errors, depending on which portion of the e-mail address is wrong. If you get the domain name wrong, the nondelivery report indicates an error, such as *destination not found* or *bad destination system address.* If the recipient's name is incorrect, the nondelivery report indicates an error, such as *recipient not found* or *no such user.*

For example, if you try to send mail to me@mydomain.cmo instead of me@mydomain.com, the delivery will fail because the domain is incorrect. However, if you try to send the mail to em@mydomain.com instead of me@mydomain.com, the delivery will fail because the recipient is incorrect.

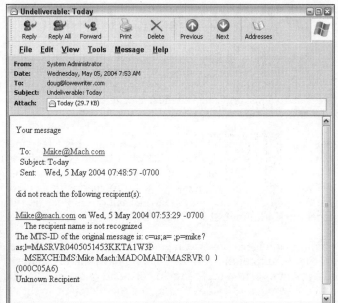

Figure 16-1:
A non-
delivery
report.

✔ **The recipient's domain MX records may be configured incorrectly.** In this case, you have sent the mail to the correct address, but the mail system can't find the recipient's mail server because of the incorrect MX record.

Some mail gateways are more tolerant of MX errors than others. As a result, a minor error in the MX configuration may not be noticed because the recipient receives most of his or her mail.

✔ **The recipient's mail server is down.** If this is the case, hopefully the recipient's system administrator will get the server back up soon so the mail can be delivered.

✔ **Your mail gateway is unable to reach the recipient's mail gateway due to communication failures.** This usually means that your mail server's Internet connection is down. After the connection has been reestablished, the mail can be resent.

✔ **The recipient's mail server rejects the mail because it doesn't trust you.** In many cases, this happens if your mail gateway has been listed at one of the Internet's many blacklist sites because of a spam problem or other abuse problem. For information about how to get off a blacklist, see the section "Help! I've been blacklisted!" later in this chapter.

Viewing the mail server's error logs

Sometimes you can garner additional information about the reason a mail message didn't get through by examining your e-mail server's error logs. For example, if your mail delivery fails because of a communication error, the mail server's error logs may help you to pinpoint the cause of the communication failure.

If you're using a Windows server with Exchange Server as your e-mail gateway, you can find the e-mail by opening the Event Viewer. E-mail events are logged in the Application log. Other mail gateways have similar logs.

How to view message headers

To make e-mail more user-friendly, modern e-mail clients hide nasty details such as the e-mail message headers that accompany messages. Sometimes, however, these headers can help track down the cause of e-mail delivery problems. E-mail headers are especially useful if you suspect that a message you receive isn't from whom it claims to be from. If you reply to a message and your reply comes back as undeliverable, you can look into the message headers to find out the actual e-mail address of the person who sent you the original message.

To display e-mail headers in Microsoft Outlook, open the message, and then choose the View➪Options command. This displays the Message Options dialog box; the message headers are shown in a scrollable text box at the bottom of this dialog box.

How to deal with spam

Spam — not the lunchmeat, but junk e-mail — is another one of the big headaches network administrators have to contend with. Left unchecked, eventually most network users' inboxes will become filled with spam. For every legitimate piece of e-mail, your users may get 10, 20, or even 50 spam e-mails. This makes it all too easy for the legitimate e-mail to get overlooked.

There are three popular methods of limiting the amount of spam that reaches your users' inboxes:

   ✔ **Filters:** *Filters* analyze incoming mail and try to identify spam according to its contents. The filter looks for words and phrases that commonly appear in spam. Unfortunately, spammers know all about these filters and are constantly figuring out ways to get their spam past the filters. In addition, sometimes the filters will incorrectly decide that a legitimate e-mail message is spam. Filters are improving all the time, however, and the latest generation of spam filters use a technique called *Bayesian analysis* that's very accurate.

✔ **Blacklists:** A *blacklist* is a list of known spammers whose mail is blocked by your mail server. There are several Internet services that publish blacklists you can connect your mail server to. For more information, log on to the Internet and search for *spam blacklist.*

✔ **Whitelists:** A *whitelist* is the opposite of a blacklist: it's a list of addresses whose mail you always want to receive.

One way to fight spam is to configure Outlook to filter spam. (The most recent version, Outlook 2003, has substantially better anti-spam features than previous versions.) Alternatively, you can purchase separate spam filtering software and install it on each client computer. However, the best solution is to set up spam filtering on your mail server. That way, spam will never make it into your users' inboxes and you won't have to worry about maintaining anti-spam software on each user's computer. If your network has more than a few users, you're much better off running centralized anti-spam software on a server than running a separate anti-spam program on each user's computer.

Help! I've been blacklisted!

Blacklists are a popular and useful way to fight spam. But what happens if your own mail server gets entered into a blacklist? In some cases, this happens because your mail server may have security holes that allow spammers to hijack your server and use it to send spam. The most common of these holes is called an open relay. An *open relay* is a mail server that can be hijacked by spammers so they can use it to send spam. If your mail server is an open relay, it can be taken over by spammers and used to deliver their mail anonymously. Because open relays are a major source of spam, many blacklists automatically blacklist servers that are configured as open relays. (There are many Web sites you can use to test if your mail server is an open relay. To find one, go to a search service such as Google and search for *open relay test.*)

Some blacklists are complaint-driven. You get listed in the blacklist if someone complains that you've been sending spam to that person. Unfortunately, it's possible to be falsely accused, so you may find yourself blacklisted even if you've done nothing wrong. And sometimes you get reported because of a misunderstanding. For example, a customer may forget that he or she *gave* you his or her e-mail address, and then complain to a blacklist when they receive your e-mail.

If you discover that you are blacklisted, the first step is to find out which blacklists you're on and why. Then correct the problems that caused you to be blacklisted — and ask the lists to retest your server so you can be removed from the lists.

Unfortunately, it's much easier to get *on* a blacklist than it is to get off of one. Once you've been blacklisted, it can easily take several weeks to get off the lists after you've corrected the problem.

The most comprehensive Web site for solving blacklist problems is `relays. osirusoft.com`. From this page, you can enter your domain name to discover whether you have been listed on any of the major blacklists. If this site reports that you are on any blacklists, you have to correct the problem that caused you to be blacklisted, and then ask each of the blacklists to retest your site and remove you from their lists. Then, recheck your domain at `relays. osirusoft.com` to make sure that you've been removed. Don't be surprised if it takes several weeks to get removed from all the blacklists.

Chapter 17

Network Troubleshooting

*F*ace it: Networks are prone to breaking.

They have too many parts. Cables. Connectors. Cards. Hubs. Switches. Routers. All these parts must be held together in a delicate balance; the network equilibrium is all too easy to disturb. Even the best-designed computer networks sometimes act as if they're held together with baling wire, chewing gum, and duct tape.

To make matters worse, networks breed suspicion. After your computer is attached to a network, users begin to blame the network every time something goes wrong, regardless of whether the problem has anything to do with the network. You can't get columns to line up in a Word document? Must be the network. Your spreadsheet doesn't add up? The @@#$% network's acting up again. The stock market's down? Arghhh!!!!!!

The worst thing about network failures is that sometimes they can shut down an entire company. It's not so bad if just one user can't access a particular shared folder on a file server. If a critical server goes down, however, your network users may be locked out of their files, their applications, their e-mail, and everything else they need to conduct business as usual. When that happens, they'll be beating down your doors and won't stop until you get the network back up and running.

In this chapter, I review some of the most likely causes of network trouble — and suggest some basic troubleshooting techniques that you can employ when your network goes on the fritz.

When Bad Things Happen to Good Computers

The following are some basic troubleshooting tips about what you should examine at the first sign of network trouble. In many (if not most) of the cases, one of the following tips will get your network back up and running.

1. **Make sure that your computer and everything attached to it is plugged in.**

   Computer geeks love it when a user calls for help and they get to tell the user that the computer isn't plugged in. They write it down in their geek logs so they can tell their geek friends about it later. They may even want to take your picture so they can show it to their geek friends. (Most "accidents" involving computer geeks are a direct result of this kind of behavior. So try to be tactful when you ask a user if he or she is sure the computer is actually turned on.)

2. **Make sure that your computer is properly connected to the network.**

3. **Note any error messages that appear on the screen.**

4. **Try the built-in Windows network troubleshooter.**

   For more information, see the section "Using the Windows Networking Troubleshooter," later in this chapter.

5. **Check the free disk space on the server.**

   When a server runs out of disk space, strange things can happen. Sometimes you'll get a clear error message indicating such a situation, but not always. Sometimes the network just grinds to a halt; operations that used to take a few seconds now take a few minutes.

6. **Do a little experimenting to find out whether the problem is indeed a network problem or just a problem with the computer itself.**

   See the section "Time to Experiment" later in this chapter for some simple things you can do to isolate a network problem.

7. **Try restarting the computer.**

   An amazing number of computer problems are cleared up by a simple restart of the computer. Of course, in many cases, the problem will recur — but then it has showed itself, and you can isolate the cause and fix the problem. Some problems are only intermittent, and a simple reboot is all that's needed.

8. **Try restarting the network server.**

   See the section "How to Restart a Network Server" later in this chapter.

How to Fix Dead Computers

If a computer seems totally dead, here are some things to check:

- ✔ Is it plugged in?

- ✔ If the computer is plugged into a surge protector or a power strip, make sure that the surge protector or power strip is plugged in *and turned on*. If the surge protector or power strip has a light, it should be glowing.

- ✔ Make sure that the computer's On/Off switch is turned on. This sounds too basic to even include here, but many computers are set up so the computer's actual power switch is always left in the On position and the computer is actually turned on or off by means of the switch on the surge protector or power strip (not kind to the computer, but common). Many computer users are surprised to find out that their computers have On/Off switches on the back of the cases.

- ✔ To complicate matters, newer computers have a Sleep feature, in which they appear to be turned off but really they're just sleeping. All you have to do to wake such a computer is jiggle the mouse a little. (I used to have an uncle like that.) It's easy to assume that the computer is turned off, press the power button, wonder why nothing happened, and then press the power button and hold it down, hoping it will take. If you hold down the power button long enough, the computer will actually turn itself off. Then, when you turn the computer back on, you'll get a message saying the computer wasn't shut down properly. Arghhh! The moral of the story: Jiggle the mouse if the computer seems to have nodded off.

- ✔ If you think the computer isn't plugged in but it looks like it is, listen for the fan. If the fan is running, the computer is getting power and the problem is more serious than an unplugged power cord. (If the fan isn't running, but the computer is plugged in and the power is on, the fan may be out to lunch; better shut the thing down before it overheats.)

- ✔ If the computer is plugged in, turned on, and still not running, plug a lamp into the outlet to make sure that power is getting to the outlet. You may need to reset a tripped circuit breaker or replace a bad surge protector. Or you may need to call the power company. (If you live in California, don't bother calling the power company. It probably won't do any good.)

Surge protectors have a limited lifespan. After a few years of use, many surge protectors continue to provide electrical power for your computer, but the components that protect your computer from power surges no longer work. If you are using a surge protector that is more than two or three years old, replace the old surge protector with a new one.

✔ The monitor has a separate power cord and switch. Make sure that the monitor is plugged in and turned on. (The monitor actually has two cables that must be plugged in. One runs from the back of the monitor to the back of the computer; the other is a power cord that comes from the back of the monitor and must be plugged into an electrical outlet.)

✔ Your keyboard, monitor, mouse, and printer are all connected to the back of your computer by cables. Make sure that these cables are all plugged in securely.

✔ Make sure that the other ends of the monitor and printer cables are plugged in properly, too.

✔ Some monitors have knobs or buttons that you can use to adjust the contrast and brightness of the monitor's display. If the computer is running but your display is dark, try adjusting these knobs. They may have been turned all the way down.

Ways to Check a Network Connection

Network gurus often say that 95 percent of all network problems are cable problems. The cables that connect client computers to the rest of the network are finicky beasts. They can break at a moment's notice, and by "break," I don't necessarily mean "to physically break in two." Sure, some broken cables look like someone got to the cable with pruning shears. However, cable problems aren't usually visible to the naked eye. Here are some tips for dealing with cable connection problems:

✔ If your network uses twisted-pair cable, you can quickly tell whether the cable connection to the network is good by looking at the back of your computer. Look for a small light located near where the cable plugs in; if this light is glowing steadily, the cable is good. If the light is dark or if it's flashing intermittently, you have a cable problem (or a problem with the network card or the hub or switch that the other end of the cable is plugged in to).

If the light is not glowing steadily, try removing the cable from your computer and reinserting it. This action may cure the weak connection.

✔ Detecting a cable problem in a network that's wired with *coaxial cable,* the kind that looks like cable-TV cable, is more difficult. The connector on the back of the computer forms a *T.* The base end of the *T* plugs into your computer. One or two coaxial cables plug into the outer ends of the *T.* If you use only one coaxial cable, you must use a special plug called a *terminator* instead of a cable at the other end of the *T.* Without the terminator, the entire network will probably cough and sputter. If you can't find a terminator, try conjuring one up from farther along in the twenty-first century. (**Warning:** Do not do this if your name happens to be Sarah Connor.)

Don't unplug a coaxial cable from the network while the network is running. Data travels around a coaxial network in the same way that a baton travels around the track in a relay race. If one person drops it, the race is over. The baton never gets to the next person. Likewise, if you unplug the network cable from your computer, the network data never gets to the other computers that are "down the line" from your computer.

If you must disconnect the cable from your computer, make sure that you disconnect the T-connector itself from the network card; don't disconnect the cable from the T-connector itself. (If you disconnect the cable from the T-connector, you'll disrupt the flow of data on the entire network.)

✔ With any luck, your network is wired so each computer is connected to the network with a short (six-foot-or-so) patch cable. One end of the patch cable plugs into the computer, and the other end plugs into a cable connector mounted on the wall. Try quickly disconnecting and reconnecting the patch cable. If that doesn't do the trick, try to find a spare patch cable that you can use.

✔ Hubs and switches are prone to having cable problems, too — especially those hubs that are wired in a "professional manner" involving a rat's nest of patch cables. Be careful whenever you enter the lair of the rat's nest. If you need to replace a patch cable, be very careful when you disconnect the suspected bad cable and reconnect the good cable in its place.

A Bunch of Error Messages Just Flew By!

Do error messages show up on-screen when your computer boots? If so, they can provide invaluable clues to determine the source of the problem.

If you see error messages when you start up the computer, keep the following points in mind:

✔ Don't panic if you see a lot of error messages. Sometimes a simple problem that's easy to correct can cause a plethora of error messages when you start your computer. The messages may look as if your computer is falling to pieces, but the fix may be very simple.

✔ If the messages fly by so fast that you can't see them, press your computer's Pause key. Your computer comes to a screeching halt, giving you a chance to catch up on your error-message reading. After you've read enough, press the Pause key again to get things moving. (On computers that don't have a Pause key, pressing Ctrl+Num Lock or Ctrl+S does the same thing.)

- ✔ If you missed the error messages the first time, restart the computer and watch them again.

- ✔ Better yet, press F8 when you see the message `Starting Windows`. This displays a menu that allows you to select from several startup options, including one that processes each line of your `CONFIG.SYS` file one at a time, prompting you before proceeding to the next command.

Double-Checking Your Network Settings

I swear that there are little green men who sneak into offices at night, turn on computers, and mess up TCP/IP configuration settings just for kicks. These little green men are affectionately (?) known as *networchons*.

Remarkably, network configuration settings sometimes get inadvertently changed so a computer, which enjoyed the network for months or even years, one day finds itself unable to access the network. So one of the first things you do, after making sure that the computers are actually on and the cables aren't broken, is a basic review of the computer's network settings. Check the following:

- ✔ At a command prompt, run `ipconfig` to make sure that TCP/IP is up and running on the computer and that the IP addresses, subnet masks, and default gateway settings look right.

- ✔ Call up the network connection's Properties dialog box and make sure that the necessary protocols are installed correctly.

- ✔ Open the System Properties dialog box (double-click System in Control Panel) and check the Computer Name tab. Make sure that the computer name is unique and the domain or workgroup name is spelled properly.

- ✔ Double-check the user account to make sure that the user really has permission to access the resources they need.

Using the Windows Networking Troubleshooter

Windows comes with a built-in troubleshooter that can often help you to pin down the cause of a network problem. Figure 17-1 shows the Windows XP version. Answer the questions asked by the troubleshooter and click Next to move from screen to screen. The Networking Troubleshooter can't solve all networking problems, but it does point out the causes of the most common problems.

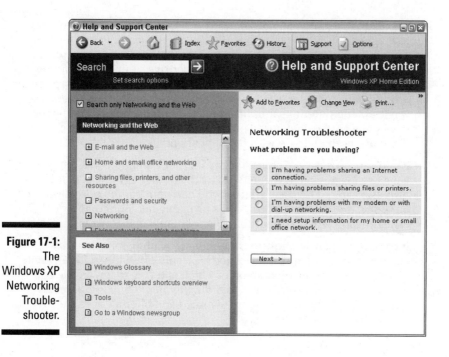

Figure 17-1:
The
Windows XP
Networking
Trouble-
shooter.

The procedure for starting the Networking Troubleshooter depends on which version of Windows you are using:

- ✔ For Windows XP, choose Start➪Help and Support➪Networking and the Web➪Fixing Network or Web problems; then click Home and Small Office Networking Troubleshooter.

- ✔ For Windows 98, click the Start button; then choose Help➪ Troubleshooting➪Windows 98 Troubleshooters, and finally click Networking.

- ✔ For Windows Me, choose Start➪Help➪Troubleshooting➪ Home Networking & Network Problems. Finally, click Home Networking Troubleshooter.

Windows 95 also came with a network troubleshooter, but it was not as thorough.

Time to Experiment

If you can't find some obvious explanation for your troubles — for example, the computer is unplugged — you need to do some experimenting to narrow down the possibilities. Design your experiments to answer one basic question: *Is this a network problem or a local computer problem?*

Here are some ways you can narrow down the cause of the problem:

- ✔ Try performing the same operation on someone else's computer. If no one on the network can access a network drive or printer, something is probably wrong with the network. On the other hand, if the error occurs on only one computer, the problem is likely with that computer. The wayward computer may not be reliably communicating with the network, may not be configured properly for the network, or the problem may have nothing to do with the network at all.

- ✔ If you can perform the operation on another computer without problems, try logging on to the network with another computer using your own username. Then see whether you can perform the operation without error. If you can, the problem is probably on your computer. If you can't, the problem may be with the way your user account is configured.

- ✔ If you can't log on at another computer, try waiting for a bit. Your account may be temporarily locked out. This can happen for a variety of reasons — the most common of which is trying to log on with the wrong password several times in a row. If you're still locked out an hour later, call the network administrator and offer a doughnut to soften the bad news.

Who's on First?

When troubleshooting a networking problem, it is often useful to find out who is actually logged on to a network server. For example, if a user is unable to access a file on the server, you can check to see whether the user is logged on. If so, you'll know that the user's account is valid, but the user may not have permission to access the particular file or folder that he or she is attempting to access. On the other hand, if the user is not logged on, the problem may lie with the account itself or with the way the user is attempting to connect to the server.

It's also useful to find out who's logged on in the event that you need to restart the server. For more information about restarting a server, see the section, "How to Restart a Network Server" later in this chapter.

The exact procedure of checking who is logged on depends on which server operating system you're using. The following paragraphs describe how to find out who's logged on to Windows NT 4 Server, Windows 2000 Server, or Windows Server 2003.

- ✔ For Windows NT 4 Server, choose Start➪Program Files➪Administrative Tools➪Server Manager. Double-click the server in the list of available servers, and then click the Users button. This brings up the dialog box shown in Figure 17-2.

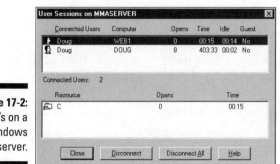

Figure 17-2:
Who's on a
Windows
NT server.

✔ For Windows 2000 Server, right-click the My Computer icon on the desktop and pick Manage from the menu that appears. This brings up the
Computer Management window. Open System Tools in the tree list, and
then open Shared Folders and select Sessions. A list of users who are
logged on appears.

✔ For Windows Server 2003, you can bring up the Computer Management
window by choosing Start⇨Administrative Tools⇨Computer
Management.

You can immediately disconnect all users in Windows NT Server by clicking
Disconnect All. In Windows 2000 Server or Windows Server 2003, right-click
Sessions in the Computer Management window and choose All Tasks⇨
Disconnect All.

How to Restart a Client Computer

Sometimes trouble gets a computer so tied up in knots that the only thing
you can do is reboot. In some cases, the computer just starts acting weird.
Strange characters appear on the screen, or Windows goes haywire and
won't let you exit a program. Sometimes the computer gets so confused
that it can't even move. It just sits there, like a deer staring at oncoming
headlights. It won't move, no matter how hard you press the Esc key or the
Enter key. You can move the mouse all over your desktop, even throw it
across the room, but the mouse pointer on-screen stays perfectly still.

When a computer starts acting strange, you need to reboot. If you must
reboot, you should do so as cleanly as possible. I know this procedure may
seem elementary, but the technique for safely restarting a client computer
is worth repeating, even if it is basic:

1. **Save your work if you can.**

   Use the File⇨Save command, if you can, to save any documents or files that you were editing when things started to go haywire. If you can't use the menus, try clicking the Save button in the toolbar. If that doesn't work, try pressing Ctrl+S — the standard keyboard shortcut for the Save command.

2. **Close any running programs if you can.**

   Use the File⇨Exit command or click the Close button in the upper-right corner of the program window. Or press Alt+F4.

3. **Choose the Start⇨Shut Down command from the taskbar.**

   For Windows XP, choose Start⇨Turn Off Computer.

   The Shut Down Windows dialog box appears.

4. **Select the Restart option and then click OK.**

   Your computer restarts itself.

If restarting your computer doesn't seem to fix the problem, you may need to turn your computer all the way off and then turn it on again. To do so, follow the previous procedure until Step 4. Choose the Shut Down option instead of the Restart option and then click OK. Depending on your computer, Windows either turns off your computer or displays a message stating that you can now safely turn off your computer. If Windows doesn't turn the computer off for you, flip the On/Off switch to turn your computer off. Wait a minute or so and then turn the computer back on.

Most newer computers won't immediately shut themselves off when you press the Power button. Instead, you must hold the Power button down for a few seconds to actually turn off the power. This is a precaution designed to prevent you from accidentally powering down your computer.

Here are a few things to try if you have trouble restarting your computer:

- ✔ If your computer refuses to respond to the Start⇨Shut Down command, try pressing Ctrl+Alt+Delete. This is called the "three-finger salute." It's appropriate to say "Queueue" as you do it.

  When you press Ctrl+Alt+Delete, Windows 9x and later versions attempt to display a dialog box that enables you to close any running programs or shut down your computer entirely. Unfortunately, sometimes Windows 9x becomes so confused that it can't display the Restart dialog box, in which case, pressing Ctrl+Alt+Delete may restart your computer.

- ✔ If Ctrl+Alt+Delete doesn't do anything, you've reached the last resort. The only thing left to do is press the Reset button on your computer.

Pressing the Reset button is a drastic action that you should take only after your computer becomes completely unresponsive. Any work you haven't yet saved to disk is lost. (Sniff.) (If your computer doesn't have a Reset button, turn the computer off, wait a few moments, and then turn the computer back on again.)

✔ If at all possible, save your work before restarting your computer. Any work you haven't saved is lost. Unfortunately, if your computer is totally tied up in knots, you probably can't save your work. In that case, you have no choice but to push your computer off the (digital) cliff.

Restarting Network Services

Once in awhile, the NOS service that supports the task that's causing you trouble inexplicably stops or gets stuck. If users can't access a server, it could be because one of the key network services has stopped or is stuck.

You can review the status of services by using the Services tool, as shown in Figure 17-3. To display it, choose Administrative Tools⇨Services. Review this list to make sure that all key services are running. If a key service is paused or stopped, restart it.

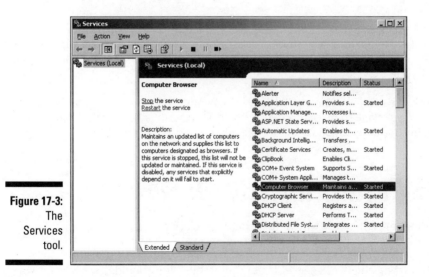

Figure 17-3:
The
Services
tool.

Which service qualifies as a *key* service depends on what roles you've defined for the server. Table 17-1 lists a few key services that are common to most Windows network operating systems. However, many servers will require additional services besides these.

Table 17-1	Key Windows services
Service	**Description**
Computer Browser	Maintains a list of computers on the network that can be accessed. If this service is disabled, the computer won't be able to use browsing services, such as My Network Places.
DHCP Client	Enables the computer to obtain its IP address from a DHCP server. If this service is disabled, the computer's IP address won't be configured properly.
DNS Client	Enables the computer to access a DNS server to resolve DNS names. If this service is disabled, the computer won't be able to handle DNS names, including Internet addresses and Active Directory names.
Server	Provides basic file and printer sharing services for the server. If this service is stopped, clients won't be able to connect to the server to access files or printers.
Workstation	Enables the computer to establish client connections with other servers. If this service is disabled, the computer won't be able to connect to other servers.

Key services usually stop for a reason, so simply restarting a stopped service probably won't solve your network's problem — at least, not for long. You should review the System log to look for any error messages that may explain why the service stopped in the first place.

If you're using Windows 2000 Server or Windows Server 2003, you can double-click a service to display a dialog box that describes the service. This can come in handy if you're not certain what a particular service does.

How to Restart a Network Server

Sometimes, the only way to flush out a network problem is to restart the network server that's experiencing trouble.

Restarting a network server is only something you should do as a last resort. Network operating systems are designed to run for months or even years at a time without rebooting. Restarting a server invariably results in a temporary shutdown of the network. If you must restart a server, try to do it during off hours if possible.

Before you restart a server, check to see whether a specific service that is required has been paused or stopped. You may be able to just restart the individual service rather than the entire server. For more information, see the section "Restarting Network Services" earlier in this chapter.

Here is the basic procedure for restarting a network server. Keep in mind that for NetWare or Windows 2000 servers, you may need to take additional steps to get things going again. Check with your network administrator to be sure.

1. **Make sure everyone is logged off the server.**

   The easiest way to do that is to restart the server after normal business hours, when everyone has gone home for the day. Then, you can just shut down the server and let the shutdown process forcibly log off any remaining users.

   To find out who's logged on, refer to the section "Who's On First?" earlier in this chapter.

2. **When you're sure the users have logged off, shut down the network server.**

   You want to do this behaving like a good citizen if possible — decently and in order. If you use Novell NetWare, type **down** on the server's keyboard and then reboot the server. For Windows servers, use the Start➪ Shut Down command.

   Windows Server 2003 won't let you shut down the server without providing a reason for the shutdown. When you press Ctrl+Alt+Delete, the Shut Down Windows dialog box appears. In this dialog box, you can select one of several predetermined reasons for planned or unplanned shutdowns from the drop-down list. You can also provide additional details about the shutdown, if you want. This dialog box won't let you shut down until you select a reason and type at least one character in the Comment text box. The information you supply here is entered into the server's System log, which you can review by using the Event Viewer.

3. **Reboot the server computer or turn it off and then on again.** Watch the server start up to make sure that no error messages appear.

4. **Tell everyone to log back on, and make sure everyone can now access the network.**

Restarting the network server is more drastic than restarting a client computer. Make sure that everyone saves his or her work and logs off the network before you do it! You can cause major problems if you blindly turn off the server computer while users are logged on. And remember, restarting a network server is a major inconvenience to every network user. Better offer treats.

Looking at Event Logs

One of the most useful troubleshooting techniques for diagnosing network problems is to review the network operating system's built-in event logs. These logs contain information about interesting and potentially troublesome events that occur during the daily operation of your network. Ordinarily, these logs run in the background, quietly gathering information about network events. When something goes wrong, you can check the logs to see whether the problem generated a noteworthy event. In many cases, the event logs will contain an entry that pinpoints the exact cause of the problem and suggests a solution.

To display the event logs in a Windows server, use the Event Viewer available from the Administrative Tools menu. For example, Figure 17-4 shows an Event Viewer from a Windows Server 2003 system. The tree listing on the left side of the Event Viewer lists five categories of events that are tracked: Application events, Security events, System events, Directory Service events, and File Replication Service events. Select one of these options to see the log that you want to view. For details about a particular event, double-click the event; this action displays a dialog box that has detailed information about the event.

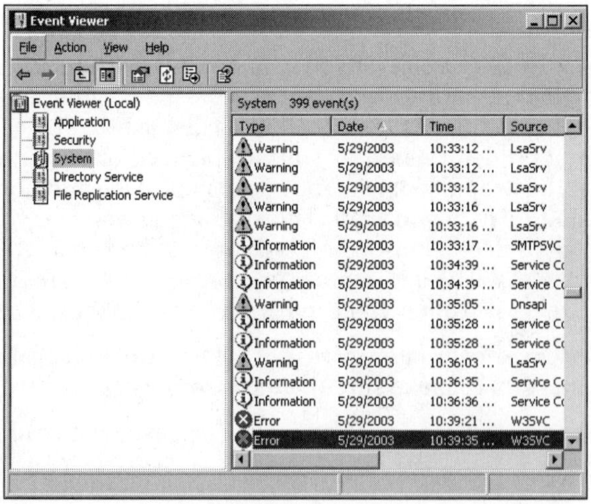

Figure 17-4:
Event logs
keep
track of
interesting
and
potentially
troublesome
events.

Documenting Your Trials and Tribulations

Even if you have a small network, I suggest that you keep a log of all the problems you experience with your network and how you solved each problem. Record the details of both the problem and the solution as specifically as possible. You'll be amazed at how useful this log can be. Not surprisingly, most network problems fall into patterns as users encounter the same or similar problems over and over again. Often, the true solution to a problem doesn't become obvious until after you think you've fixed the problem two or three times. (Or maybe four or five times!)

For a large network, you'll probably want to invest in problem management software that tracks each problem through the entire process of trouble-shooting, from initial report to final resolution. For small- and medium-sized networks, it's probably sufficient to put together a three-ring binder with pre-printed forms. Or, record your log in a Word document or Excel spreadsheet.

Regardless of how you track your network problems, the tracking log should include the following information:

- ✔ The real name and the network username of the person reporting the problem.
- ✔ The date the problem was first reported.
- ✔ An indication of the severity of the problem. Is it merely an inconvenience, or is a user unable to complete his or her work because of the problem? Does a workaround exist?
- ✔ The name of the person assigned to resolve the problem.
- ✔ A description of the problem.
- ✔ A list of the software involved, including versions.
- ✔ A description of the steps taken to solve the problem.
- ✔ A description of any intermediate steps that were taken to try to solve the problem, along with an indication of whether those steps were "undone" when they didn't help solve the problem.
- ✔ The date the problem was finally resolved.

Chapter 18

How to Stay on Top of Your Network and Keep the Users Off Your Back

*N*etwork managers really have a rotten deal. Users come to you whenever anything goes wrong, regardless of whether the problem has anything to do with the network. They knock on your door if they can't log in, if they've lost a file, or if they can't remember how to use the microwave. They probably even ask you to show them how to program their VCRs.

This chapter brushes you up on a few basic things you can do to simplify your life as a network manager.

Training Your Users

After you first get your network up and running, invite all the network users to Network Obedience School, so you can teach them how to behave on the network. Show them the basics of accessing the network, make sure they understand about sharing files, and explain the rules to them.

A great way to prepare your users for this session is to ask them to read the first six chapters of this book. Remember, I wrote those chapters with the network user in mind, so they explain the basic facts of network life. If your users read those chapters first, they are in a much better position to ask good questions during obedience school.

Here are some more ways to make the training process painless for you and your users:

- ✔ **Write up a summary of what your users need to know about the network, on one page if possible.** Include everyone's user ID, the names of the servers, network drive assignments and printers, and the procedure for logging in to the network. Make sure that everyone has a copy of this Network Cheat Sheet.

- ✔ **Emphasize the etiquette of network life.** Make sure everyone understands that all that free space on the network drive isn't personal space — it's shared, and should be used sparingly. Explain the importance of treating other people's files with respect. Suggest that users check with their fellow users before sending a three-hour print job to the network printer.

- ✔ **Don't bluff your way through your role as network manager.** If you're not a computer genius, don't pretend to be one just because you know a little more than everyone else. Be up front with your users. Tell them that everyone is in this together, and you're going to do your best to try to solve any network problems that may come up.

Organizing a Library

One of the biggest bummers about being the network manager is that every network user expects you to be an expert at every computer program he or she uses. That's a manageable enough task when you have only two network users and the only program they use is Microsoft Word. But if you have a gaggle of users who use a bevy of programs, being an expert at all them is next to impossible.

The only way around this dilemma is to set up a well-stocked computer library that has all the information you may need to solve problems that come up. When a user bugs you with some previously undiscovered bug, you can say with confidence, "I'll get back to you on that one."

Your library should include the following:

- ✔ **A copy of your network binder:** All the information you need about the configuration of your network should be in this binder. (Don't put the original copy of the network binder in the library. Keep the original under lock and key in your office. And keep an extra copy off site in a safe place.)

- ✔ **A copy of the manuals for every program used on the network:** Most users ignore the manuals, so they won't mind if you "borrow" them for the library. If a user won't part with a manual, at least make a note of the manual's location so you know where to find it.

- ✔ **A copy of the *Windows Resource Kit* for every version of Windows in use on your network:** You can get the *Windows Resource Kit* at any bookstore that has a well-stocked section of computer books.

- ✔ **A copy of the network software manual or manuals.**

- ✔ **At least 20 copies of this book:** (Hey, I have bills to pay.) Seriously, your library should contain books appropriate to your level of expertise. Of course, *For Dummies* books are available on just about every major computer subject. Devoting an entire shelf to these yellow-and-black books isn't a bad idea.

Keeping Up with the Computer Industry

The computer business changes fast, and your users probably expect you to be abreast of all the latest trends and developments. "Hey," they ask, "what do you think about the new version of SkyWriter? Should we upgrade, or should we stick with Version 23?"

"We want to build an Intranet Web site. What's the best Web page editor for under $200?"

"My kid wants me to buy video-editing software. Which one is better, the VideoPro 2005 or the MovieMaker 9000?"

The only way to give halfway intelligent answers to questions like these is to read about the industry. Visit your local newsstand and pick out a few computer magazines that appeal to you.

- ✔ Subscribe to at least one general-interest computer magazine and one magazine specifically written for network users. That way you can keep abreast of general trends, plus the specific stuff that applies just to networks.

- ✔ Subscribe to e-mail newsletters that have information about the systems you use.

- ✔ Look for magazines that have a mix of good how-to articles and reviews of new products.

- ✔ Don't overlook the value of the advertisements in many of the larger computer magazines. Some people (I'm one of 'em) subscribe to certain magazines to read the ads as much as to read the articles.

- ✔ Keep in mind that most computer magazines are very technical. Try to find magazines written to your current level. You may discover that after a year or two, you outgrow one magazine and are ready to replace it with one that's more technical.

The Guru Needs a Guru, Too

No matter how much you know about computers, plenty of people know more than you do. This rule seems to apply at every rung of the ladder of computer experience. I'm sure that a top rung exists somewhere, occupied by the world's best computer guru. However, I'm not sitting on that rung, and neither are you. (Not even Bill Gates is sitting on that rung. In fact, Bill Gates got to where he is today by hiring people on higher rungs.)

As the local computer guru, one of your most valuable assets can be a knowledgeable friend who's a notch or two above you on the geek scale. That way, when you run into a real stumper, you have a friend you can call for advice. Here are some tips for handling your own guru:

- In dealing with your own guru, don't forget the Computer Geek's Golden Rule: "Do unto your guru as you would have your own users do unto you." Don't pester your guru with simple stuff that you just haven't spent the time to think through. If you *have* thought it through and can't come up with a solution, however, give your guru a call. Most computer experts welcome the opportunity to tackle an unusual computer problem. It's a genetic defect.

- If you don't already know someone who knows more about computers than you do, consider joining your local PC users' group. The group may even have a subgroup that specializes in your networking software — or may be devoted entirely to local folks who use the same networking software that you use. Odds are good that you're sure to make a friend or two at a users' group meeting. Also, you can probably convince your boss to pay any fees required to join the group.

- If you can't find a real-life guru, try to find an online guru. Check out the various computing newsgroups on the Internet. Subscribe to online newsletters that are automatically delivered to you via e-mail.

Helpful Bluffs and Excuses

As network administrator, you just won't be able to solve a problem sometimes, at least not immediately. You can do two things in this situation. The first is to explain that the problem is particularly difficult and that you'll have a solution as soon as possible. The second solution is to look the user in the eyes and, with a straight face, try one of these phony explanations:

- Blame it on the version of whatever software you're using. "Oh, they fixed that with version 39."

- Blame it on cheap, imported memory chips.

✔ Blame it on Democrats. Or Republicans. Or hanging chads. Whatever.

✔ Blame it on Enron executives.

✔ Hope that the problem wasn't caused by stray static electricity. Those types of problems are very difficult to track down. Tell your users that not properly discharging themselves before using their computers can cause all kinds of problems.

✔ You need more memory.

✔ You need a bigger disk.

✔ You need an Itanium to do that.

✔ Blame it on Jar-Jar Binks.

✔ You can't do that in Windows XP.

✔ You can *only* do that in Windows XP.

✔ You're not using Windows XP, are you?

✔ Could be a virus.

✔ Or sunspots.

✔ All work and no beer make Homer something something something . . .

Part IV
Network Operating Systems

In this part . . .

You get an overview of the most popular network operating systems used for server computers. You'll learn the basics of working with Windows Server 2003 (Windows Server 2000 is similar), NetWare 6 (including the latest version, 6.5), and Linux. You also get a brief introduction to the world of Macintosh networking. Happy networking! And hey, be careful out there.

Chapter 19

Windows Server 2003

● ●

In This Chapter

▶ Getting ready for the installation

▶ Installing a network operating system

▶ Setting up a share on a file server

▶ Using basic troubleshooting tools

● ●

*T*his chapter presents a whirlwind tour of working with Windows Server 2003, the latest and greatest server operating system from Microsoft. I can't possibly show you everything there is to know about Windows Server 2003 in one chapter, so instead I'll focus on the tasks that come up most often, such as configuring user accounts, resetting passwords, setting up file shares, and so on. You'll find more detailed information about Windows Server 2003 in my book, *Networking All In One Desk Reference For Dummies* or in *Windows 2003 Server For Dummies* by Ed Tittel and James Michael Stewart, both published by Wiley, of course.

Note that much of the information applies to Windows 2000 Server as well. Although the exact procedures may vary, Windows 2000 Server is similar enough to Windows Server 2003 that you should be able to get through most of the procedures without much trouble.

Installing and Configuring Windows Server 2003

The following sections briefly describe the process of installing and configuring Windows Server 2003.

Planning for installation

For the most part, installing Windows Server 2003 is simply a matter of answering the questions posed by the Setup program. The key to a successful installation, then, is knowing what questions to expect and what answers to provide. This section should help you prepare.

Meeting the minimum requirements

Before you install a Windows Server operating system, you should make sure that the computer meets the minimum requirements. Table 19-1 lists the official minimum requirements for Windows Server 2003 — as well as what I consider more realistic minimums if you expect to get satisfactory performance from the server as a moderately-well-used file server.

Table 19-1	Minimum hardware requirements for Windows Server 2003	
Item	*Official Minimum*	*A More Realistic Minimum*
CPU	133MHz Pentium	1GHz Pentium 4
RAM	128MB	512MB
Free disk space	1.5GB	5GB

Besides meeting the minimum requirements, you should also check to make sure that your specific hardware has been checked out and approved for use with Windows Server 2003. Microsoft publishes an official list of supported hardware, called the *Hardware Compatibility List,* or *HCL*. You can find the HCL at

```
www.microsoft.com/whdc/hcl/default.mspx
```

The Windows Server 2003 distribution CD-ROM includes a feature called the Check System Compatibility option that automatically checks your hardware against the HCL.

The Windows Server 2003 distribution disc includes a file called Relnotes. asp, located in the Docs file. You should read this file before you start Setup, just to make sure any of the specific procedures or warnings it contains applies to your situation.

Choosing the installation mode

Windows offers two installation modes that you should choose from before you begin setup: full installation or upgrade installation. A *full installation* deletes any existing operating system it finds on the computer and configures the new operating system from scratch. An *upgrade* installation keeps the settings of the previous Windows Server operating system version already installed.

Choosing the licensing mode

You can purchase Microsoft operating systems on a per-server or a per-user basis. You'll need to know which plan you have when you install the operating system. *Per-server* licensing allows a certain number of simultaneous client connections. This is a good choice if you have a large number of users, but only a small number of them use the server at a given time. In most cases, *per-user* licensing is a better idea: Each user has a license to use the Windows server, so all your users can use the server simultaneously.

Choosing the file system and partitioning scheme

Windows servers provide three choices for the file system to format the server's disk: FAT, FAT32, and NTFS. In most cases, you should elect to use NTFS. Well, actually, you should use NTFS in almost all cases. Come to think of it, you should *always* use NTFS.

You should also plan ahead how you're going to partition your hard drives. *Partitioning* enables you to divide a physical disk into one or more separate units called *partitions*. Each disk can have up to four partitions. All four of the partitions can be *primary partitions*, each of which can be formatted with a file system, such as NTFS or FAT32. Or, you can create up to three primary partitions and one *extended partition*, which can then be subdivided into one or more *logical drives*. Then, each logical drive can be formatted with a file system.

There are two common ways to partition a Windows server:

- ✔ **Allocate the entire disk as a single partition that will be formatted with NTFS.** The operating system will be installed into this partition, and disk space that isn't needed by the operating system or other network applications can be shared.

- ✔ **Divide the disk into two partitions.** Install the operating system and any other related software (such as Exchange Server or a backup utility) on the first partition. If the first partition will contain just the operating system, 10GB is a reasonable size, although you can get by with as little as 4 GB if space is at a premium. Then, use the second partition for application data or network file shares.

Plan your TCP/IP configuration

Before you install the operating system, you should have a plan for how you will implement TCP/IP on the network. In particular, decide such things as the IP subnet address and mask, the domain name, the host name for the server, whether the server will use DHCP or have a static IP address and perhaps itself be a DHCP server, and so on. (If all this seems like gobbledygook, refer to Chapters 24 and 25 for more information.)

Choose workgroups or domains

You'll need to decide whether to use domains or workgroups. A *domain* is a grouping of user accounts and various network resources under the control of a single directory database. A *workgroup* is a less formal association of computers on a network that makes it easy to locate shared files and printers. Workgroups don't have a sophisticated directory database, so they can't enforce strict security.

Workgroups are normally used only for very small networks. In fact, any network large enough to have a dedicated server computer that runs Windows Server 2003 is too large to use workgroups. So here's a word to the wise: If you're installing a Windows server, I recommend that you always opt for domains.

Assuming you opt for domains, you need to make two basic decisions:

- ✔ **What will the domain name be?** If you have a registered Internet domain name, such as mydomain.com, you may want to use it for your network's domain name. Otherwise, you can make up any name you want.

- ✔ **What computer or computers will be the domain controllers for the domain?** If this is the first server in a domain, you must designate it as a domain controller. If you already have a server acting as a domain controller, you can either add this computer as an additional domain controller, or designate it as a *member server*. A member server is simply a server that belongs to the domain but isn't responsible for authenticating logons and other duties that only domain controllers have to worry about.

Before You Install . . .

After you've made the key planning decisions for your Windows server installation, you should take a few precautionary steps before you actually start the Setup program. The following paragraphs describe the tasks you should complete before you perform an upgrade installation. Note that all these steps except the last one apply only to upgrades. If you're installing a Windows server on a new system, you can skip the first three.

- ✔ **Back up:** Do a complete backup of the server before you begin. Although Windows Setup is reliable, sometimes something serious goes wrong that results in lost data. (Note that you don't have to back up the drive to external media, such as tape. If you can find a network disk share with enough free space, back up to it.)

✔ **Check the event logs:** Look at the event logs of the existing server computer to check for recurring errors. You may discover that you have a problem with a SCSI device or that you have a problem with your current TCP/IP configuration. Better to find out now rather than in the middle of Setup.

✔ **Uncompress data:** If you've used DriveSpace or any other disk-compression software to compress a drive (as people did in the days before multi-gigabit drives), you'll have to uncompress the drive before you run Setup. Windows Server 2003 doesn't support DriveSpace or other disk-compression programs.

✔ **Disconnect UPS devices:** If you have installed an Uninterruptible Power Supply (UPS) device on the server and connected it to your computer via a serial cable, you should temporarily disconnect the serial cable before you run Setup. After setup is complete, you can reconnect the serial cable.

Running Setup

Now that you've planned your installation and prepared the computer, you're ready to run the Setup program. To start the Setup program, insert the distribution CD in the computer's CD-ROM drive and restart the computer. After a few moments, the Windows Setup Wizard fires up. It begins by asking whether you want to perform a new or upgrade installation, as shown in Figure 19-1. Choose the option you want, click Next, and continue answering the questions posed by the Setup Wizard. You'll be asked to enter the 25-character product key that verifies that you have a legal copy of the software, plus a bevy of configuration options (such as the type of file system you want to use and the partition structure to create).

Figure 19-1:
Welcome to
Windows
Setup!

Eventually, Setup will format your disk drive (if you're performing a new installation) and copy the Windows files to the drive. This part of the setup takes awhile — and runs in text mode, so you can't play Solitaire while you wait. I suggest you bring along your favorite book. Start on Chapter 1.

After all the files have been copied, Setup reboots your computer again and returns you to the more attractive GUI Setup program. Then, Setup examines all the devices on the computer and installs any necessary device drivers. You can read Chapter 2 of your book during this time.

After the drivers are all set up, Setup continues by asking other configuration questions such as your region, language, name, licensing mode, the password for the Administrator account, domain name, and so on.

Completing the installation

Setup gets a working Windows operating system up and running on your server. When that's done, however, you still have plenty of configuration information to specify before you can say your server is installed. Follow these steps to complete the installation and configuration of your server:

1. **Log on to Windows.**

   To log on to Windows, press Ctrl+Alt+Delete. When the Log On to Windows dialog box appears, type the Administrator password and click OK.

2. **Activate Windows.**

   The Product Activation feature is annoying to be sure, but Microsoft claims that it helps to reduce piracy. You have 30 days to activate Windows, but you may as well do it now.

   Windows displays a pop-up reminder in the bottom-right corner of the desktop. When you click the reminder, the Activation Wizard appears. Follow the wizard's steps to activate Windows.

3. **Configure your server roles.**

   The first time your new Windows server boots up, the Configure Your Server Wizard appears automatically, as shown in Figure 19-2. The following list describes the roles that you can configure for the server by using this wizard:

   - **File Server:** Lets you share disk folders that can be accessed over the network.

   - **Print Server:** Lets you share printers over the network.

   - **Application Server:** Installs Microsoft's Web server, Internet Information Service (also known as IIS).

- **Mail Server:** Installs a basic POP3 and SMTP server for e-mail.

- **Terminal Server:** Allows other users to run applications on the server via the network.

- **Remote Access/VPN Server:** Enables dialup and VPN connections.

- **Domain Controller:** Enables Active Directory and designates the server as a domain controller.

- **DNS Server:** Enables the DNS server for DNS name resolution.

- **DHCP Server:** Enables the DHCP server to dynamically assign IP addresses to client computers.

- **Streaming Media Server:** Enables the Streaming Media Server.

- **WINS Server:** Enables the WINS server for Windows-based name resolution.

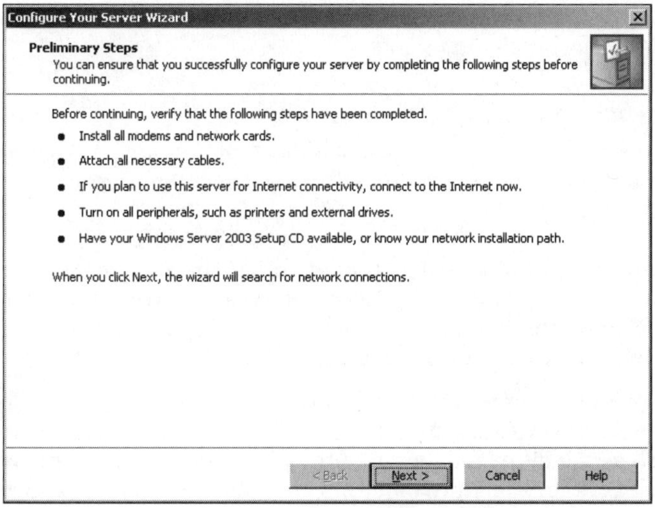

Figure 19-2:
Configuring
server roles.

Managing User Accounts

Every user who accesses a network must have a *user account*. User accounts let you control who can access the network and who can't. In addition, user accounts let you specify what network resources each user can use. Without user accounts, all your resources would be open to anyone who casually dropped by your network.

Understanding Windows User Accounts

User accounts are one of the basic tools for managing a Windows server. As a network administrator, you'll spend a large percentage of your time dealing with user accounts: creating new ones, deleting expired accounts, resetting passwords for forgetful users, granting new access rights, and so on. Before I get into the specific procedures of creating and managing user accounts, this section presents an overview of user accounts and how they work.

Local accounts versus domain accounts

A *local account* is a user account stored on a particular computer; the account applies only to that computer. Typically, each computer on your network will have a local account for each person who uses that computer.

In contrast, a *domain account* is a user account that's stored by Active Directory and can be accessed from any computer that's a part of the domain. Domain accounts are centrally managed. This chapter deals primarily with setting up and maintaining domain accounts.

User account properties

Every user account has a number of important *account properties* that specify the characteristics of the account. The three most important account properties are:

- **Username:** A unique name that identifies the account. The user must enter the username when logging in to the network. The username is public information. In other words, other network users can (and often should) find out your username.

- **Password:** A secret word that must be entered in order to gain access to the account. You can set up Windows so it enforces password policies, such as the minimum length of the password, whether the password must contain a mixture of letters and numerals, and how long the password remains current before the user must change it.

- **Group membership:** Indicates the group or groups to which the user account belongs. Group memberships are the key to granting access rights to users so they can access various network resources, such as file shares or printers, or to perform certain network tasks, such as creating new user accounts or backing up the server.

Many other account properties record information about the user, such as the user's contact information, whether the user is allowed to access the system only at certain times or from certain computers, and so on. I describe some of these features in later sections of this chapter, and some are described in more detail in Chapter 4 of this book.

The Administrator account

Windows comes with a built-in account named Administrator that has complete access to all the features of the server. As a network administrator, you'll frequently log on using the Administrator account to perform maintenance chores.

Because the Administrator account is so powerful, you should always enforce good password practices for it. In other words, don't use your dog's name as the Administrator account password. Instead, pick a random combination of letters and numbers. Then change the password periodically. (For an account of password policymaking that only a spymaster or a network administrator could love, take a good look at Chapter 13.)

Write down the Administrator account password, and keep it in a secure location. Note that by "secure location," I don't mean "taped to the front of the monitor." Keep it in a safe place where you can retrieve it if you forget it, but where it won't easily fall into the hands of someone looking to break into your network.

Creating a New User

To create a new domain user account in Windows Server 2003, follow these steps:

1. **Choose Start➪Administrative Tools➪Active Directory Users and Computers.**

    This fires up the Active Directory Users and Computer management console, as shown in Figure 19-3.

2. **Right-click the domain that you want to add the user to; then choose New➪User.**

    This summons the New User Wizard, as shown in Figure 19-4.

3. **Type the user's first name, middle initial, and last name.**

    As you type the name, the New User Wizard automatically fills in the Full Name field.

4. **Change the Full Name field if you want it to appear some way other than proposed.**

    For example, you may want to reverse the first and last names so the last name appears first.

5. **Type the user logon name.**

    This name must be unique within the domain.

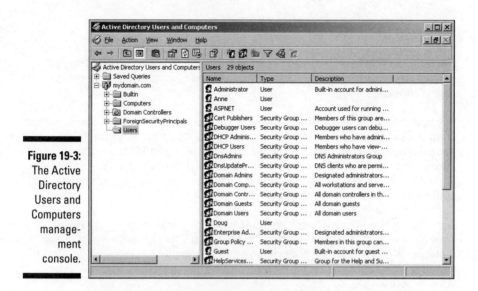

Figure 19-3:
The Active
Directory
Users and
Computers
manage-
ment
console.

Figure 19-4:
Creating a
new user.

Pick a naming scheme to follow when creating user logon names. For example, use the first letter of the first name followed by the complete last name, the complete first name followed by the first letter of the last name, or any other scheme that suits your fancy.

6. **Click Next.**

   The second page of the New User Wizard appears. It asks for the user's password.

7. **Type the password twice.**

   You're asked to type the password twice, so type it correctly. If you don't type it identically in both boxes, you're asked to correct your mistake.

8. **Specify the password options that you want to apply.**

The following password options are available:

- **User must change password at next logon.**

- **User cannot change password.**

- **Password never expires.**

- **Account is disabled.**

For more information about these options, see the section "Setting account options," later in this chapter.

9. **Click Next.**

You're taken to the final page of the New User Wizard, which simply summarizes the information you've entered so far.

10. **Verify that the information is correct; then click Finish to create the account.**

If the account information is not correct, click the Back button, and correct the error.

You're done! Now you can customize the user's account settings. At a minimum, you'll probably want to add the user to one or more groups. You may also want to add contact information for the user or set up other account options.

Setting user properties

After you've created a user account, you can set additional properties for the user by right-clicking the new user and choosing Properties. This brings up the User Properties dialog box, which has about a million tabs that you can use to set various properties for the user. Figure 19-5 shows the General tab, which lists basic information about the user, such as the user's name, office location, phone number, and so on.

The following sections describe some of the administrative tasks that you can perform via the various tabs of the User Properties dialog box.

Changing the user's contact information

Several tabs of the User Properties dialog box contain contact information for the user. In particular:

- **Address:** Lets you change the user's street address, post-office box, city, state, ZIP code, and so on.

- **Telephones:** Lets you specify the user's phone numbers.

- **Organization:** Lets you record the user's job title and the name of his or her boss.

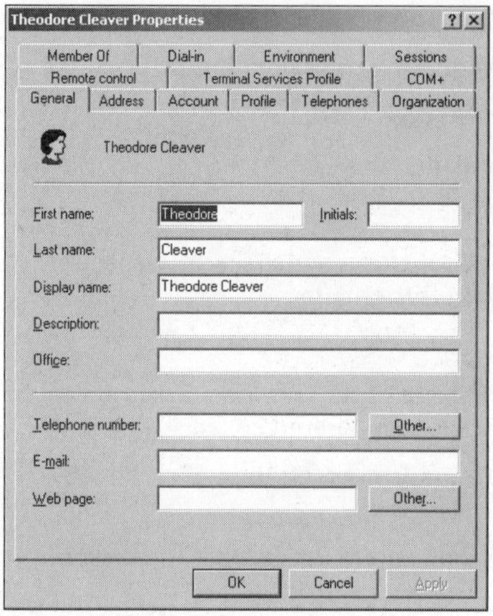

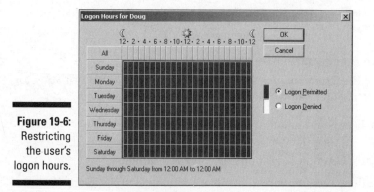

Figure 19-5:
The General
tab.

Setting account options

The Account tab of the User Properties dialog box features a variety of interesting options that you can set for the user. From this dialog box, you can change the user's logon name. In addition, you can change the password options that you set when you created the account and set an expiration date for the account and set password options such as requiring the user to change passwords at the next logon, or prohibiting the user from changing the password.

Specifying logon hours

You can restrict the hours during which the user is allowed to log on to the system by clicking the Logon Hours button from the Account tab of the User Properties dialog box. This brings up a dialog box shown in Figure 19-6.

Figure 19-6:
Restricting
the user's
logon hours.

Initially, the Logon Hours dialog box is set to allow the user to log on at any time of day or night. To change the hours that you want the user to have access, click a day and time or a range of days and times and choose either Logon Permitted or Logon Denied.

Restricting access to certain computers

Normally, a user can use his or her user account to log on to any computer that's a part of the user's domain. However, you can restrict a user to certain computers by clicking the Logon To button in the Account tab of the User Properties dialog box. This brings up a dialog box that lets you specify which computers the user can log on to the network from.

Resetting user passwords

By some estimates, the single most time-consuming task of most network administrators is resetting user passwords. It's easy to sniff at users as forgetful idiots, but put yourself in their shoes. We insist that they set their password to something incomprehensible, such as 94kD821eL384K, that they change it a week later to something more unmemorable, such as dJUQ63DWd8331, and that they don't write it down. Then we get mad when they forget their passwords.

So when a user calls and says he or she forgot his or her password, the least we can do is be cheerful when we reset if for them. After all, they've probably already spent 15 minutes trying to remember it before they finally gave up and admitted failure.

Here's the procedure to reset the password for a user's domain account:

1. **Log on as an administrator.**

   You have to have administrator privileges in order to perform this procedure.

2. **Choose Start➪Administrative Tools➪Active Directory Users and Computers.**

   The Active Directory Users and Computer management console appears.

3. **Click Users in the console tree.**

4. **In the Details pane, right-click the user who forgot his or her password and choose Reset Password.**

5. **Type the new password in both password boxes.**

   You have to type the password twice to ensure that you type it correctly.

6. **If desired, check the User Must Change Password at Next Logon option.**

   If you check this option, the password that you assign will work for only one logon. As soon as the user logs on, he or she will be required to change the password.

7. **Click OK.**

   That's all there is to it! The user's password is now reset.

Deleting a User

Deleting a user account is surprisingly easy. Just follow these steps:

1. **Log on as an administrator.**

   You have to have administrator privileges in order to perform this procedure.

2. **Choose Start⇨Administrative Tools⇨Active Directory Users and Computers.**

   The Active Directory Users and Computer management console appears.

3. **Click Users in the console tree.**

4. **In the details pane, right-click the user that you want to delete and choose Delete.**

   Windows asks whether you really want to delete the user, just in case you're kidding.

5. **Click Yes and poof! The user is history.**

   The account, anyway.

Working with groups

A *group* is a special type of account that represents a set of users who have common network access needs. Groups can dramatically simplify the task of assigning network access rights to users. Rather than assigning access rights to each user individually, groups let you assign rights to the group itself. Then those rights automatically extend to any user account that you add to the group.

The following sections describe some of the key concepts that you need for using groups effectively — and some of the most common procedures you'll employ when setting up groups on your server.

Group types

Two distinct types of groups exist, and they reflect two different ways of look-ing at what a group is for:

- ✔ **Security groups:** Most groups are security groups, which extend access rights only to members of the group. For example, if you want to allow a group of users to access your high-speed color laser printer, you can create a group called ColorPrintUsers. Then, you can grant permission to use the printer to the ColorPrintUsers group. Finally, you can add individual users to the ColorPrintUsers group.

- ✔ **Distribution groups:** Distribution groups aren't used as much as secu-rity groups. They are designed as a way to send e-mail to a group of users by specifying the group as the recipient.

Group scope

Three distinct group scopes exist:

- ✔ **Domain local:** A group with *domain local scope* can have members from any domain. However, the group can be granted permissions only from the domain in which the group is defined.

- ✔ **Global:** A group with *global scope* can have members only from the domain in which the group is defined. However, the group can be granted permissions in any domain in the forest. (A *forest* is a high-level grouping of domains.)

- ✔ **Universal scope:** Groups with *universal scope* are available in all domains that belong to the same forest.

As you can probably guess, universal scope groups are usually found only on very large networks.

One common way to use domain local and global groups is like this:

- ✔ Use domain local groups to assign access rights for network resources. For example, to control access to a high-speed color printer, create a domain local group for the printer. Grant the group access to the printer, but don't add any users to the group.

- ✔ Use global groups to associate users with common network access needs. For example, create a global group for users who need to access color printers. Then, add each user who needs access to a color printer mem-bership in the group.

- ✔ Finally, add the global group to the domain local group. Doing so extends printer access to all members of the global group.

This technique gives you the most flexibility when your network grows.

Default groups

Both Windows 2000 Server and Window Server 2003 come with a number of predefined groups. Although you shouldn't be afraid to create your own groups when you need them, there's no reason to create your own group if you find a default group that meets your needs.

Some of these groups are listed in the Builtin container in the Active Directory Users and Computers management console. Others are found in the Users container.

Creating a group

If none of the built-in groups meet your needs, you can create your own group by following these steps:

1. **Log on as an administrator.**

   You have to have administrator privileges to perform this procedure.

2. **Choose Start⇨Administrative Tools⇨Active Directory Users and Computers.**

   The Active Directory Users and Computer management console appears.

3. **Right-click the domain to which you want to add the group; then choose New⇨Group.**

4. **Type the name for the new group.**

5. **Choose the group scope.**

   The choices are Domain Local, Global, or Universal. For groups that will be granted access rights to network resources, use Domain Local. Use Global for groups to which you'll add users and Domain Local groups. Use Universal groups only if you have a large network with multiple domains.

6. **Choose the group type.**

   The choices are Security and Distribution. In most cases, you specify Security.

7. **Click OK.**

   The group is created.

Adding a member to a group

Groups are collections of objects, called *members*. The members of a group can be user accounts or other groups. When you create a group, it has no members. As a result, the group isn't very useful until you add at least one member.

Follow these steps to add a member to a group:

1. **Log on as an administrator.**

You have to have administrator privileges in order to perform this procedure.

2. **Choose Start➪Administrative Tools➪Active Directory Users and Computers.**

   The Active Directory Users and Computer management console appears.

3. **Open the folder that contains the group to which you want to add members; then double-click the group.**

   The Group Properties dialog box appears.

4. **Click the Members tab.**

5. **Type the name of a user or other group that you want to add to this group; then click Add.**

   The member is added to the list.

6. **Repeat Step 5 for each user or group that you want to add.**

   Keep going until you've added everyone!

7. **Click OK.**

That's all there is to it.

The Group Properties dialog box also has a Member Of tab that lists each group that the current group is a member of.

Adding members to a group is only half of the process of making a group useful. The other half is adding access rights to the group so the members of the group can actually *do* something.

Managing a File Server

The following sections present the basics of managing a Windows Server 2003 file server. First you decipher how permissions and shares work together to allow users to access shared data. Then you get a look at setting up a share and granting access to it.

Understanding permissions

Before I get into the details of setting up a file server, you need to have a solid understanding of the concept of permissions. *Permissions* are what allow users to access shared resources on a network. Simply sharing a resource such as a disk folder or a printer doesn't guarantee that a given user will be able to access that resource. Windows makes this decision for each resource, based on the permissions assigned to various groups, and on the group memberships of the user. If the user belongs to a group that has been granted permission to access the resource, the access will be allowed. If not, access will be denied.

In theory, this sounds pretty simple. In practice, however, it can get pretty complicated. The following paragraphs explain some of the nuances of how access control and permissions work:

- Every object — that is, every file and folder — on an NTFS volume has a set of permissions called the *Access Control List,* or *ACL,* associated with it.

- The ACL identifies the users and groups who can access the object and specify what level of access that the user or group has. For example, a folder's ACL may specify that one group of users can read files in the folder, while another group can read and write files in the folder, and a third group is denied access to the folder altogether.

- Container objects — files and volumes — allow their ACLs to be inherited by the objects that they contain. As a result, if you specify permissions for a folder, those permissions extend to the files and child folders that appear within it.

- The permissions that can be applied to files and folders include such things as listing directory contents, reading files, modifying files, and executing programs.

- It's best to assign permissions to groups rather than to individual users. Then, if a particular user needs access to a particular resource, add that user to a group that has permission to use the resource.

Understanding shares

A *share* is simply a folder made available multiple users via the network. Each share has the following elements:

- **Share name:** The name by which the share is known over the network. To be compatible with older computers, you should stick to eight-character share names whenever possible.

- **Path:** The path to the folder on the local computer that's being shared, such as C:\Accounting.

- **Description:** A one-line description of the share.

- **Permissions:** A list of users or groups who have been granted access to the share.

Configuring the file-server role

If you haven't already configured Windows Server 2003 to function as a file server, you can do so by following these steps:

1. **Log on as an administrator.**

   You need administrator rights in order to make the changes called for by this wizard.

2. **Choose Start⇨Administrative Tools⇨Manage Your Server.**

   The Manage Your Server screen appears, as shown in Figure 19-7. This screen shows the various roles that you've configured for the server. If the File Server role already appears, you can skip the rest of this procedure — you've already configured the computer to be a file server.

3. **Choose Add or Remove a Role.**

   A screen appears, suggesting that you take some preliminary steps such as connecting network cables and installing modems. Read this list just to make sure you've done it all already.

4. **Click Next until you get to the Server Role page.**

   The next page displays a list of the various roles that can be configured for the server.

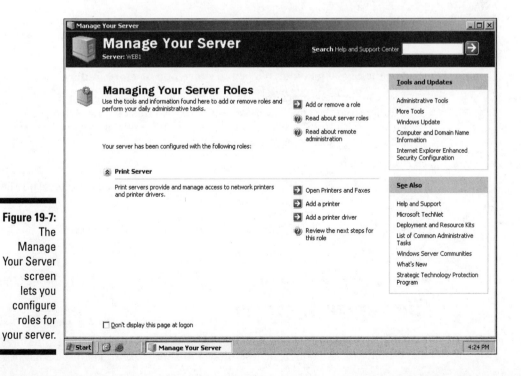

Figure 19-7: The Manage Your Server screen lets you configure roles for your server.

5. **Select File Server; then click Next.**

The File Server Disk Quotas page appears. This page lets you set up disk quotas to track and limit the amount of disk space used by each user. The default setting is to limit each user to a paltry 5 MB of disk space. Microsoft recommends that you set this limit low and then change it for users who need more space.

This page also lets you specify the consequences that occur if a user exceeds the quota. By default, no consequences are specified, so the quota is just a tracking device. If you want, you can tell Windows to refuse to let the user have more space than the quota specifies, or you can specify that an event should be logged to let you know that a user has exceeded the quota.

6. **Specify the disk quota settings that you want to use; then click Next.**

The Indexing Service page appears next. This page lets you indicate whether you want to activate the Windows Indexing Service for the file server. In most cases, activating this service is a bad idea; it can dramatically slow down the performance of the server. Few users take advantage of the Indexing Service, but if you need it, it's available here.

7. **Check Yes if you want to use the Indexing Service, or leave No checked to disable Indexing. Then click Next.**

A summary page appears, listing the options that you've selected.

8. **Click Next.**

The computer grinds and whirs for a moment as it configures the file server. In a moment, the Share a Folder Wizard appears. This wizard allows you to set up the initial file shares for the server.

9. **Use the Share a Folder Wizard to share one or more folders.**

For the complete procedure for using this wizard, see the section "Sharing a folder from the File Server Manager," later in this chapter. After you're finished with the Share a Folder Wizard, a final screen appears to congratulate you for setting up the file server successfully.

10. **Click Finish.**

You're returned to the Manage Your Server page, which now lists the File Server role as active.

That's it. You have now configured the computer to be a file server.

Sharing a folder from the File Server Manager

To be useful, a file server should offer one or more *shares* — folders that have been designated as publicly accessible via the network. You can see a list of the current shares available from a file server by firing up the File Server Manager and clicking Shares in the console tree. The File Server Manager displays the share name, description, and network path for each share that you've already created.

To create additional shares, use the Share a Folder Wizard as described in the following procedure.

1. **Choose Start⇨Administrative Tools⇨Manage Your Server; then choose Manage File Server.**

   This brings up the File Server Management console as shown in Figure 19-8.

2. **Select Shares from the console tree; then choose Action⇨New Share.**

   The Share a Folder Wizard comes to life and displays a welcome page.

3. **Click Next.**

   The wizard asks you what folder you want to share.

4. **Type the path that leads to the folder that you want to share over the network; then click Next.**

   If you aren't sure of the path, you can click Browse. This action calls up a dialog box that lets you search the server's hard drive for a folder to share. You can also create a new folder from this dialog box if the folder that you want to share doesn't yet exist. After you've selected or created the folder to share, click OK to return to the wizard.

   The next page of the Wizard asks for a name and description for the share.

5. **Type the name that you want to use for the share in the Share Name box and a description of the share in the Description box.**

   The default name is the name of the folder being shared. If the folder name is long, you can use a more succinct name here.

   The description is strictly optional but it can sometimes help users determine the intended contents of the folder.

6. **Click Next.**

   A confirmation page appears to indicate that the share was successfully created.

7. **If you want to create another share, check the Run the Wizard Again checkbox, click Finish, and return to Step 4. Otherwise, click Finish to dismiss the wizard.**

   If you click Finish, you're returned to the File Server Management console. The share or shares that you created will now appear in the list.

File Server Management

File | Action | View | Favorites | Window | Help

Manage Shared Folders

File Server Management
  Shares (Local)
  Sessions (Local)
  Open Files (Local)
  Disk Defragmenter
  Disk Management(Lo...

Add a Shared Folder
Backup File Server
Send Console Message
Configure Shadow Copies
Refresh
More Information

Share Name	Description	Folder Path
Accounting		C:\Accounting
ADMIN$	Remote Admin	C:\WINDOWS
C$	Default share	C:\
Development		C:\Development
Inetpub		C:\Inetpub
IPC$	Remote IPC	
NETLOGON	Logon server share	C:\WINDOWS\SYSVOL\sysvol\myc
print$	Printer Drivers	C:\WINDOWS\system32\spool\dri
SCREENS		C:\Documents and Settings\Admin
Shared		C:\Shared
SYSVOL	Logon server share	C:\WINDOWS\SYSVOL\sysvol
Users	Roaming profiles	C:\Users
wwwroot$	Used for file share acces...	C:\Inetpub\wwwroot

Figure 19-8:
The File
Server
Manage-
ment
console.

TIP

If you think wizards should be confined to Harry Potter movies, you can set up a share without bothering the wizard. Open a My Computer or Explorer window and navigate to the folder you want to share, then right click the folder and choose Sharing and Security. A Properties dialog box appears, with the Sharing tab already selected. You can then use the controls on this dialog box to create a share.

Granting permissions

When you first create a file share, all users are granted read-only access to the share. If you want to allow users to modify files in the share or allow them to create new files, you need to add additional permissions. Here's how to do this via the File Server Manager:

1. **Click Shares in the console tree.**

   A list of all the server's shares appears.

2. **Right-click the share you want to set permissions for; then choose Properties. Then click the Share Permissions tab.**

   The dialog box shown in Figure 19-9 appears. This dialog box lists all the users and groups to whom you've granted permission for the folder.

When you select a user or group from the list, the check boxes at the bottom of the list change to indicate which specific permissions you've assigned to each user or group.

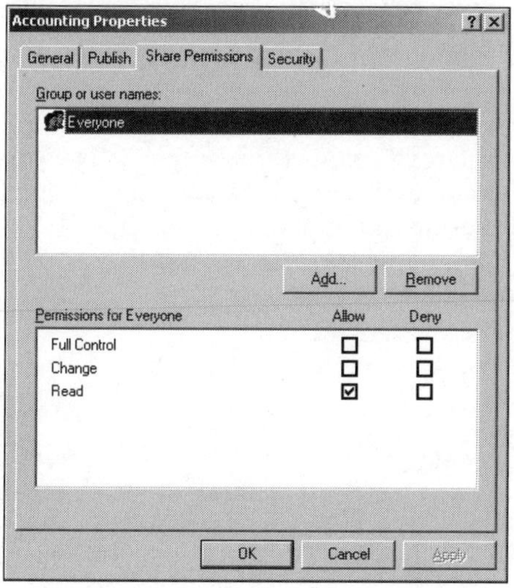

Figure 19-9:
The Share
Permissions
tab.

3. **Click Add.**

   A dialog box entitled "Select Users, Computers, or Groups" appears. You can use this dialog box to indicate which users or groups should be allowed to access the share.

4. **Type the name of the user or group to whom you want to grant permission; then click OK.**

   You're returned to the Share Permissions tab, which shows the new user or group added.

   If you're not sure of the name, click Advanced. This action brings up a dialog box that lets you search for users or groups.

5. **Check the appropriate Allow or Deny check boxes to specify which permissions to allow for the user or group.**

6. **Repeat Steps 3 through 5 for any other permissions that you want to add.**

7. **When you're done, click OK.**

Here are a few other thoughts to ponder concerning adding permissions:

✔ If you want to just grant full access to everyone for this folder, don't bother adding another permission. Instead, click the Everyone group to select it and then check the Allow box for each permission type.

✔ You can remove a permission by selecting the permission and then clicking Remove.

✔ If you'd rather not fuss with the File Server Manager, you can set the permissions from My Computer. Right-click the shared folder, and choose Sharing and Security; then click Permissions. You can then follow the preceding procedure, picking up at Step 3.

✔ The permissions assigned in this procedure apply only to the share itself. The underlying folder can also have permissions assigned to it. If that's the case, whichever of the restrictions is more restrictive will always apply. For example, if the Share Permissions grant a user Full Control permission, but the folder permission grants the user only Read permission, the user will be given Read permission for the folder.

Troubleshooting

Windows Server 2003 is extremely reliable. Get it configured right in the first place, and it'll chug along without incident. (That is, at least until something goes wrong. Which is inevitable.) The following sections present a couple of Windows tools you can use to help pin down and fix trouble when it shows up.

Using the Event Viewer

Windows has a built-in event-tracking feature that automatically logs a variety of interesting system events. Usually, when something goes wrong with your server, you can find at least one and maybe dozens — or even hundreds — of events in one of the logs. All you have to do is open the Event Viewer, and check the logs for suspicious-looking entries.

To display the event logs, choose Start➪Administrative Tools➪Event Viewer. This brings up the Event Viewer, as shown in Figure 19-10. The tree on the left side of the Event Viewer lists the five categories of events that are tracked:

✔ **Application:** Lists events that were generated by application programs. In most cases, these are events that the application's developers purposely wrote to the event log, to inform you of error conditions or developing trouble.

✔ **Security:** Lists security-related events, such as unsuccessful logon attempts, changes to security policy, and so on. For information about how to change the events that are written to the security log, see Chapter 4 of this book.

✔ **System:** This is where you find events related to hardware or operating-system failures. For example, if you're having trouble with a hard drive, you should check here for events related to the hard drive.

✔ **Directory Service:** Active Directory events are recorded here.

✔ **DNS Server:** If you're having trouble with your DNS service, look at this log to find the details.

✔ **File Replication Service:** Here is where you find events logged by File Replication Service.

Select one of these options to see the log you want to view. In Figure 19-10, I clicked the System Events log and scrolled down the list a little to find some messages related to a DHCP problem.

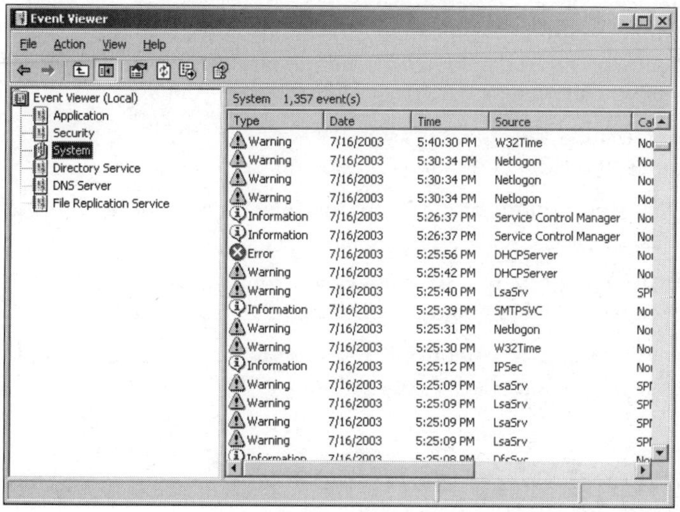

Figure 19-10: The Event Viewer lets you examine events.

Notice the cute little icons next to each item in the log. They indicate whether the message is merely informative or is trying to alert you to a warning or error condition.

To see the details for a particular event, double-click the event. This brings up a dialog box that displays the details about the event. In some cases, you may be able to diagnose a problem just by reading the error message displayed in this dialog box. In other cases, this information just points you in the right direction — it tells you *what* went wrong, but you still have to figure out *why*.

Using the Computer Management Console

The Start➪Administrative Tools➪Computer Management command leads you to the Computer Management Console, which is a tool that's often useful when tracking down problems in a Windows Server 2003 system. Poke around the console tree in Computer Management and here's what you'll find:

- **Event Viewer:** Refer to the section "Using the Event Viewer" earlier in this chapter for more information.

- **Shared Folders:** Here you can manage your shared folders, current sessions, and open files. For more information, see Chapter 4 of this book.

- **Performance Logs and Alerts:** Refer to Chapter 14 for more information on Performance Monitor.

- **Device Manager:** A handy tool for diagnosing problems with hardware devices. Device Manager lists all the hardware devices currently installed on the computer. You can double-click a device to bring up a Properties dialog box that displays information about the status of the device and lets you change drivers or configuration settings.

- **Removable Storage:** Lets you track removable storage media such as tapes and CDs, and manage tape and CD libraries.

- **Disk Defragmenter:** Lets you optimize the way data is stored on your disks.

- **Disk Management:** Lets you work with disk partitions, format disks, create mirror sets, and perform other disk operations.

- **Services and Applications:** Lets you manage services and applications that you've installed on the computer, such as DHCP, DNS, IIS, and so on.

Working with services

The last troubleshooting tool I want to describe is the Services console, which you can access by choosing Start➪Administrative Tools➪Services. As Figure 19-11 shows, the Services console displays a list of all services currently running on your system.

If a Windows server feature isn't working properly, the problem is often that something has caused one of the services associated with the feature to stop. You can often correct the problem by calling up the Services console and restarting the service. To do that, just select the service, and then click the Start the Service link.

Of course, this action doesn't correct the underlying cause of the problem. If the service stopped because of a one-time error, simply restarting the service may be all that you need to do. In many cases, though, the problem that disrupted the service will resurface and cause the service to stop again.

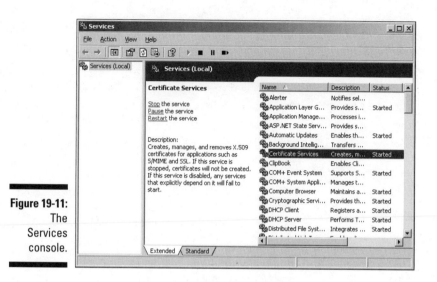

Figure 19-11:
The
Services
console.

Always look at the Services console before rebooting your server in an effort to correct a problem. Very few problems require a reboot in Windows Server 2003. Instead, you can often correct the problem by restarting just the affected service.

Chapter 20

NetWare 6 and 6.5

● ●

In This Chapter

▶ Getting ready to install NetWare

▶ Installing a network operating system

▶ Setting up the client software

▶ Looking at Novell's management tools

▶ Creating and maintaining user accounts

▶ Working with login scripts

● ●

This chapter presents an introduction to installing, configuring, and managing NetWare 6, both versions 6.0 and the latest version, 6.5. I can't possibly cover everything there is to know about managing a NetWare system in one short chapter, so I'll focus on planning for a NetWare server and installing a server. Then, I'll give you an overview of the various administration tools that are available for managing a NetWare server. Half the trick of managing a NetWare network is knowing which of the many administration tools to use for a particular management task.

Planning a NetWare Installation

Before you actually install a NetWare operating system, you need to do some preliminary planning and preparation, as described in the following paragraphs:

⊩ **Checking system requirements:** Before you install a NetWare operating system, make sure that the computer meets minimum system requirements. As Table 20-1 shows, Novell offers a set of official minimum requirements for NetWare 6.5 — and I've put what I consider more *realistic* minimum requirements right next to 'em. If you expect your server to get a fair amount of use and still offer satisfactory performance, all I can say is, "Get realistic."

Table 20-1	Minimum hardware requirements for NetWare 6.5	
Item	**Official minimum**	**A more realistic minimum**
CPU	Pentium II, any speed	Pentium III, at least 700MHz
RAM	512 MB	1 GB
Free disk space	2 GB	5 GB
Video	Super VGA	Super VGA is good enough
Network	Any network board	100BaseT bus mastering PCI card
CD	Any CD-ROM drive	A bootable CD-ROM drive

✔ **Reading the Readme file:** The Readme file for NetWare is available online at www.novell.com/documentation/lg/nw6p/. You should read this file before you start Setup just to make sure that any of the specific procedures or warnings that it contains apply to your situation.

✔ **Deciding whether to upgrade or install:** NetWare offers two installation modes from which you should choose before you begin setup: full installation or upgrade installation. A *full installation* deletes any existing operating system that it finds on the computer and configures the new operating system from scratch. If you do a full installation onto a disk that already has an operating system installed, the full installation offers to keep any existing data files it finds on the disk.

An upgrade installation upgrades previous versions of NetWare as old as NetWare 4.11, provided you've kept up with support packs.

✔ **Planning your partitions:** *Partitioning* enables you to divide a physical disk into one or more separate units called *partitions*. NetWare requires at least two partitions before you can install it: A bootable DOS partition, which must be at least 200 MB (400 MB is better), and the SYS partition where NetWare will live. This partition must be at least 2.2GB, but 4GB is a more reasonable size for the SYS partition.

You'll usually create at least one additional partition on the server for application data, file server storage, and so on. It's best to create these additional partitions later, however. For now, you can concentrate on getting NetWare up and running.

✔ **Deciding your TCP/IP configuration:** Before you install the operating system, you should have a plan for how you will implement TCP/IP on the network. You'll need to know the following:

 • The public IP subnet address and mask for your network

 • The domain name

 • The host name for the server

- Whether the server will obtain its IP address from DHCP or use a static IP address (and if it uses a static address, you'll need to know that address)

- Whether the server itself will be a DHCP server

- The default gateway for the server (that is, the IP address of the network's Internet router)

- Whether the server will be a DNS server

✔ **Planning your tree:** NetWare has its own directory service called *eDirectory*, which is a direct descendant of the venerable *Novell Directory Services* (also known as *NDS*) from NetWare 5. When you install a NetWare server, you have to decide where the server will fit in the scheme of your existing eDirectory tree. If this is the first NetWare server on your network, you have to create a new eDirectory eDirectory tree.

Before you install the server, you should determine the following items of information for your eDirectory tree:

- The name of the eDirectory tree.

- The name of the organization. This is usually your company name.

- The name of the organizational unit, if any. eDirectory lets you subdivide your organization into units, such as divisions or regions. If your company is small, you may not need organizational units.

- The location within the eDirectory tree where the server will be located – either the organization or an organizational unit.

✔ **Running the NetWare Deployment Manager:** If your network already has at least one NetWare server, you should run a special program called the NetWare Deployment Manager to prepare the network for the new server. To do so, insert the NetWare 6.5 installation CD into any Windows client computer and then run NWDEPLOY.EXE.

Installing NetWare

When you've planned your installation and prepared the computer, you're ready to begin the installation. Start by inserting the installation CD in the server's CD-ROM drive and restarting the computer. This will cause the computer to boot from the installation CD and start the NetWare Setup wizard. The wizard begins by asking a few preliminary questions, such as what language you want to install in, and whether your CD-ROM drive is an IDE or a SCSI drive. You'll then be asked how you want to partition the server's drives. The Setup wizard will wipe your disk clean, create a new boot partition, then restart your computer from the new partition.

When your computer starts back up, it formats the boot partition and begins to initialize itself. This takes a few minutes, so be patient. Eventually, the setup program will ask whether you want to perform a Default or Manual installation. A Default installation uses default values for such settings as the size of the sys volume and the drivers to use for your network cards. Manual installation lets you choose these options yourself. If this is your first NetWare installation, Default is probably a safe choice. If you're a NetWare veteran, choose Manual and set the options however you want.

Next, NetWare begins copying files. Lots of them. Now would be a good time to take a walk.

When all the files have been copied, the installation program continues by asking configuration information such as the name of the server, the IP configuration information, and so on. It then asks you to choose a server type from one of several common server patterns. For example, you can choose to create a basic file server, a backup server, a Web server, or another server type. If one of the patterns isn't exactly what you want, you can choose to customize the server by picking any combination of components you want. You'll then be asked configuration questions that are specific to the type of server you chose.

Time to stretch and take another walk as the Installation wizard configures all the components required for the type of server you selected. When the entire installation process is complete, you can remove the installation CD from the server's CD-ROM drive and restart the computer. The server is now ready to use.

Installing Client Software

Now that you've set up a NetWare server, you also have to configure your client computers to access it. All versions of Windows include built-in support for NetWare servers, so you don't have to do anything special to access NetWare servers if you're happy with Microsoft's client files. However, Novell has a product called Novell Client that is a huge improvement over Windows' native NetWare support. If you're going to go to all the trouble of installing a NewWare server, you may as well get the best client support.

The easiest way to install the Novell client software is to insert the Novell Client CD in the client computer and open the INSTALL.HTML file in the CD drive's root directory. This launches an HTML-based installation routine that's easy to use.

If you don't have the Novell Client CD, you can download the Novell Client from Novell's Web site (www.novell.com). Then, you can place the Novell Client installation files on a network disk and install the Novell Client software on each client computer via the network.

Looking at Novell's Administration Tools

One of the best things about NetWare is that it has a lot of tools for administering the server. Unfortunately, many of these tools provide overlapping functions. With NetWare, if there's one way to do something, you can bet there are three or four others as well.

You can use many administration tools from either the server's console or remotely from any workstation on the network. This makes it possible to manage an entire network from the comfort of your own cubicle. You rarely have to venture into the computer room. You may want to go there once in awhile just to hear the hum of your servers and to remind yourself how much you appreciate remote management.

The following sections describe the major network-administration tools you'll use as you manage a NetWare network.

ConsoleOne

ConsoleOne is an all-in-one client-based management program. You can install ConsoleOne on any workstation. It's Java-based, which means it can run on almost any workstation platform. However, Java is pretty demanding on your computer's resources, so you shouldn't try to run it on an older system. Use it only on newer systems that have plenty of RAM. Novell says the minimum is 64 MB, but it recommends 128 MB.

You can install ConsoleOne on a Windows computer from the CD, or you can download it from Novell's download site (`download.novell.com`). After you've installed it, you can start it by double-clicking the ConsoleOne icon on your desktop.

You can also install it on a NetWare or Windows server. To run ConsoleOne from a network location, map a drive to the directory where you installed ConsoleOne; then run `consoleone.exe`. You may want to create a desktop shortcut to this file so you don't have to hunt and peck for it each time you need to use it.

Figure 20-1 shows ConsoleOne in action. When you first start ConsoleOne, it may not look this interesting. The tree pane on the left may contain just the Tree icon until you log on. You do that by clicking the eDirectory Authenticate button or by choosing File⇨Authenticate. After you've logged on, the tree expands to resemble Figure 20-1.

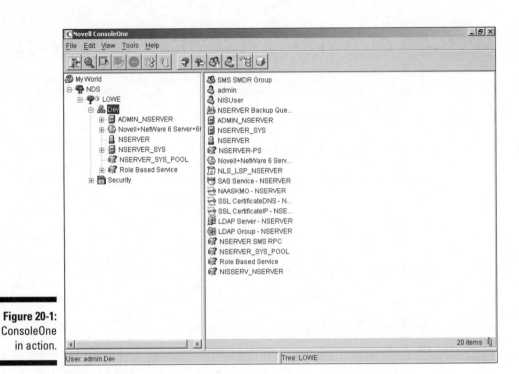

Figure 20-1:
ConsoleOne
in action.

Here are some additional thoughts to keep in mind as you ponder whether ConsoleOne is the tool for you:

✔ ConsoleOne has the same look and feel on whatever platform you run it, whether at the server, on your Windows 2000 or XP Professional desktop, or on a Linux or UNIX box.

✔ ConsoleOne has the best support for eDirectory.

✔ ConsoleOne is still pretty new, so it doesn't support every feature that's available in NetWare. Specifically, ConsoleOne lacks full support for print services and some older services.

Web Manager

Web Manager is a portal to a series of Web-based management tools that you can access from any computer on the network that has a relatively current Web browser (at least Internet Explorer 5.0 or NetWare 4.5). To access it, point your browser at port 2200 of the server on a secure connection by using the server's IP address or DNS name. For example, either of the following options call up the Web Manager page for my test NetWare server:

```
https//:192.168.1.60:2200
https//:Nserver.LoweWriter.com:2200
```

Figure 20-2 shows Web Manager in action. The next four sections describe three Web-based management tools that you can access from Web Manager: eDirectory, Remote Manager, iManager, and RConsoleJ.

eDirectory Administration

The Novell eDirectory Administration tool lets you manage eDirectory information remotely from a Web-based interface, as shown in Figure 20-3. You use this tool to create and modify basic eDirectory objects — including user accounts, groups, organizations, and organizational units. You can access the eDirectory Administration tool from the Web Manager page.

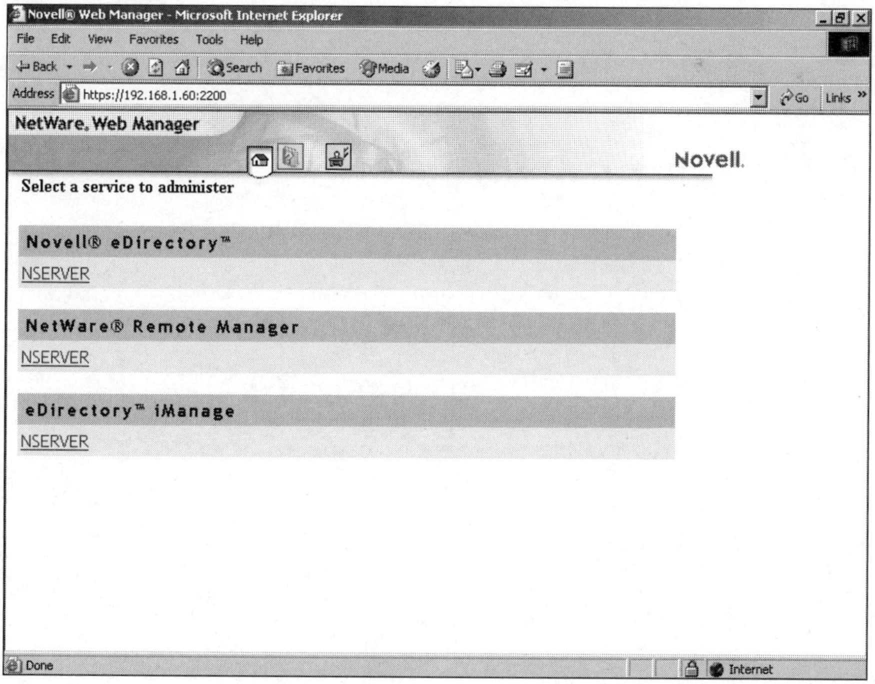

Figure 20-2: Web Manager provides links to Web-based management tools.

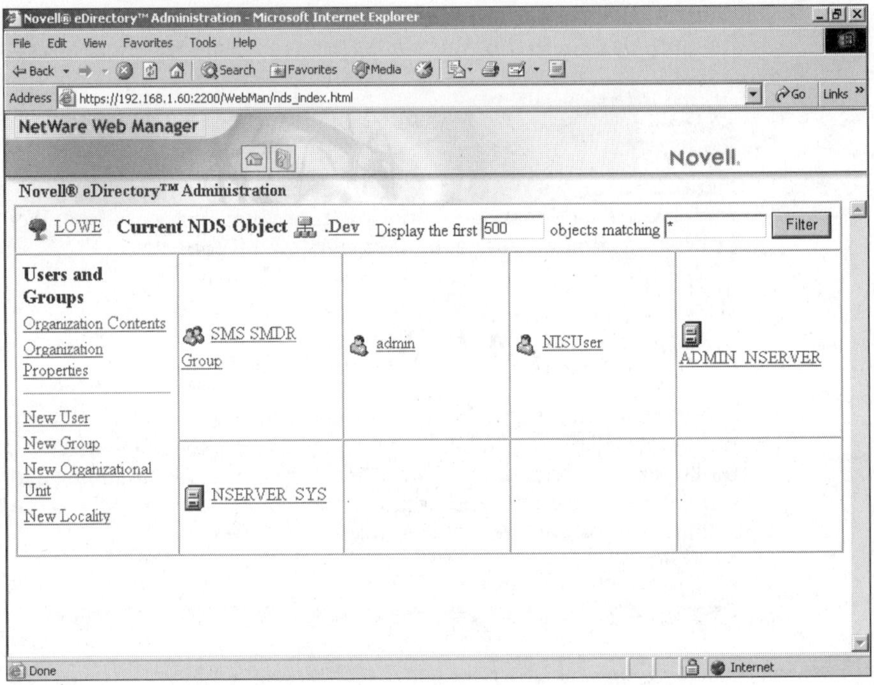

Figure 20-3: eDirectory Administrator lets you manage eDirectory objects.

Remote Manager

Remote Manager is a server-based Web tool that lets you manage a NetWare server's configuration. Figure 20-4 shows the Remote Manager Volume Management page, which lets you manage volumes on a remote server. You can get to Remote Manager from the Web Manager page.

The left pane of the Remote Manager page is a menu that lets you access the following administration features:

- **Diagnose Server:** These tools let you diagnose problems with the server. The choices are Health Monitor, Profile/Debug, Run Config, and Report.

- **Manage Server:** These tools let you manage the server's configuration. The choices are Volumes, Console Screens, Connections, Set Parameters, Schedule Tasks, Console Commands, View Memory Config, View Statistics, and Down /Restart.

- **Manage Applications:** These tools let you manage server applications. The choices are List Modules, Protected Memory, System Resources, NetWare Registry, Winsock 2.0, Protocol Information, and Java Application Information.

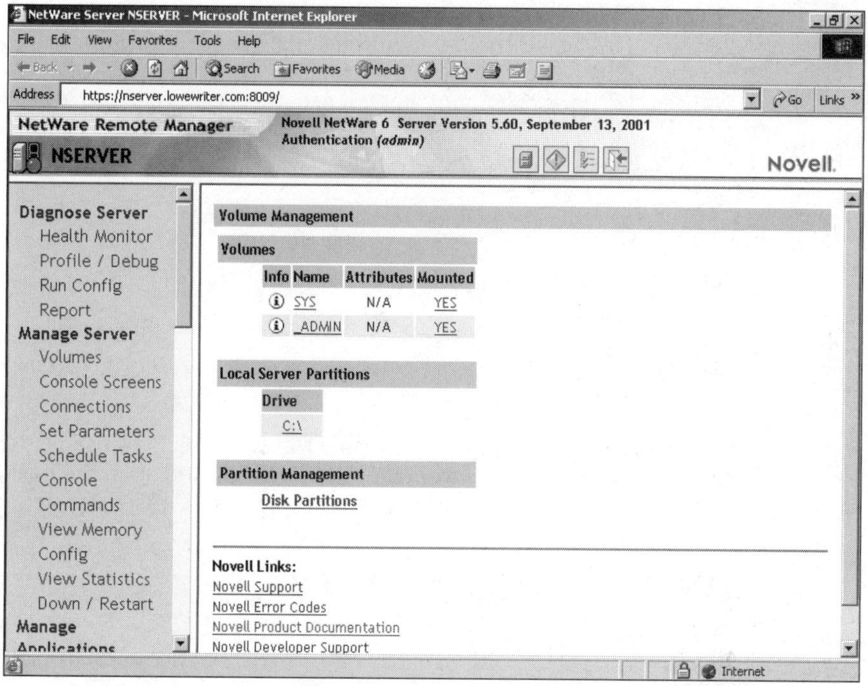

Figure 20-4:
The Remote
Manager
Volume
Manage-
ment page.

✔ **Manage Hardware:** These tools let you manage the server's hardware. The choices are: Processors, Disk /LAN Adapters, PCI Devices, and Other Resources.

✔ **Manage eDirectory:** These tools give you access to eDirectory. The choices are: Access Tree Walker, View eDirectory Partitions, eDirectory iMonitor, DS Trace, NFAP Security, and NFAP Import Users.

✔ **User Server Groups:** These tools let you set up server groups to make servers easier to manage. The options are Build Group and Load Group File.

✔ **Access Other Servers:** These tools let you manage other servers. The choices are Managed Server List and Basic File Access.

✔ **NetWare Usage:** These tools let you capture and display server usage information. The options are Usage Information and Configuration.

iManager

Novell's iManager is another Web-based tool. Because it's Web-based, you can use it from any computer on the network. iManager is shown in Figure 20-5.

iManager was introduced with NetWare 6, but NetWare 6.5 introduces a new version of iManager that offers more complete functionality than the previous version. In fact, the new iManager provides all the features of ConsoleOne, so you can use it for just about any important server-administration task.

You can call up iManager directly by using this address:

```
https://server's_IP_address/nps/iManager.html
```

After you get to iManager, I suggest that you bookmark it.

RConsoleJ

RConsoleJ is a remote server console through which you can enter old-fashioned server commands from a remote workstation. If you're a command-line junkie, this is the tool to use. Figure 20-6 shows RConsoleJ in action.

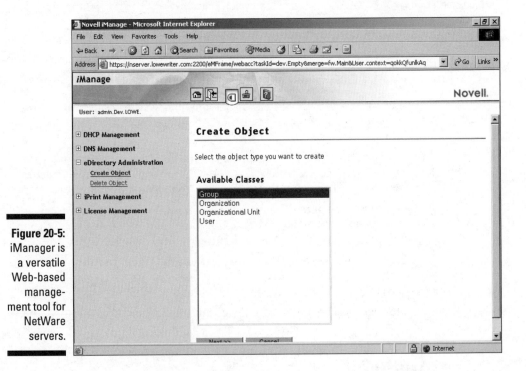

Figure 20-5: iManager is a versatile Web-based management tool for NetWare servers.

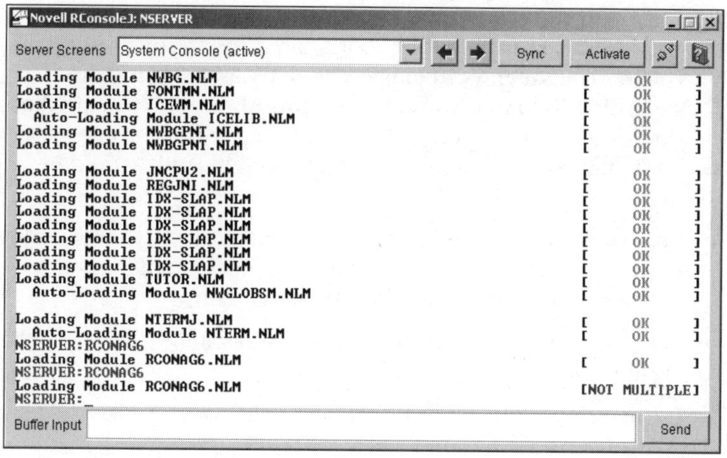

Figure 20-6:
RConsoleJ
lets you
enter server
console
commands
from a
remote
location.

Managing NetWare Users

Every user who accesses a NetWare server must have an account defined by a *user-object* defined in an eDirectory directory tree. The following sections present an overview of how user accounts work and how you can create and maintain them.

Understanding User Accounts

Every user account lives on the network as an object that has a several important properties that specify its characteristics. The three most important object properties are

- **Username:** A unique name that identifies the user. The user must enter the username when logging on to the network. The username is public information. In other words, other network users can (and often should) find out your username.

- **Password:** A secret word that must be entered in order to gain access to the object. You can set up NetWare so it enforces password policies, such as the minimum length of the password and how long the password remains current before the user must change it.

- **Group membership:** Indicates which group or groups to which the user object belongs. Group memberships are the key to granting access rights to users so they can access various network resources, such as file shares or printers, or perform certain network tasks, such as creating new user objects or backing up the server.

Here are some additional user object properties to ponder:

- **Home directory:** A directory on a NetWare server where the user can store files. Usually, this directory is a subdirectory of a directory named Home or Users, and the subdirectory name is the same as the username. Thus, the home directory for a user named Wally would be `\Home\Wally` or `\Users\Wally`.

- **User restrictions:** These properties restrict how the user may access the network, such as what time of day the user can access the network or what types of passwords the user can create.

- **Security equal to:** You can specify that a user's security rights should be granted to another user.

- **Logon script:** You can use logon scripts to customize the user's network environment.

- **Trustee rights:** The user can be granted access to other objects.

- **File and folder rights:** The user can be granted access to specific files or folders.

The admin object

NetWare come with built-in object named `admin` that has complete access to all the features of the server. As a network administrator, you'll frequently log on as `admin` to perform maintenance chores.

The `admin` user account is more powerful than a locomotive. As a network administrator (the next best thing to a superhero), you should always enforce good password practices for the `admin` object. Don't use pets' names, kids' birthdays, or (for that matter) any intelligible word as the `admin` user's password. Instead, pick a random combination of letters and numbers. Then change the password periodically — and review the password-policy guidelines in Chapter 13 every now and then.

I almost never say this, but yeah, okay, in just this one case: Write down the `admin` password (preferably when nobody's looking), and *keep it in a secure location*. Note that by "secure location," I don't mean a sticky note pasted on the CPU. Keep it in a safe place where you can retrieve it if you forget it, but where it won't easily fall into the hands of someone looking to break into your network.

Creating a new user

You can create a new user object (that is, account) in many ways in NetWare 6.*x*. You can create new users with ConsoleOne, eDirectory Administrator,

Remote Manager, and several other tools. In the following procedure, I show you how to do it by using ConsoleOne. The procedures for other tools are similar.

1. **Open ConsoleOne and log on if asked.**

   The ConsoleOne screen appears.

2. **Right-click the organization you want to add the user to, then choose New⇨User.**

   This summons the New User dialog box.

3. **Type the username in the Name field and the user's last name in the Surname field.**

   These are the only two fields required. After you enter them, the OK button is enabled.

4. **If you want to create a home directory for the user, check the Create Home Directory checkbox, and then enter the path where you want the directory to be created.**

   For example, enter **\SYS\Home** to create the home directory as a sub-directory of Home directory on the SYS volume.

5. **Select the password option that you want.**

   You can choose one of two ways to create the password:

   - **Prompt during creation:** You are prompted for the password immediately after completing this dialog box.

   - **Prompt user on first login:** The user is required to supply a password the first time that he or she uses the account.

6. **If you want to specify other user properties now, check the Define Additional Properties check box.**

   If you leave this box unchecked, you can easily set the additional properties later.

7. **If you want to create another user after you've finished with this user, check the Create Another User checkbox.**

   This option simplifies the task of creating multiple users.

8. **Click OK.**

   You're prompted for the password.

9. **Type the password twice.**

   You're asked to type the password twice to verify accuracy. If you don't type if identically in both boxes, you'll be asked to correct your mistake.

10. **Click Set Password.**

    The user account is created. If you checked the Define Additional Properties check box, you are taken to the Properties page for the user as described in the next section. If you checked the Create Another User check box, the New User dialog box reappears so you can create another user. Otherwise, you're returned to the main ConsoleOne window.

Now that you've created a user (it's alive! it's alive!), you'll want to customize the user's properties. At the minimum, you'll probably want to add the user to one or more groups. You may also want to add restrictions or set other properties. You can do that by right-clicking the user object and choosing Properties. This brings up the User Properties dialog box, which has tabs you can use to access various options for the user account. The General tab of this dialog box lists basic information abut the user, such as the user's name, office location, phone number, and so on. The other tabs let you set additional options for the user's account.

Resetting user passwords

Users frequently forget their passwords. It's not really their fault. After all, we're the ones who tell them so use passwords like `iD5Kk139no0` or `UD584jj239D` instead of more memorable ones like `PASSWORD`. So we shouldn't be surprised or annoyed when they forget.

Here's the quick procedure to reset a password from ConsoleOne:

1. **Call up the Properties page for the user.**

2. **Open the Password Restrictions page under the Restrictions tab.**

3. **Click the Change Password button.**

   A dialog box appears, asking for the new password.

4. **Type the new password in both password boxes.**

   You have to type the password twice to ensure that you type it correctly.

5. **Click OK.**

   That's all there is to it! The user's password is now reset.

Creating NetWare Login Scripts

In a NetWare network, login scripts are the main way you set up each user's networking environment. With a login script, you can automatically map network drives, display messages, and execute programs. The beauty of login scripts is that you can create just a few login scripts and use them for all your users. In other words, using login scripts lets you automate much of your network setup.

Understanding login scripts

A *login script* is nothing more than a text file that contains a sequence of special login commands that are executed when a user logs in to a NetWare network. In most cases, the main job of the login script is to set up drive mappings that make it convenient for network users to access the applications and data that they need. For example, if all the users in a marketing department need access to the directory SYS:\DATA\MKTG, you could use login scripts to map this directory to drive M: for every marketing department user.

You can execute four types of login scripts when a user logs in:

- **Container script:** The container in which the user is defined (that is, the organization or organizational unit object) can have an associated login script. If so, this is the first script that is executed when any user defined in the organization or organizational unit logs on. This script lets you set up global drive mappings that you want to be common for all the users on your network.

- **Profile script:** Profiles can also have login scripts. If you have assigned a user to a profile, the profile's login script is executed after the container login script. Profiles are how you can create separate login scripts for different types of users within your network.

- **User script:** Users can have individualized login scripts. If a user has a login script, it's executed after the profile script is executed.

- **Default script:** If the user doesn't have a user script, the default script is run in its place after any container and profile scripts are executed.

To give you a feel for what a login script does, here's a simple example:

```
MAP DISPLAY OFF
MAP ERRORS OFF
MAP M:=SYS:\DATA\SALES
MAP N:=SYS:\DATA\MKTG
MAP O:=SYS:\DATA\FIN
```

This login file simply maps three subdirectories of the SYS volume to drives M:, N:, and O:. That way, the user can access sales data on drive N:, marketing data on drive O:, and financial data on drive P:.

In all likelihood, most users require access to only one of these drive mappings. You can create a more customized login script by adding IF statements to determine what groups the user is a member of and to map the drives accordingly:

```
MAP DISPLAY OFF
MAP ERRORS OFF
IF MEMBER OF ".SALES.Dev" THEN MAP M:=SYS:DATA\SALES
IF MEMBER OF ".MKTG.Dev" THEN MAP N:=SYS:DATA\MKTG
IF MEMBER OF ".FIN.Dev" THEN MAP O:=SYS:DATA\FIN
```

As you work more with login scripts, you'll discover many ways that you can customize them to automate your users' network configuration.

Creating login scripts

Despite their mighty powers, it's well to remember that login scripts are actually simple text files that reside on a server and are associated with container, profile, and user objects. The following procedure shows how to create a container script using ConsoleOne. The procedure for creating other types of scripts is similar.

1. **Open ConsoleOne and log in as an administrator.**

   You need some authority to mess with people's login scripts.

2. **Expand the tree down to the organization or organizational unit where the user objects are defined.**

3. **Right-click the organization or organizational unit to create a container script or the user object for which you want to create a user script and select Properties.**

   The Properties dialog box for the container or the user is displayed.

4. **Click the Login Script tab.**

   The Login Script property page is displayed. Figure 20-7 shows what this page looks like for a container script. It's nearly identical for a user script.

5. **Type the login script in the text box.**

   You can use any of the commands described later in this chapter in your script.

6. **When you're done, click OK.**

   The login script is saved.

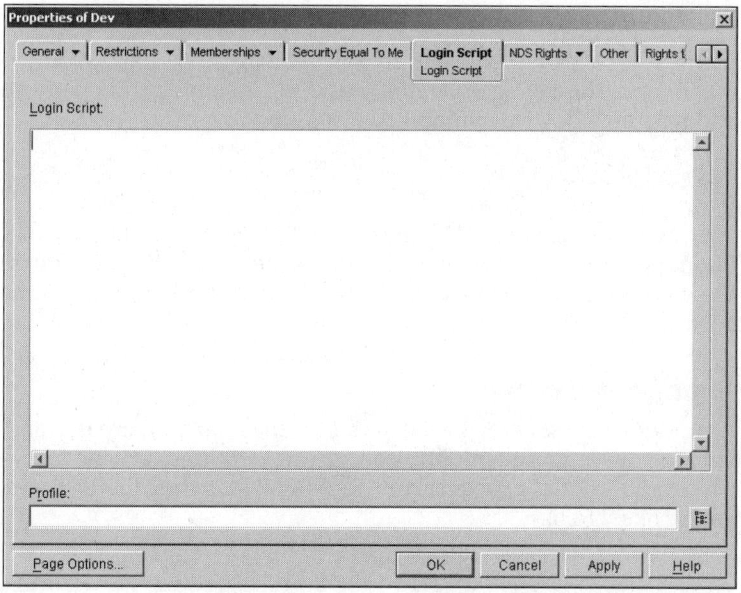

Figure 20-7:
Creating a
login script.

Working with login-script commands

The following sections describe the commands that you'll use most often
when you're creating login scripts.

The display command

The display command displays the contents of a file in the user's login
window. Normally, the login text flies by so fast that users don't see it anyway,
but you can add a Pause command to the login script to force the login script
to stop so the user has a chance to read the display.

One possible use of the display command is to let you set up a message file
that's displayed whenever users log on. For example, you can create a file
named ANNOUNCE.TXT in SYS:\PUBLIC. Then, you can include this line in the
container login script:

```
display SYS:PUBLIC\ANNOUNCE.TXT
```

Note that if the file doesn't exist, nothing is displayed.

The exit command

The exit command terminates the login script. You'll usually use it in combination with an if command to terminate the login procedure if some unusual
condition arises.

The fire phasers command

Being a *Star Trek* fan, this has always been my personal favorite login command, even though it's essentially useless. It sounds a beep or other sound, and has the following syntax:

```
fire [phasers] [n] [soundfile]
```

Why do I say it's useless? Because usually Windows is playing its own symphonic startup sound right around the time your login procedure decides to fire its phasers. So the login beep usually gets swallowed up in the Windows sound.

Identifier variables

Identifier variables are special variables that NetWare creates and are available to your login scripts. You can use an identifier variable just about anywhere you want in a login script. Table 20-2 lists the identifier variables that you're likely to use.

Table 20-2	Commonly Used Identifier Variables
Variable	*Description*
AM_PM	Either a.m. or p.m.
CN	The user's full eDirectory name
DAY	The day of the month (01 through 31)
DAY_OF_WEEK	The day of the week (Monday, Tuesday, and so forth)
FILE_SERVER	The file server name
FULL_NAME	The user's unique username
GREETING_TIME	Morning, afternoon, or evening
HOUR	Hour (1 through 12)
HOUR24	Hour (1 through 24)
LAST_NAME	The surname from the user object
LOGIN_NAME	The user's unique login name
MEMBER OF "group"	True if the user is a member of the specified group
MINUTE	Minute (00 through 59)
MONTH	The month number (01 through 12)
MONTH_NAME	The name of the month (January, February, and so forth)

Variable	Description
NDAY_OF_WEEK	The weekday number (1 through 7, where Sunday is 1)
NOT MEMBER OF "*group*"	True if the user is not a member of the specified group
PASSWORD_EXPIRES	The number of days until the user's password expires
SHORT_YEAR	The last two digits of the year
SMACHINE	A short machine name

The if command

The if command lets you include conditional logic in your login scripts. You can use it in two ways. The first is a single line if, like this:

```
if condition then command
```

For example, this line maps a hard drive if the user is a member of the SALES group:

```
if member of ".SALES.DEV" then map m:=SYS:DATA\SALES
```

Or, for more complicated login scripts, you can use the multi-line if-then-else statement with this syntax:

```
if condition then
    commands
[else
    commands ]
end
```

For example, here's an if command that maps several drives and displays a flattering message if the administrator logs in:

```
if "%1"="ADMIN" then
    map W:=SYS:\SYSTEM
    map X:=SYS:\ETC
    write "Hello, boss. You look great today!"
else
    write "Hello ordinary non-administrator user!"
end
```

The condition test in an If statement can compare identifier variables, login parameters, environment variables, or literals.

The map command

The map command is the main reason you need to create login scripts. It lets you associate an MS-DOS drive letter with a directory on a NetWare volume. The basic syntax is this:

```
map drive:=path
```

You have two ways to specify the drive:

- As a drive letter, as in

  ```
  map m:=SYS:Public
  ```

  Here, drive M: is mapped to SYS:Public.

- A relative network drive, like this:

  ```
  map *1:=SYS:Public
  map *2:=SYS:Public\Data
  ```

  Here, the first network drive will be mapped to SYS:Public and the second network drive will be mapped to SYS:\Public\Data. When you use this notation, the drive letter depends on which drive letter is configured to be the first drive available for the network.

The pause command

The pause command causes the login script to stop until the user presses a key. This is the only way to make sure that the user has time to read any messages created by the display or write commands.

The set command

The set command lets you create environment variables that are used by some application programs. The syntax of the set statement is this:

```
set variable=value
```

For example, this line creates an environment variable named messages, whose value is yes:

```
set messages="yes"
```

To use the value of an environment variable, enclose it in angle brackets (< >), like this:

```
if <messages>="yes" then pause
```

The write command

The `write` command displays a line in the login message dialog box. It has a simple syntax:

```
write "message"
```

If you want to include an identifier in the output, use a percent sign (%) before the identifier:

```
write %LAST_NAME
```

You can string together several identifiers and text strings by separating them with semicolons:

```
write "Hello ";%LAST_NAME
```

Chapter 21

Using a Linux Server

*L*inux, the free operating system based on Unix, is becoming more and more popular as an alternative to expensive server operating systems such as Windows Server 2003 and NetWare. In fact, by some estimates, there are more computers now running the Linux operating system than there are running the Macintosh operating system. You can use Linux as a Web server for the Internet or for an intranet, and you can use it as a firewall or a file and print server on your local-area network.

Linux was started in 1991 by a Linus Torvalds, who was at the time an under-graduate student at the University of Helsinki in Finland. Linus thought it would be fun to create his own operating system for his brand-new PC, based on Unix. In the nearly ten years since Linux was first conceived, Linux has become a full-featured operating system that is fast and reliable.

In this chapter, you find out the basics of setting up a Linux server on your network and using it as a file server, as a Web server for the Internet or an intranet, as an e-mail server, and as a router and firewall to help connect your network to the Internet.

Linux is a complicated operating system. Learning how to use it can be a daunting task, especially if your only prior computer experience is with Windows. Fortunately, Wiley Publishing, Inc. has a plethora of *For Dummies* books that make learning Linux less painful. Check out *Linux For Dummies*, 2nd Edition by Jon "maddog" Hall, *Linux For Dummies Quick Reference*, 2nd Edition by Phil Hughes, and *Linux Administration For Dummies* by Michael Bellomo.

Comparing Linux with Windows

If your only computer experience is with Windows, you are in for a steep learning curve when you first get into Linux. There are many fundamental differences between the Linux operating system and Windows. Here are some of the more important differences:

✔ **Linux is a multiuser operating system.** That means more than one user can log on and use a Linux computer at the same time. Two or more users can log on to a Linux computer from the same keyboard and monitor by using virtual consoles, which let you switch from one user session to another with a special key combination. Or, users can log on to the Linux computer from a terminal window running on another computer on the network.

In contrast, most versions of Windows are single-user systems. Only one user at a time can log on to a Windows computer and run commands. (Windows 2000 and 2003 can be configured as a multiuser system with terminal services.)

✔ **Linux does not have a built-in graphical user interface (GUI) as Windows does.** Instead, the GUI in Linux is provided by an optional component called *X Window System.* You can run Linux without X Window, in which case you interact with Linux by typing commands. If you prefer to use a GUI, you must install and run X Window.

X Window is split into two parts: a server component, called an *X server,* which handles the basic chores of managing multiple windows and providing graphics services for application programs, and a user interface component, called a *window manager,* which provides user interface features such as menus, buttons, toolbars, a taskbar, and so on. Several different window managers are available, each with a different look and feel. With Windows, you're stuck with the user interface that Microsoft designed. With Linux, you can use the user interface of your choosing.

✔ **Linux cannot run Windows programs.** That means you cannot run Microsoft Office on a Linux system; instead, you must find a similar program that is written specifically for Linux. Many Linux distributions come with an office suite called StarOffice, which provides word processing, spreadsheet, presentation, graphics, database, e-mail, calendar, and scheduling software. And the documents created by StarOffice are compatible with Microsoft Office. Thousands of other programs are available for Linux. (There are Windows emulator programs — the best-known is Wine — that can run some Windows programs on Linux. But the emulators can run only some Windows programs, and it runs them slower than they would run on a Windows system.)

✔ **Linux doesn't do Plug and Play the way Windows does.** Although the major Linux distributions come with configuration programs that can automatically detect and configure the most common hardware components, Linux does not have built-in support for Plug-and-Play hardware devices. As a result, you're more likely to run into a hardware-configuration problem with Linux than with Windows.

✔ **Linux uses a different system for accessing disk drives and files than Windows does.** For an explanation of how the Linux file system works, see the "I can't see my C drive!" sidebar that's coming up in this chapter.

✔ **Linux runs better on older hardware than the current incarnations of Windows do.** Linux is an ideal operating system for an older Pentium computer with at least 32MB of RAM and 2GB of hard-drive space. If you're fond of antiques, however, you can (with a bit of juggling) get Linux to run well on even a 486 computer with as little as 4MB of RAM and a few hundred MB of disk space.

I can't see my C drive!

Well, no, but that's normal. Linux and Windows have completely different ways of referring to your computer's disk drives and partitions. The differences can take some getting used to for experienced Windows users.

Windows uses a separate letter for each drive and partition on you system. For example, if you have a single drive formatted into three partitions, Windows identifies the partitions as drives C, D, and E. Each of these drives has its own `root` directory, which can in turn contain additional directories used to organize your files. As far as Windows is concerned, drives C, D, and E are completely separate drives, even though the drives are actually just partitions on a single drive.

Linux does not use drive letters. Instead, Linux combines all the drives and partitions into a single directory hierarchy. In Linux, one of the partitions is designated as the *root partition*. The `root` is roughly analogous to the C drive on a Windows system. Then, the other partitions can be *mounted* on the `root` partition and treated as if they were directories on the `root` partition. For example, you might designate the first partition as the `root` partition and then mount the second partition as `/user` and the third partition as `/var`. Then any files stored

in the `/user` directory would actually be stored in the second partition, and files stored in the `/var` directory would be stored on the third partition.

The directory which a drive mounts to is called the drive's *mount point.*

Notice that Linux uses regular forward slash characters (/) to separate directory names rather than the backward slash characters (\) used by Windows. Typing backslashes instead of regular slashes is one of the most common mistakes made by new Linux users.

While we're on the subject, Linux uses a different convention for naming files, too. In Windows, file names end in a three-letter extension that is separated from the rest of the file name by a period. The extension is used to indicate the file type. For example, files that end in `.exe` are program files, but files that end in `.doc` are word-processing documents.

Linux doesn't use file-name extensions, but periods are often used in Linux file names to separate different parts of the name — and the last part often indicates the file type. For example, `ldap.conf`, and `pine.conf` are both configuration files.

Choosing a Linux Distribution

Because the kernel (that is, the core operating functions) of the Linux operating system is free, several companies have created their own *distributions* of Linux, which include the Linux operating system along with a bundle of packages to go along with it, such as administration tools, Web servers, and other useful utilities, as well as printed documentation. These distributions are inexpensive — ranging from $25 to $100 — and are well worth the small cost.

The following are some of the more popular Linux distributions:

- ✔ **Red Hat** is by most counts the most popular Linux distribution. Red Hat comes in several versions depending on the size of your network. For more information, visit `www.redhat.com`.

- ✔ **Linux-Mandrake** is another popular Linux distribution, one that is often recommended as the easiest for first-time Linux users to install.

- ✔ **SuSE** (pronounced "Soo-zuh," like the famous composer of marches) is a popular Linux distribution that comes on six CD-ROM disks and includes more than 1,500 Linux application programs and utilities, including everything you need to set up a network, Web, e-mail, or electronic commerce server. You can find more information at `www.suse.com`.

- ✔ **Caldera OpenLinux** emphasizes Linux's role as an electronic commerce server for the Internet with its OpenLinux distributions. With Caldera, you get just about everything you need to set up an online Web store. Check out `www.caldera.com` for more information.

- ✔ **Slackware,** one of the oldest Linux distributions, is still popular — especially among Linux old-timers. A full installation of Slackware gives you all the tools you need to set up a network or Internet server. See `www.slackware.com` for more information.

All distributions of Linux include the same core components — the Linux kernel, an X Server, popular windows managers such as GNOME and KDE, compilers, Internet programs such as Apache, Sendmail, and so on. However, not all Linux distributions are created equal. The manufacturer of each distribution creates its own installation and configuration programs to install and configure Linux.

The installation program is what makes or breaks a Linux distribution. All the distributions I list in this section have easy-to-use installation programs that automatically detect the hardware that is present on your computer and configure Linux to work with that hardware, eliminating most (if not all) manual configuration chores. The installation programs also let you select the Linux packages you want to install, and let you set up one or more user accounts besides the `root` account.

The most enjoyable installation program overall comes with the Caldera distribution: It lets you play PacMan while it copies files from the CD-ROM to your hard drive!

Installing Linux

All the Linux distributions described in the section "Choosing a Linux Distribution" include an installation program that simplifies the task of installing Linux on your computer. The installation program asks you a series of questions about your hardware, what components of Linux you want to install, and how you want to configure certain features. Then it copies the appropriate files to your hard drive and configures your Linux system.

If the thought of installing Linux gives you hives, you can buy computers with Linux preinstalled, just as you can buy computers with Windows already installed.

Before you begin to install Linux, you should make a list of all the hardware components on your computer and how they are configured. Be as specific as you can: Write down each component's manufacturer and model number, as well as configuration information such as the component's IRQ and I/O address, if appropriate.

Next, decide how you want to partition your hard drive for Linux. Although Windows is usually installed into a single disk partition, Linux installations typically require three or more hard-drive partitions:

- ✔ **A boot partition:** This should be small — 16MB is recommended. The boot partition contains the operating system kernel and is required to start Linux properly on some computers.

- ✔ **A swap partition:** This should be about twice the size of your computer's RAM. For example, if the computer has 64MB of RAM, allocate a 128MB swap partition. Linux uses this partition as an extension of your computer's RAM.

- ✔ **A** root **partition:** This, in most cases, uses up the remaining free space on the disk. The root partition contains all the files and data used by your Linux system.

You can also create additional partitions if you wish. The installation program includes a disk-partitioning feature that lets you set up your disk partitions and indicate the mount point for each partition. (For more information about disk partitions, see the sidebar "I can't see my C drive!" earlier in this chapter.)

Linux is happy to share your hard drive with another operating system, such as Windows. However, you may have to repartition your disk to install Linux without erasing your existing operating system. If you need to repartition your hard drive, I recommend you pick up a copy of PowerQuest's PartitionMagic (www.powerquest.com) or a similar partitioning program, which will allow you to juggle your partitions without losing your existing operating system.

You'll also need to decide which optional Linux packages to install along with the Linux kernel. If you have enough drive space, I recommend you install all the packages that come with your distribution. That way, if you decide you need to use a package, you won't have to figure out how to install the package outside of the installation program. If you're tight on space, make sure that you at least install the basic network and Internet server packages, including Apache, Sendmail, FTP, and Samba.

Finally, you'll need to set the password for the root account and, in most distributions, choose whether to create one or more user accounts. I suggest you create at least one user account during installation, so you can log on to Linux as a user rather with the root account. That way, you can experiment with Linux commands without accidentally deleting or corrupting an important system file.

On Again, Off Again

Any user who accesses a Linux system, whether locally or over a network, must be authenticated by a valid user account on the system. The following sections lay out the whys, hows, and wherefores of logging on and and logging off a Linux system — and how to shut down the system.

Logging on

When Linux boots up, it displays a series of startup messages as it starts the various services that comprise a working Linux system. Assuming you selected X server when you installed Linux, you're eventually greeted by the login screen. To log on to Linux, enter your user ID on this screen, press Enter, enter your password, and press Enter again.

As a part of the installation process, the Setup Agent created a user account for you. You should use this user account rather than the root user account whenever possible. Use the root account only when you are making major changes to the system's configuration. When you're doing routine work, log on as an ordinary user to avoid accidentally corrupting your system.

When you log on, Linux grinds its gears for a moment, then displays the GNOME desktop, which I describe later in this chapter.

If you didn't install X server, you'll see a text-mode login prompt that resembles this:

```
Red Hat Linux release 9 (Shrike)
Kernel 2.4.20-6 on an i586

LSERVER login:
```

The login prompt displays the Linux version (Red Hat Linux release 9), the kernel version it's based on (2.4.20-6), the CPU architecture (i586), and the server's hostname (LSERVER). To log in, type your user ID, press Enter, then type the password and press Enter again.

When you've successfully logged in, you'll be greeted by a semi-friendly prompt similar to this:

```
Last login: Sun Jul 20 20:00:56 on :0
[doug@LSERVER doug]$
```

The prompt character in the standard Linux shell is a dollar sign ($) rather than a greater-than sign (>) as it is in MS-DOS or Windows. Also, notice that prompt indicates your user name and server (doug@LSERVER) as well as the name of the current directory (doug).

Even if you've installed X server, you can still log in to a command shell by pressing Ctrl+Alt+F1. This switches you to a virtual console.

Logging off

Once you've logged on, you'll probably want to know how to log off. If you logged on to GNOME, you can log off by clicking the main menu and choosing the Log Out command. A dialog box asks whether you're sure you want to log out. Click OK.

In a command shell, there are three ways to log out:

✔ Enter the logout command.

✔ Enter the exit command.

✔ Press Ctrl+D.

Shutting down

As with any operating system, you should never turn off the power to a Linux server without first properly shutting down the system. You can shut down a Linux system using one of these three techniques:

- Press Ctrl+Alt+Delete.
- From GNOME, click the main menu and choose Log Out. Then, when the confirmation dialog box appears, select Shut Down or Restart and click OK.
- From a command shell, enter the `halt` command.

Using GNOME

Although you can do all your Linux configuration chores from the command line, Red Hat Linux includes a number of GNOME-based configuration tools for many configuration tasks. Although you can do most of your Linux configuration from GNOME, you do need to use a command line once in a while.

Figure 21-1 shows a typical GNOME desktop with the Text Editor application open. As you can see, the GNOME desktop looks a lot like Microsoft Windows. In fact, many of the basic skills for working with Windows — such as moving or resizing windows, minimizing or maximizing windows, and using drag-and-drop to move items between windows — work almost exactly the same in GNOME. So you should feel right at home.

The following paragraphs describe some of the key features of the GNOME desktop:

- On the desktop itself, several icons let you access common features. The Home icon takes you to your home directory. The Start Here icon provides access to commonly used configuration utilities. And the Trash icon is similar to the Recycle Bin in Windows.
- The area at the bottom of the desktop is called the *panel*. It works much like the taskbar in Windows. At the extreme left of the panel is a Red Hat icon. Click the hat to access the Main Menu, which works like the Start menu in Windows. You can start an application by choosing the application in the Main Menu.

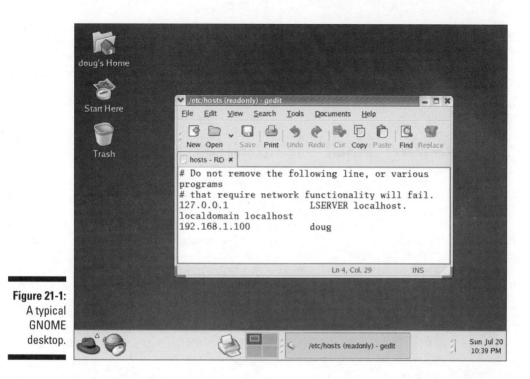

✔ The down arrow at the top-left corner of each window reveals a menu of things you can do with the window. Try the Roll Up command; it reduces a window to its title bar, but leaves the window on the desktop. To restore the window, click the down arrow and choose Unroll. This menu also lets you move the window to a different workspace.

✔ Workspaces, you ask? A *workspace* is like a separate desktop where you can keep open windows to reduce the clutter on your screen. The panel contains a tool called the Workspace Switcher, which lets you switch from one active workspace to another by clicking one of the rectangles in the grid.

Getting to a Command Shell

There are two basic ways to get to a *command shell* (the program that provides the command line) when you need to run Linux commands directly. The first is to press Ctrl+Alt+F*x* (that is, one of the function keys) to switch to one of the virtual consoles. Then you can log on and run commands to your heart's content. When you're done, press Ctrl+Alt+F7 to return to GNOME.

Or, you can open a command shell directly in GNOME by choosing Main Menu➪System Tools➪Terminal. This opens a command shell in a window that appears on the GNOME desktop. Because this shell runs within the user account GNOME is logged in as, you don't have to log on. You can just start typing commands. When you're done, type **Exit** to close the window.

Managing User Accounts

One of the most common network administration tasks is adding a user account. The Setup program may create a single user account for you when you first install Linux. But you'll probably need to create additional accounts.

Each Linux user account has the following information associated with it:

- ✔ **User name:** The name the user types to log on to the Linux system.

- ✔ **Full name:** The user's full name.

- ✔ **Home directory:** The directory in which the user will be placed when he or she logs in. In Red Hat Linux, the default home directory is `/home/username`. For example, if the user name is `blowe`, the home directory will be `/home/blowe`.

- ✔ **Shell:** The program used to process Linux commands. Several shell programs are available. In most distributions, the default shell is `/bin/bash`.

- ✔ **Group:** You can create group accounts, which make it easy to apply identical access rights to groups of users.

- ✔ **User ID:** The internal identifier for the user.

You can add a new user by using the `useradd` command. For example, to create a user account named `slowe` and using default values for the other account information, open a Terminal window (or switch to a virtual console) and type this command:

```
# useradd slowe
```

The `useradd` command has many optional parameters you can use to set account information, such as the user's home directory and shell.

Fortunately, most Linux distributions come with special programs that simplify routine system-management tasks. Red Hat Linux is no exception. It comes with program called Red Hat User Manager. To start this program, choose Main Menu➪System Tools➪User and Groups.

To create a user account using Red Hat User Manager, click the Add User button. This brings up a dialog box that asks for the user's name, password, and other information. Fill out this dialog box, and then click OK.

The Red Hat User Manager also lets you create groups. You can simply the task of administering users by applying access rights to groups rather than individual users. Then, when a user needs access to a resource, you can add the user to the group that has the needed access.

To create a group, click the Add Group button. A dialog box appears, asking for the name of the new group. Type the name you want, and then click OK.

To add a user to a group, click the Groups tab in the Red Hat User Manager. Then, double-click the name of the group you want to add users to. This brings up the Group Properties dialog box. Click the Group Users tab, and then check off the users you want to belong to the group.

Network Configuration

In many cases, configuring a Linux server for networking is a snap. When you install Linux, the Installation program automatically detects your network adapters and installs the appropriate drivers. Then you're prompted for basic network-configuration information, such as the computer's IP address, hostname, and so on.

However, you may need to manually change your network settings after installation. Or you may need to configure advanced networking features that aren't configured during installation. In the following sections, you get a look at the basic procedures for configuring Linux networking services.

Using the Red Hat Network Configuration program

Before you can use a network interface to access a network, you have to configure the interface's basic TCP/IP options, such as its IP address, host name, DNS servers, and so on. In this section, I'll show you how to do that by using the Red Hat's Network Configuration program. You can access this program by choosing Main Menu⇨System Settings⇨Network. (Most other Linux distributions have similar programs.)

The Network Configuration program lets you configure the basic TCP/IP settings for a network interface by pointing and clicking your way through tabbed windows. You can call up this program by choosing Main Menu⇨ System Settings⇨Network.

The main window of the Network Configuration lists all the network interfaces installed in your computer. You can select any of the interfaces and click Edit to bring up a window similar to the one shown in Figure 21-2. This window lets you set the configuration options for the network interface, such as its IP address and other TCP/IP-configuration information.

Restarting your network

Whenever you make a configuration change to your network, you must restart the Linux networking services before the change can take effect. If you find that requirement annoying, just be thankful that you don't have to restart the entire computer. Simply restarting the network services is sufficient.

Figure 21-2:
The
Ethernet
Device
window is
where you
configure
basic
TCP/IP
settings.

You can restart the network services from a GNOME desktop by following these steps:

1. **Choose Main Menu⇨System Settings⇨Server Settings⇨Services.**

   The Service Configuration window appears.

2. **Select the Network service.**

   You'll have to scroll down the list of services to find it.

3. **Click the Restart button.**

   The service is stopped, then started again. When its finished, a small dialog box displaying the message "Network restart successful" is displayed.

4. **Click OK.**

   You're returned to the Service Configuration program.

5. **Close the Service Configuration program.**

   That's all!

If you prefer working in a command shell, you can restart the network by entering the command `service network restart`. Doing so results in a display similar to the following:

```
Shutting down interface eth0:               [  OK  ]
Shutting down loopback interface:           [  OK  ]
Setting network parameters:                 [  OK  ]
Bringing up loopback interface:             [  OK  ]
Bringing up interface eth0:                 [  OK  ]
```

Doing the Samba Dance

Until now, you probably thought of Samba as a Brazilian dance with intricate steps and fun rhythms. But in the Linux world, Samba refers to a file- and printer-sharing program that allows Linux to mimic a Windows file-and-print server so Windows computers can use shared Linux directories and printers. If you want to use Linux as a file or print server in a Windows network, you'll have to learn how to dance the Samba.

Understanding Samba

Because Linux and Windows have such different file systems, you can't create a Linux file server simply by granting Windows users access to Linux directories. Windows client computers wouldn't be able to access files in the Linux directories. There are just too many differences between the file systems — these, for example:

✔ Linux file names are case-sensitive; Windows file names are not. For example, in Windows, `File1.txt` and `file1.txt` are the same file. In Linux, they are different files.

✔ Linux file names can contain periods. In Windows, only one period is allowed — and it separates the file name from the file extension.

✔ Windows has file attributes such as Read-only and Archive. Linux doesn't have these.

More fundamentally, Windows networking uses a protocol called *SMB,* which stands for *Server Message Block,* to manage the exchange of file data between file servers and clients.

Linux doesn't have SMB support built in. That's why Samba is required.

Samba is a program that mimics the behavior of a Windows-based file server by implementing the SMB protocol. So when you run Samba on a Linux server, the Windows computers on your network see the Linux server as if it were a Windows server.

Like a Windows server, Samba works by creating and designating certain directories as shares. A *share* is simply a directory that is made available to other users via the network. Each share has the following elements:

- ✔ **Share name:** The name by which the share is known over the network. Share names should be eight-character share names whenever possible.

- ✔ **Path:** The path to the directory on the Linux computer that's being shared, such as \Users\Doug.

- ✔ **Description:** A one-line description of the share.

- ✔ **Access:** A list of users or groups who have been granted access to the share.

Samba also includes a client program that lets a Linux computer access Windows file servers.

Installing Samba

If you didn't install Samba when you installed Linux, you'll have to install it now. There are two basic ways to do that. One is to use Red Hat's GNOME-based package management tool to install Samba. Just insert the Red Hat distribution CD in the CD drive, and click Yes when you're asked whether you want to run the autorun program. Then, when the Package Management window appears, select the Windows File Server group, which installs the Samba packages for you.

Beware: One sure way to render a Samba installation *absolutely useless* is to enable the default Linux firewall settings on the computer that runs Samba. The Linux firewall is designed to prevent users from accessing network services such as Samba. It's designed to be used between the Internet and your local network, not between Samba and your local network. Although it is possible to configure the firewall to allow access to Samba only to your internal network, a much better option is to run the firewall on a separate computer. That way the firewall computer can concentrate on being a firewall, the file-server computer can concentrate on serving up files, and peace can reign in the valley once again.

Starting and stopping Samba

Before you can use Samba, you must start its two daemons, smbd and nmbd. Both can be started at once by starting the smb service. From a command shell, use this command:

```
service smb start
```

Whenever you make a configuration change such as adding a new share or a creating a new Samba user, you should stop and restart the service with these commands:

```
service smb restart
```

If you prefer, you can stop and start the service with separate commands:

```
service smb stop
service smb start
```

If you're not sure that Samba is running, enter this command:

```
service smb status
```

You'll get a message indicating whether the smbd and nmbd daemons are running.

To configure Samba to start automatically when you start Linux, use this command:

```
chkconfig -level 35 smb on
```

To make sure the chkconfig command worked right, enter this command:

```
chkconfig -list smb
```

You should see output similar to the following:

```
Smb        0:off  1:off  2:off  3:on   4:off  5:on   6:off
```

You can also start and stop Samba using the Service Configuration tool. Scroll down the list of services until you find the smb service. You can use the three buttons in the toolbar at the top of the window to start, stop, or restart a service.

Using the Red Hat Samba Server Configuration tool

Red Hat Linux includes a handy GNOME-based configuration tool that simplifies the task of configuring Samba. To start it, choose Main Menu⇨ System Settings⇨Server Settings⇨Samba Server. When you do, the Samba Server Configuration window appears, as shown in Figure 21-3. This tool lets you configure basic server settings and manage shares.

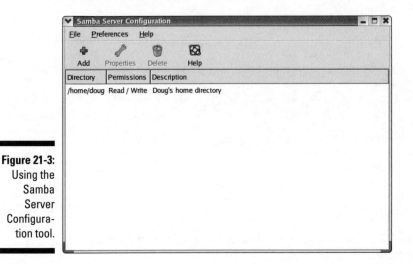

Figure 21-3: Using the Samba Server Configuration tool.

To make your Samba server visible on the network, choose Preferences⇨ Server Settings. This brings up a dialog box that lets you set the workgroup name (which much match the workgroup or domain name you want the Samba server to belong to) and a description for the server, as well as some basic security settings that control how users can access the Samba server.

You can set four basic types of security for your Samba server:

- ✔ **Domain:** This mode configures the Samba server to use a Windows domain controller to verify the user. If you specify this option, you must provide the name of the domain controller in the Authentication Server field. Also, you must set Encrypted Passwords to Yes if you use Domain mode.

- ✔ **Server:** This mode configures Samba to use another Samba server to authenticate users. If you have more than one Samba server, this feature lets you set up user accounts on just one of the servers. Then, in the Authentication Server field, specify the name of the Samba server that you want to perform the authentication.

✔ **Share:** This mode authorizes users separately for each share they attempt to access.

✔ **User:** This is the default mode. It requires that users provide a valid username and password when they first connect to a Samba server. That authentication then grants them access to all shares on the server, subject to the restrictions of the account they are authorized under.

You must create a separate Samba user account for each network user who needs to access the Samba server. In addition, you must first create a Linux user account for each user. The Samba user account maps to an existing Linux user account; you must create the Linux user account first.

To create a Samba user account, choose Preferences⇨Samba Users from the Samba Server Configuration window. This brings up the Samba Users dialog box. You can use this dialog box to add, edit, or delete users.

To be useful, a file server should offer one or more *shares* — directories that have been designated as publicly accessible via the network. Again, you use the Samba Server Configuration program to manage your shares. To add a share, click the Add button in the Samba Server Configuration program's toolbar. This brings up the Add Share dialog box. You can then enter the path for the directory you want to share, as well as a description for the share and whether you want to allow read-only or read-write access. You can also click the Access tab if you want to set limits on access (for example, to specific users).

When you create a new share using the Samba Configuration program, the share should be immediately visible to other network users. If not, try restarting the Samba server, as described in the section "Starting and Stopping Samba" earlier in this chapter.

Chapter 22

Macintosh Networking

This book dwells on networking PCs as if IBM were the only game in town. (Hah! They wish.) To be politically correct, I should at least acknowledge the existence of an altogether different breed of computer: the Apple Macintosh.

This chapter presents what you need to know to hook up a Macintosh network, use a Macintosh network, and mix Macintoshes and PCs on the same network. This chapter is not a comprehensive tome on networking Macintoshes, but it should be enough to get you started.

What You Need to Know to Hook Up a Macintosh Network

The following sections present some key things you should know about networking Macintosh computers before you start plugging in cables.

AppleTalk and Open Transport

Every Macintosh ever built, even an original 1984 model, includes networking support. Of course, newer Macintosh computers have better built-in networking features than older Macintosh computers. The newest Macs include built-in 10/100Mbps Ethernet adapters and sophisticated networking support built in to the operating system — similar to the networking features that come with Windows XP. The beauty of Macintosh networking is that the network card is built in, so you don't have to worry about installing and configuring the network.

Macintosh computers use a set of networking protocols collectively known as *AppleTalk*. Because AppleTalk is built in to every Mac, it has become an inarguable networking standard among Macintosh users. You don't have to worry about the differences between different network operating systems, because all Macintosh networking is based on AppleTalk.

AppleTalk has gone through several major revisions since it was first introduced back in 1984. Originally, AppleTalk supported only small networks that operated only over low-speed connections. In 1989, Apple enhanced AppleTalk to support larger networks and faster connections.

In 1996, with the release of MacOS System 7.5.3, Apple folded AppleTalk into a grander networking scheme known as Open Transport. The idea behind Open Transport is to bring all the different types of communications software used on Macintoshes under a common umbrella — and make them easy to configure and use. Currently, two types of networking are handled by Open Transport:

- **Open Transport/AppleTalk:** Handles local-area networks (LANs) according to the AppleTalk protocols. Open Transport/AppleTalk is a beefed-up version of AppleTalk that's more efficient and flexible.

- **OpenTransport/TCP:** Handles TCP/IP communications, such as Internet connections.

Open Transport is standard fare on all new Macintosh computers; old Macintosh computers can be upgraded to Open Transport, provided they're powerful enough. (The minimum system requirements for Open Transport are a 68030 processor, 5 MB of RAM, and MacOS System 7.5.3.)

AppleTalk enables you to subdivide a network into *zones,* which are similar to workgroups in Windows for Workgroups. Each zone consists of the network users who regularly share information.

Although basic support for networking is built in to every Macintosh, you still have to purchase cables to connect the computers to one another. You have several types of cables to choose from. You can use AppleTalk with two different cabling schemes that connect to the Macintosh printer port, or you can use AppleTalk with faster Ethernet interface cards.

Mac OS X Server

Apple offers a dedicated network operating system known as Mac OS X Server (the *X* is pronounced "Ten," not "Ex"), which is designed for PowerMac G3 or later computers. Mac OS X Server is based on a Unix operating-system kernel known as Mach. As a result, Mac OS X Server can handle many network-server tasks as efficiently as any other network operating system, including Windows 2000, NetWare, and Unix.

(Mac OS X Server is the server version of the Mac OS X operating system, which is the current operating system version for client Macintosh computers.)

The Mac OS X Server includes the following features:

- ✔ Apache Web server
- ✔ NetBoot, a feature that simplifies the task of managing network client computers
- ✔ File services using AFP
- ✔ WebObjects, a high-end tool for creating Web sites
- ✔ QuickTime Streaming Server, which lets the server broadcast multimedia programs over the network

What You Need to Know to Use a Macintosh Network

Here are some of the most common questions that come up after you install the network cable. Note that the following sections assume that you're working with AppleTalk networking using Mac OS X. The procedures may vary somewhat if you're using Open Transport networking or an earlier version of the Macintosh Operating System.

Configuring a Mac for networking

Before you can access the network from your Mac, you must configure your Mac for networking by activating AppleTalk and assigning your network name and password.

Activating AppleTalk

After all the cables are in place, you have to activate AppleTalk. Here's how:

1. **Choose the Chooser desk accessory from the Apple menu.**

2. **Click the Active button.**

3. **Close the Chooser.**

That's all there is to it.

Assigning your name and password

Next, assign an owner name, a password, and a name for your computer. This process allows other network users to access your Mac. Here's how:

1. **Choose the File Sharing control panel from the Apple menu (Apple⇨ Control Panels⇨File Sharing).**

2. **Type your name in the Owner Name field.**

3. **Type a password in the Owner Password field.**

   Don't forget what the password is.

4. **Type a descriptive name for your computer in the Computer Name field.**

   Other network users will know your computer by this name.

5. **Click the Close button.**

Piece of cake, eh?

Accessing a network printer

Accessing a network printer with AppleTalk is no different than accessing a printer when you don't have a network. If more than one printer is available on the network, you use the Chooser to select the printer you want to use. Chooser displays all the available network printers — just pick the one you want to use. And keep the following points in mind:

✔ **Be sure to enable Background Printing for the network printer.** If you don't, your Mac is tied up until the printer finishes your job — that can be a long time if someone else sent a 500-page report to the printer just before you. When you enable Background Printing, your printer output is captured to a disk file and then sent to the printer later while you continue with other work.

   To enable Background Printing:

   1. **Choose Apple⇨Chooser desk accessory.**

   2. **Select the printer you want to use from the Chooser.**

   3. **Click the Background Printing On button.**

✔ **Do not enable Background Printing if a dedicated print server has been set up.** In that case, print data is automatically spooled to the print server's disk so your Mac doesn't have to wait for the printer to become available.

Sharing files with other users

To share files on your Mac with other network users, you must set up a shared resource. You can share an entire disk or just individual folders and restrict access to certain users, if you want.

Before you can share files with other users, you must activate the AppleTalk file-sharing feature. Here's how:

1. **Choose the File Sharing control panel from the Apple Menu.**
2. **Click the Start button in the File Sharing section of the control panel.**
3. **Click the Close button.**

To share a file or folder, click the file or folder once. Then open the File menu, choose Get Info, and then choose Sharing from the submenu that appears. You can also use the Sharing section of the Info window to set access privileges to restrict access to the file or folder.

Accessing shared files

To access files on another Macintosh, follow this procedure:

1. **Choose the Chooser from the Apple menu.**
2. **Click the AppleShare icon from the Chooser window.**
3. **Click the name of the computer you want to access. (If your network has zones, you must first click the zone you want to access.)**
4. **Click OK.**

   A login screen appears.

5. **If you have a user account on the computer, click the Registered User button and enter your user name and password. Otherwise click the Guest button and then click OK.**

   A list of shared folders and disks appears.

6. **Click the folders and disks you want to access.**

   A check box appears next to each item on the list. If you check this box, you connect to the corresponding folder or disk automatically each time you start your computer.

7. **Click OK.**

With Mac OS 8.5 and later, you can also use the Network Browser, found in the Apple menu, to access network drives or folders. Just open the Network Browser from the Apple menu, double-click the server that contains the shared disk or folder, and then double-click the drive or folder you want to use.

What You Need to Know to Network Macintoshes with PCs

Life would be too boring if Macs *really* lived on one side of the tracks and PCs lived on the other. If your organization has a mix of both Macs and PCs, odds are you eventually want to network them together. Fortunately, you have several ways to do so:

- ✔ If your network has a OS X Server, you can use the Windows client software that comes with OS X Server to connect any version of Windows to the server. Doing so enables Windows users to access the files and printers on the Macintosh server.

- ✔ If you have a Windows server, you can use a feature called Services for Macintosh to allow Macintosh computers to access files and printers managed by the Windows server without having to install special client software on the Macintosh computers.

- ✔ If you use NetWare, you must purchase separate NetWare client software for your Macintosh computers. After you install this client software, the Macs can access files and printers managed by your NetWare servers.

The biggest complication that occurs when you mix Macintosh and Windows computers on the same network is that the Mac OS and Windows have slightly different rules for naming files. For example, Macintosh file names are limited to 31 characters, but Windows filenames can be up to 255 characters. And although a Macintosh filename can include any characters *other than a colon,* Windows filenames can't include backslashes, greater-than or less-than signs, and a few other oddball characters.

The best way to avoid filename problems is to stick with short names (under 31 characters) and limit your filenames to letters, numbers, and common symbols such as the hyphen or pound sign. Although you can translate any filenames that violate the rules of the system being used into a form that is acceptable to both Windows and the Macintosh, doing so sometimes leads to cryptic or ambiguous filenames. But hey, network administration is as much an art as a science.

Part V
TCP/IP and the Internet

The 5th Wave   By Rich Tennant

In this part . . .

You get a look at how to safely connect your network to the Internet — and how to configure the Internet's most important protocol, TCP/IP. These chapters are the most technical ones in this book, so the journey through these chapters may be a bit rocky. In the long run, you'll thank me. But for now, wear comfortable shoes.

Chapter 23

Connecting Your Network to the Internet

In This Chapter

▶ Looking at DSL and cable

▶ Examining T1 and T3 connections

▶ Using a router

▶ Securing your connection with a firewall

▶ Using the firewall that comes with Windows XP

So you've decided to connect your network to the Internet. All you have to do is run to the local computer discount store, buy a modem, and plug it in, right? Wrong. Unfortunately, connecting to the Internet involves more than just installing a modem. For starters, you have to make sure that a modem is the right way to connect — other methods are faster but more expensive. Then you have to select and configure the software you use to access the Internet. And finally, you have to lie awake at night worrying whether hackers are breaking into your network via its Internet connection.

Connecting to the Internet

Connecting to the Internet is not free. For starters, you have to purchase the computer equipment necessary to make the connection. Then, you have to obtain a connection from an *Internet Service Provider,* or *ISP.* The ISP charges you a monthly fee that depends on the speed and capacity of the connection.

The following sections describe the most commonly used methods of connecting network users to the Internet.

Dial-up connections

A *dial-up connection* connects your computer to an Internet provider over a standard telephone connection. A dial-up connection depends on a device called a *modem* to convert the computer's digital signals to a form that can be transmitted over a telephone line. When you want to connect to the Internet, the modem accesses the phone line, dials the number for your Internet provider, and connects you.

Dial-up connections may be the least expensive way to connect to the Internet, but they're also the slowest. The standard speed for modems is 56 Kbps, which means that the modem can send about 56,000 bits of information per second over a standard phone connection.

Frankly, dial-up connections to the Internet are rapidly becoming a thing of the past. Even home users are replacing their slow dial-up connections by high-speed connections such as cable or DSL. Just as I like to tell my kids about how we used to have "party lines" on our phones, which meant that we could use the phone only if our neighbors weren't already using it, my kids will someday tell their kids about the good old days when they had "modems" on their phones to connect to the Internet and they could actually hear the modem call the Internet, and how excited they would get when they heard the Internet answer with a screech and a buzz. Ah, those were the days. . . .

Connecting with cable or DSL

If your network users will use the Internet frequently, you may want to consider one of two popular, high-speed methods of connecting to the Internet: cable or DSL. Cable and DSL connections are often called *broadband connections,* for technical reasons you don't really want to know.

Cable Internet access works over the same cable that brings 40 billion TV channels into your home, whereas DSL is a digital phone service that works over a standard phone line. Both offer three major advantages over normal dial-up connections:

  ✔ **Cable and DSL are much faster than dial-up connections.** A cable connection can be anywhere from 10 to 200 times faster than a dial-up connection, depending on the service you get. And the speed of a DSL line is comparable to cable. (Although DSL is a dedicated connection, cable connections are shared among several subscribers. The actual speed of a cable connection may slow down when several subscribers use the connection simultaneously.)

✔ **With cable and DSL, you are always connected to the Internet.** You don't have to connect and disconnect each time you want to go online. No more waiting for the modem to dial your service provider and listening to the annoying modem shriek as it attempts to establish a connection.

✔ **Cable and DSL do not tie up a phone line while you are online.** With cable, your Internet connection works over TV cables rather than phone cables. And with DSL, the phone company installs a separate phone line for the DSL service, so your regular phone line is not affected.

Unfortunately, there's no such thing as a free lunch, and the high-speed, always-on connections offered by cable and DSL do not come without a price. For starters, you can expect to pay a higher monthly access fee for cable or DSL. In most areas of the United States, cable runs about $50 per month for residential users; business users can expect to pay more, especially if more than one user will be connected to the Internet via the cable.

The cost for DSL service depends on the access speed you choose. In some areas, residential users can get a relatively slow DSL connection for as little as $30 per month. For higher access speeds or for business users, DSL can cost substantially more.

Cable and DSL access are not available everywhere. If you live in an area where cable or DSL is not available, you can still get high-speed Internet access via a satellite hookup. With satellite access, you still need a modem and a phone line to send data from your computer to the Internet. The satellite is used only to receive data from the Internet. Still, a satellite setup like this is much faster than a modem-only connection.

Connecting with high-speed private lines: T1 and T3

If your network is large and high-speed Internet access is a high priority, contact your local phone company (or companies) about installing a dedicated high-speed digital line. These lines can cost you plenty (on the order of hundreds of dollars per month), so they're best suited for large networks in which 20 or more users are accessing the Internet simultaneously.

A T1 line has a connection speed of up to 1.544 Mbps. A T3 line is faster yet: It transmits data at an amazing 44.184 Mbps. Of course, T3 lines are also considerably more expensive than T1 lines.

If you don't have enough users to justify the expense of an entire T1 or T3 line, you can lease just a portion of the line. With a *fractional T1 line,* you can get connections with speeds of 128 Kbps to 768 Kbps, and with a *fractional T3 line,* you can choose speeds ranging from 4.6 Mbps to 32 Mbps.

Setting up a T1 or T3 connection to the Internet is stuff best left to professionals. Getting this type of connection to work is far more complicated than setting up a basic LAN.

You may be wondering whether T1 or T3 lines are really any faster than cable or DSL connections. After all, T1 runs at 1.544 Mbps and T3 runs at 44.184 Mbps, and cable and DSL claim to run at comparable speeds. But there are many differences that justify the substantial extra cost of a T1 or T3 line. In particular, a T1 or T3 line is a dedicated line — not shared by any other users. T1 and T3 are higher-quality connections, so you actually get the 1.544 or 44.184 connection speeds. In contrast, both cable and DSL connections usually run at substantially less than their advertised maximum speeds because of poor-quality connections.

Sharing an Internet connection

After you have chosen a method to connect to the Internet, you can turn your attention to setting up the connection so more than one user on your network can share it. The best way to do that is by using a separate device called a *router.* An inexpensive router for a small network can be had for under $100. Routers suitable for larger networks will, naturally, cost a bit more.

Because all communications between your network and the Internet must go through the router, the router is a natural place to provide the security measures necessary to keep your network safe from the many perils of the Internet. As a result, a router used for Internet connections often doubles as a firewall, as described in the section "Using a firewall" later in this chapter.

Securing Your Connection with a Firewall

If your network is connected to the Internet, a whole host of security issues bubble to the surface. You probably connected your network to the Internet so your network's users could get out to the Internet. Unfortunately, however, your Internet connection is a two-way street. Not only does it enable your network's users to step outside the bounds of your network to access the Internet, it also enables others to step in and access your network.

And step in they will. The world is filled with hackers who are looking for networks like yours to break into. They may do it just for the fun of it, or they may do it to steal your customers' credit-card numbers or to coerce your mail server into sending thousands of spam messages on behalf of the bad guys. Whatever their motive, rest assured that your network will be broken into if you leave it unprotected.

Using a firewall

A *firewall* is a security-conscious router that sits between the Internet and your network with a single-minded task: preventing *them* from getting to *us*. The firewall acts as a security guard between the Internet and your LAN. All network traffic into and out of the LAN must pass through the firewall, which prevents unauthorized access to the network.

Some type of firewall is a must-have if your network has a connection to the Internet, whether that connection is broadband (cable modem or DSL), T1, or some other high-speed connection. Without it, sooner or later a hacker will discover your unprotected network, tell his friends about it, and within a few hours your network will be toast.

You can set up a firewall using two basic ways. The easiest way is to purchase a *firewall appliance,* which is basically a self-contained router with built-in firewall features. Most firewall appliances include a Web-based interface that enables you to connect to the firewall from any computer on your network using a browser. You can then customize the firewall settings to suit your needs.

Alternatively, you can set up a server computer to function as a firewall computer. The server can run just about any network operating system, but most dedicated firewall systems run Linux.

Whether you use a firewall appliance or a firewall computer, the firewall must be located between your network and the Internet, as shown in Figure 23-1. Here, one end of the firewall is connected to a network hub, which is, in turn, connected to the other computers on the network. The other end of the firewall is connected to the Internet. As a result, all traffic from the LAN to the Internet (and vice versa) must travel through the firewall.

The term *perimeter* is sometimes used to describe the location of a firewall on your network. In short, a firewall is like a perimeter fence that completely surrounds your property and forces all visitors to enter through the front gate.

In large networks, it is sometimes hard to figure out exactly where the perimeter is located. If your network has two or more WAN connections, make sure that every one of those connections connects to a firewall and not directly to the network. You can do this by providing a separate firewall for each WAN connection or by using a firewall with more than one WAN port.

Some firewall routers can also enforce virus protection for your network. For more information about virus protection, see Chapter 16.

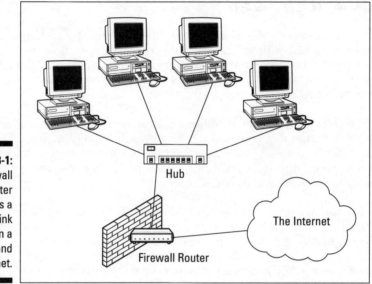

Figure 23-1:
A firewall
router
creates a
secure link
between a
network and
the Internet.

The built-in firewall in Windows XP

If you are using a Windows XP as a router to share an Internet connection for a small network, you can use the built-in firewall feature to provide basic packet-filtering firewall protection. Here are the steps that activate this feature in Windows XP:

1. **Choose Start⇨Control Panel.**

   The Control Panel appears.

2. **Click the Network Connections link.**

   If Control Panel appears in Classic view rather than Category view, you won't see a Network Connections link. Instead, just double-click the Network Connections icon.

3. **Double-click the Local Area Connection icon.**

   A dialog box showing the connection's status appears.

4. **Click the Properties button.**

   The Connection Properties dialog box appears.

5. **Click the Advanced Tab; then check the Protect My Computer option.**

   This option enables the firewall.

6. **Click OK.**

   That's all there is to it.

Do *not* enable the Windows Internet firewall if you are using a separate firewall router to protect your network. Because the other computers on the network are connected directly to the router and not to your computer, the firewall won't protect the rest of the network. Additionally, as an unwanted side effect, the rest of the network will lose the capability of accessing your computer.

Chapter 24

Understanding IP Addresses

In This Chapter

▶ Getting a handle (or two) on the binary system

▶ Digging into IP addresses

▶ Finding out how subnetting works

▶ Understanding private and public IP addresses

▶ Looking at network address translation

One of the most basic components of TCP/IP is IP addressing. Every device on a TCP/IP network must have a unique IP address. In this chapter, I explore the ins and outs of these IP addresses. Enjoy!

This is far and away the most technical chapter in this book. We'll examine the binary system, the details of how IP addresses are constructed and how subnetting works. You don't need to understand every nuance of IP addressing to set up a simple TCP/IP system. However, the more you understand the information in this chapter, the more TCP/IP will start to make sense. Be brave.

Understanding Binary

Before you can understand the details of how IP addressing works, you need to understand how the binary numbering system works, because binary is the basis of IP addressing. If you already understand binary, please skip right over this section to "Introducing IP Addresses," later in this chapter. I don't want to bore you with stuff that's too basic.

Counting by ones

Binary is a counting system that uses only two numerals: 0 and 1. In the decimal system to which most people are accustomed, you use 10 numerals: 0 through 9. In an ordinary decimal number, such as 3,482, the rightmost digit represents ones; the next digit to the left, tens; the next, hundreds; the next, thousands; and so on. These digits represent powers of ten: first 10^0 (which is 1); next, 10^1 (10); then 10^2 (100); then 10^3 (1,000); and so on.

In binary, you have only two numerals rather than ten, which is why binary numbers look somewhat monotonous, as in 110011, 101111, and 100001.

The positions in a binary number (called *bits* rather than *digits*) represent powers of two rather than powers of ten: 1, 2, 4, 8, 16, 32, and so on. To figure the decimal value of a binary number, you multiply each bit by its corresponding power of two and then add the results. The decimal value of binary 10101, for example, is calculated as follows:

```
  1 _ 2⁰ = 1 _   1 =    1
+ 0 _ 2¹ = 0 _   2 =    0
+ 1 _ 2² = 1 _   4 =    4
+ 0 _ 2³ = 0 _   8 =    0
+ 1 _ 2⁴ = 1 _  16 =   16
                       21
```

Fortunately, converting a number between binary and decimal is something a computer is good at — so good, in fact, that you're unlikely ever to need to do any conversions yourself. The point of learning binary is not to be able to look at a number such as 1110110110110 and say instantly, "Ah! Decimal 7,606!" (If you could do that, Barbara Walters would probably interview you, and they would even make a movie about you — starring Dustin Hoffman and a vintage Buick.)

Instead, the point is to have a basic understanding of how computers store information and — most important — to understand how the hexadecimal counting system works (which is described in the following section).

Here are some of the more interesting characteristics of binary and how the system is similar to and differs from the decimal system:

✔ The number of bits allotted for a binary number determines how large that number can be. If you allot eight bits, the largest value that number can store is 11111111, which happens to be 255 in decimal.

✔ To quickly figure how many different values you can store in a binary number of a given length, use the number of bits as an exponent of two. An eight-bit binary number, for example, can hold 2^8 values. Because 2^8 is 256, an eight-bit number can have any of 256 different values — which is why a byte, which is eight bits, can have 256 different values.

✔ This "powers-of-two" thing is why computers don't use nice, even, round numbers in measuring such values as memory or disk space. A value of 1K, for example, is not an even 1,000 bytes — it's 1,024 bytes because 1,024 is 2^{10}. Similarly, 1MB is not an even 1,000,000 bytes, but rather is 1,048,576 bytes, which happens to be 2^{20}.

Doing the logic thing

One of the great things about binary is that it is very efficient at handling special operations called *logical operations*. Four basic logical operations exist, though additional operations are derived from the basic four operations. Three of the operations — AND, OR, and XOR — compare two binary digits (bits). The fourth (NOT) works on just a single bit.

The following list summarizes the basic logical operations:

- ✔ **AND:** An AND operation compares two binary values. If both values are 1, the result of the AND operation is 1. If one or both of the values are 0, the result is 0.

- ✔ **OR:** An OR operation compares two binary values. If at least one of the values is 1, the result of the OR operation is 1. If both values are 0, the result is 0.

- ✔ **XOR:** An XOR operation compares two binary values. If exactly one of them is 1, the result is 1. If both values are 0 or if both values are 1, the result is 0.

- ✔ **NOT:** The NOT operation doesn't compare two values. Instead, it simply changes the value of a single binary value. If the original value is 1, NOT returns 0. If the original value is 0, NOT returns 1.

Logical operations are applied to binary numbers that have more than one binary digit by applying the operation one bit at a time. The easiest way to do this manually is to line the two binary numbers on top of one another, and then write the result of the operation beneath each binary digit. The following example shows how you would calculate 10010100 AND 11001101:

```
      10010100
AND   11011101
      10010100
```

As you can see, the result is 10010100.

Introducing IP Addresses

An *IP address* is a number that uniquely identifies every host on an IP network. IP addresses operate at the Network layer of the TCP/IP protocol stack, so they are independent of lower-level Data Link layer MAC addresses, such as Ethernet MAC addresses.

IP addresses are 32-bit binary numbers, which means that theoretically, a maximum of something in the neighborhood of 4 billion unique host addresses can exist throughout the Internet. You'd think that would be enough, but TCP/IP places certain restrictions on how IP addresses are allocated. These restrictions severely limit the total number of usable IP addresses, and today, about half of the total available IP addresses have already been assigned. However, new techniques for working with IP addresses have helped to alleviate this problem, and a new standard for 128-bit IP addresses (known as *IPv6*) is on the verge of winning acceptance.

Networks and hosts

IP stands for *Internet Protocol,* and its primary purpose is to enable communications between networks. As a result, a 32-bit IP address actually consists of two parts:

- The *network ID* (or *network address*) identifies the network on which a host computer can be found.
- The *host ID* (or *host address*) identifies a specific device on the network indicated by the network ID.

Most of the complexity of working with IP addresses has to do with figuring out which part of the complete 32-bit IP address is the network ID and which part is the host ID. The original IP specification uses a system called *address classes* to determine which part of the IP address is the network ID and which part is the host ID. A newer system, known as *classless IP addresses,* is rapidly taking over the address classes system. You come to grips with both systems later in this chapter.

The dotted-decimal dance

IP addresses are usually represented in a format known as *dotted-decimal notation.* In dotted-decimal notation, each group of eight bits, known as an *octet,* is represented by its decimal equivalent. For example, consider the following binary IP address:

```
11000000101010001000100000011100
```

The dotted-decimal equivalent to this address is:

```
192.168.136.28
```

Here, 192 represents the first eight bits (11000000), 168 the second set of eight bits (10101000), 136 the third set of eight bits (10001000), and 28 the last set of eight bits (00011100). This is the format in which you'll usually see IP addresses represented.

Classifying IP addresses

When the original designers of the IP protocol created the IP addressing scheme, they could have assigned an arbitrary number of IP address bits for the network ID. The remaining bits would then be used for the host ID. For example, suppose that the designers decided that half of the address (16 bits) would be used for the network and the remaining 16 bits would be used for the host ID. The result of that scheme would be that the Internet could have a total of 65,536 networks and each of those networks could have 65,536 hosts.

In the early days of the Internet, this scheme probably seemed like several orders of magnitude more than would ever be needed. However, the IP designers realized from the start that few networks would actually have tens of thousands of hosts. Suppose that a network of 1,000 computers joins the Internet and is assigned one of these hypothetical network IDs. Because that network uses only 1,000 of its 65,536 host addresses, more than 64,000 IP addresses would be wasted.

As a solution to this problem, the idea of IP address *classes* was introduced. The IP protocol defines five different address classes: A, B, C, D, and E. The first three classes, A through C, each use a different size for the network ID and host ID portion of the address. Class D is for a special type of address called a *multicast address.* Class E is an experimental address class that isn't used.

The first four bits of the IP address are used to determine into which class a particular address fits, as follows:

- ✔ If the first bit is a zero, the address is a Class A address.
- ✔ If the first bit is one, and if the second bit is zero, the address is a Class B address.
- ✔ If the first two bits are both one, and if the third bit is zero, the address is a Class C address.
- ✔ If the first three bits are all one, and if the fourth bit is zero, the address is a Class D address.
- ✔ If the first four bits are all one, the address is a Class E address.

Because Class D and E addresses are reserved for special purposes, I focus the rest of the discussion here on Class A, B, and C addresses. Table 24-1 summarizes the details of each address class.

Table 24-1			IP Address Classes		
Class	Address Range	Starting Bits	Length of Network ID	Number of Networks	Number of Hosts
A	1-126.x.y.z	0	8	126	16,777,214
B	128-191.x.y.z	10	16	16,384	65,534
C	192-223.x.y.z	110	24	2,097,152	254

Class A addresses

Class A addresses are designed for very large networks. In a Class A address, the first octet of the address is the network ID and the remaining three octets are the host ID. Because only eight bits are allocated to the network ID, and the first of these bits is used to indicate that the address is a Class A address, only 126 Class A networks can exist in the entire Internet. However, each Class A network can accommodate more than 16 million hosts.

Only about 40 Class A addresses are actually assigned to companies or organizations. The rest are either reserved for use by the IANA (*Internet Assigned Numbers Authority*) or are assigned to organizations that manage IP assignments for geographic regions such as Europe, Asia, and Latin America.

Just for fun, Table 24-2 lists some of the better-known Class A networks. You'll probably recognize many of them. In case you're interested, you can find a complete list of all the Class A address assignments at www.iana.org/assignments/ipv4-address-space.

Table 24-2	Some Well-Known Class A Networks		
Net	Description	Net	Description
3	General Electric Company	32	Norsk Informasjonsteknology
4	Bolt Beranek and Newman Inc.	33	DLA Systems Automation Center
6	Army Information Systems Center	35	MERIT Computer Network
8	Bolt Beranek and Newman Inc.	38	Performance Systems International
9	IBM	40	Eli Lilly and Company
11	DoD Intel Information Systems	43	Japan Inet

Net	Description	Net	Description
12	AT&T Bell Laboratories	44	Amateur Radio Digital Communications
13	Xerox Corporation	45	Interop Show Network
15	Hewlett-Packard Company	46	Bolt Beranek and Newman Inc.
16	Digital Equipment Corporation	47	Bell-Northern Research
17	Apple Computer Inc.	48	Prudential Securities Inc.
18	MIT	51	Department of Social Security of UK
19	Ford Motor Company	52	E.I. duPont de Nemours and Co., Inc.
20	Computer Sciences Corporation	53	Cap Debis CCS (Germany)
22	Defense Information Systems Agency	54	Merck and Co., Inc.
25	Royal Signals and Radar Establishment	55	Boeing Computer Services
26	Defense Information Systems Agency	56	U.S. Postal Service
28	Decision Sciences Institute (North)	57	SITA
29-30	Defense Information Systems Agency		

Class B addresses

In a Class B address, the first two octets of the IP address are used as the network ID and the second two octets are used as the host ID. Thus, a Class B address comes close to our hypothetical scheme of splitting the address down the middle, using half for the network ID and half for the host ID. It isn't identical to this scheme, however, because the first two bits of the first octet are required to be 10, so as to indicate that the address is a Class B address. Thus, a total of 16,384 Class B networks can exist. All Class B addresses fall within the range 128.x.y.z to 191.x.y.z. Each Class B address can accommodate more than 65,000 hosts.

The problem with Class B networks is that even though they are much smaller than Class A networks, they still allocate far too many host IDs. Very few networks have tens of thousands of hosts. Thus, careless assignment of Class B addresses can lead to a large percentage of the available host addresses being wasted on organizations that don't need them.

What about IPv6?

Most of the current Internet is based on version 4 of the Internet Protocol, also known as IPv4. IPv4 has served the Internet well for more than 20 years. However, the growth of the Internet has put a lot of pressure on IPv4's limited 32-bit address space. This chapter describes how IPv4 has evolved to make the best possible use of 32-bit addresses, but eventually all of the addresses will be assigned — the IPv4 address space will be filled to capacity. When that happens, the Internet will have to migrate to the next version of IP, known as IPv6.

IPv6 is also called *IP next generation,* or *IPng,* in honor of the favorite television show of most Internet gurus, *Star Trek: The Next Generation.*

IPv6 offers several advantages over IPv4, but the most important is that it uses 128 bits for Internet addresses rather than 32 bits. The number of host addresses possible with 128 bits

is a number so large it would make Carl Sagan proud. It doesn't just double or triple the number of available addresses. Just for the fun of it, here is the number of unique Internet addresses provided by IPv6:

340,282,366,920,938,463,463,374,607,431,768,211,456

This number is so large it defies understanding. If the IANA were around at the creation of the universe and started handing out IPv6 addresses at a rate of one per millisecond, they would now, 15 billion years later, have not yet allocated even one percent of the available addresses.

Unfortunately, the transition from IPv4 to IPv6 has been a slow one. Thus, the Internet will continue to be driven by IPv4 for at least a few more years.

Class C addresses

In a Class C address, the first three octets are used for the network ID and the fourth octet is used for the host ID. With only eight bits for the host ID, each Class C network can accommodate only 254 hosts. However, with 24 network ID bits, Class C addresses allow for more than 2 million networks.

The problem with Class C networks is that they are too small. Although few organizations need the tens of thousands of host addresses provided by a Class B address, many organizations need more than a few hundred. The large discrepancy between Class B networks and Class C networks is what led to the development of *subnetting,* which is described in the next section.

Subnetting

Subnetting is a technique that lets network administrators use the 32 bits available in an IP address more efficiently by creating networks that aren't limited to the scales provided by Class A, B, and C IP addresses. With subnetting, you can create networks with more realistic host limits.

Subnetting provides a more flexible way to designate which portion of an IP address represents the network ID and which portion represents the host ID. With standard IP address classes, only three possible network ID sizes exist: 8 bits for Class A, 16 bits for Class B, and 24 bits for Class C. Subnetting lets you select an arbitrary number of bits to use for the network ID.

Two reasons compel us to use subnetting. The first is to allocate the limited IP address space more efficiently. If the Internet were limited to Class A, B, or C addresses, every network would be allocated 254, 65 thousand, or 16 million IP addresses for host devices. Although many networks with more than 254 devices exist, few (if any) exist with 65 thousand, let alone 16 million. Unfortunately, any network with more than 254 devices would need a Class B allocation and probably waste tens of thousands of IP addresses.

The second reason for subnetting is that even if a single organization has thousands of network devices, operating all of those devices with the same network ID would slow the network down to a crawl. The way TCP/IP works dictates that all of the computers with the same network ID must be on the same physical network. The physical network comprises a single *broadcast domain*, which means that a single network medium must carry all of the traffic for the network. For performance reasons, networks are usually segmented into broadcast domains that are smaller than even Class C addresses provide.

Subnets

A *subnet* is a network that falls within another (Class A, B, or C) network. Subnets are created by using one or more of the Class A, B, or C host bits to extend the network ID. Thus, instead of the standard 8-, 16-, or 24-bit network ID, subnets can have network IDs of any length.

Figure 24-1 shows an example of a network before and after subnetting has been applied. In the unsubnetted network, the network has been assigned the Class B address 144.28.0.0. All of the devices on this network must share the same broadcast domain.

In the second network, the first four bits of the host ID are used to divide the network into two small networks, identified as subnets 16 and 32. To the outside world (that is, on the other side of the router), these two networks still appear to be a single network identified as 144.28.0.0. For example, the outside world considers the device at 144.28.16.22 to belong to the 144.28.0.0 network. As a result, a packet sent to this device will be delivered to the router at 144.28.0.0. The router then considers the subnet portion of the host ID to decide whether to route the packet to subnet 16 or subnet 32.

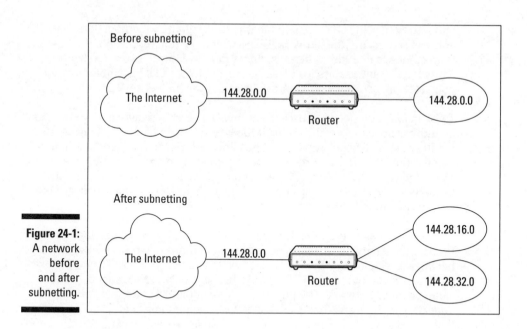

Figure 24-1:
A network
before
and after
subnetting.

Subnet masks

In order for subnetting to work, the router must be told which portion of the host ID to use for the subnet's network ID. This little sleight-of-hand is accomplished by using another 32-bit number, known as a *subnet mask*. Those IP address bits that represent the network ID are represented by a 1 in the mask, and those bits that represent the host ID appear as a 0 in the mask. As a result, a subnet mask always has a consecutive string of ones on the left, followed by a string of zeros.

For example, the subnet mask for the subnet shown in Figure 2-3, where the network ID consists of the 16-bit network ID plus an additional 4-bit subnet ID, would look like this:

```
11111111 11111111 11110000 00000000
```

In other words, the first 20 bits are ones, the remaining 12 bits are zeros. Thus, the complete network ID is 20 bits in length, and the actual host ID portion of the subnetted address is 12 bits in length.

To determine the network ID of an IP address, the router must have both the IP address and the subnet mask. The router then performs a bitwise operation called a *logical AND* on the IP address in order to extract the network ID. To perform a logical AND, each bit in the IP address is compared to the corresponding bit in the subnet mask. If both bits are 1, the resulting bit in the network ID is set to 1. If either of the bits are 0, the resulting bit is set to 0.

For example, here's how the network address is extracted from an IP address using the 20-bit subnet mask from the previous example:

```
                    144  .   28  .   16  .   17
IP address:   10010000 00011100 00100000 00001001
Subnet mask:  11111111 11111111 11110000 00000000
Network ID:   10010000 00011100 00100000 00000000
                    144  .   28  .   16  .   0
```

Thus, the network ID for this subnet is 144.28.16.0.

The subnet mask itself is usually represented in dotted-decimal notation. As a result, the 20-bit subnet mask used in the previous example would be represented as 255.255.240.0:

```
Subnet mask:  11111111 11111111 11111111 11111111
                    255  .   255  .   240  .   0
```

Don't confuse a subnet mask with an IP address. A subnet mask doesn't represent any device or network on the Internet. It's just a way of indicating which portion of an IP address should be used to determine the network ID. (You can spot a subnet mask right away because the first octet is always 255, and 255 is not a valid first octet for any class of IP address.)

The great subnet roundup

You should know about a few additional restrictions that are placed on subnet masks. In particular:

- ✔ The minimum number of network ID bits is eight. As a result, the first octet of a subnet mask is always 255.

- ✔ The maximum number of network ID bits is 30. You have to leave at least two bits for the host ID portion of the address to allow for at least two hosts. If you used all 32 bits for the network ID, that would leave no bits for the host ID. Obviously, that won't work. Leaving just one bit for the host ID won't work, either. That's because a host ID of all ones is reserved for a broadcast address — and all zeros refers to the network itself. Thus, if you used 31 bits for the network ID and left only one for the host ID, host ID 1 would be used for the broadcast address and host ID 0 would be the network itself, leaving no room for actual hosts. That's why the maximum network ID size is 30 bits.

- ✔ Because the network ID is always composed of consecutive bits set to 1, only nine values are possible for each octet of a subnet mask (including counting 0). For your reference, these values are listed in Table 24-3.

Table 24-3		The Eight Subnet Octet Values	
Binary octet	*Decimal*	*Binary octet*	*Decimal*
00000000	0	11111000	248
10000000	128	11111100	252
11000000	192	11111110	254
11100000	224	11111111	255
11110000	240		

IP block parties

A subnet can be thought of as a range or block of IP addresses that have a common network ID. For example, the CIDR `192.168.1.0/28` represents the following block of 14 IP addresses:

```
192.168.1.1     192.168.1.2     192.168.1.3     192.168.1.4
192.168.1.5     192.168.1.6     192.168.1.7     192.168.1.8
192.168.1.9     192.168.1.10    192.168.1.11    192.168.1.12
192.168.1.13    192.168.1.14
```

Given an IP address in CIDR notation, it's useful to be able to determine the range of actual IP addresses that the CIDR represents. This is a straightforward matter when the octet within which the network ID mask ends happens to be 0, as in the preceding example. You just determine how many host IDs are allowed based on the size of the network ID and count them off.

However, what if the octet where the network ID mask ends is not 0? For example, what are the valid IP addresses for `192.168.1.100/28`? In that case, the calculation is a little harder. The first step is to determine the actual network ID. You can do that by converting both the IP address and the subnet mask to binary, and then extracting the network ID as in this example:

```
                192  .  168  .    1  .  100
IP address:   11000000 10101000 00000001 01100100
Subnet mask:  11111111 11111111 11111111 11110000
Network ID:   11000000 10101000 00000001 01100000
                192  .  168  .    1  .   96
```

As a result, the network ID for `192.168.1.100/28` is `192.168.1.96`.

Next, determine the number of allowable hosts in the subnet based on the network prefix. You can look up this number in Table 24-1. For a 28-bit network prefix, the number of hosts is 14.

To determine the first IP address in the block, add 1 to the network ID. Thus, the first IP address in our example is `192.168.1.97`. To determine the last IP address in the block, add the number of hosts to the network ID. In our example, the last IP address is `192.168.1.110`. As a result, the CIDR `192.168.1.100/28` designates the following block of IP addresses:

```
192.168.1.97    192.168.1.98    192.168.1.99    192.168.1.100
192.168.1.101   192.168.1.102   192.168.1.103   192.168.1.104
192.168.1.105   192.168.1.106   192.168.1.107   192.168.1.108
192.168.1.109   192.168.1.110
```

Private and public addresses

Any host with a direct connection to the Internet must have a globally unique IP address. However, not all hosts are connected directly to the Internet. Some are on networks that are not connected to the Internet. Some hosts are hidden behind firewalls, so their Internet connection is indirect.

Several blocks of IP addresses are set aside just for this purpose — for use on private networks that are not connected to the Internet, or to use on networks hidden behind a firewall. Three such ranges of addresses exist, as summarized in Table 24-4. Whenever you create a private TCP/IP network, you should use IP addresses from one of these ranges.

Table 24-4	Private Address Spaces	
CIDR	**Subnet mask**	**Address range**
10.0.0.0/8	255.0.0.0	10.0.0.1 – 10.255.255.254
172.16.0.0/12	255.255.240.0	172.16.1.1 – 172.31.255.254
192.168.0.0/16	255.255.0.0	192.168.0.1 – 192.168.255.254

Network Address Translation

Many firewalls use a technique called *network address translation* (or *NAT*) to hide the actual IP address of a host from the outside world. When that's the case, the NAT device must use a globally unique IP to represent the host to the Internet, but behind the firewall, the host can use any IP address it wants. As packets cross the firewall, the NAT device translates the private IP address to the public IP address and vice versa.

One of the benefits of NAT is that it helps to slow down the rate at which the IP address space is assigned. That's because a NAT device can use a single public IP address for more than one host. It does this by keeping track of outgoing packets so it can match up incoming packets with the correct host. To understand how this works, consider the following sequence of steps:

1. A host whose private address is 192.168.1.100 sends a request to 216.239.57.99, which happens to be www.google.com. The NAT device changes the source IP address of the packet to 208.23.110.22, the IP address of the firewall. That way, Google will send its reply back to the firewall router. The NAT records that 192.168.1.100 sent a request to 216.239.57.99.

2. Now another host, at address 192.168.1.107, sends a request to 207.46.134.190, which happens to be www.microsoft.com. The NAT device changes the source of this request to 208.23.110.22 so Microsoft will reply to the firewall router. The NAT records that 192.168.1.107 sent a request to 207.46.134.190.

3. A few seconds later, the firewall receives a reply from 216.239.57.99. The destination address in the reply is 208.23.110.22, the address of the firewall. To determine to whom to forward the reply, the firewall checks its records to see who is waiting for a reply from 216.239.57.99. It discovers that 192.168.1.100 is waiting for that reply, so it changes the destination address to 192.168.1.100 and sends the packet on.

Actually, the process is a little more complicated than that, because it's very likely that two or more users may have pending requests from the same public IP. In that case, the NAT device uses other techniques to figure out to which user each incoming packet should be delivered.

Chapter 25

Configuring Your Network for DHCP

*E*very host on a TCP/IP network must have a unique IP address. Each host must be properly configured so it knows its IP address. When a new host comes online, it must be assigned an IP address within the correct range of addresses for the subnet — one that's not already in use. Although you can manually assign IP addresses to each computer on your network, that task quickly becomes overwhelming if the network has more than a few computers.

That's where *DHCP,* the *Dynamic Host Configuration Protocol,* comes into play. DHCP automatically configures the IP address for every host on a network, thus assuring that each host has a valid unique IP address. DHCP even automatically reconfigures IP addresses as hosts come and go. As you can imagine, DHCP can save a network administrator many hours of tedious configuration work.

In this section, you learn the ins and outs of DHCP: what it is, how it works, and how to set it up.

Understanding DHCP

DHCP allows individual computers on a TCP/IP network to obtain their configuration information — in particular, their IP address — from a server. The DHCP server keeps track of which IP addresses have already been assigned so when a computer requests an IP address, the DHCP server will offer it an IP address that is not already in use.

The alternative to DHCP is to assign each computer on your network a *static IP address.* Static IP addresses are OK for networks with just a handful of computers. But for networks with more than a few computers, using static IP addresses is a huge mistake. Eventually, some poor harried administrator (guess who) will make the mistake of assigning two computers the same IP address. Then, you'll have to manually check each computer's IP address to find the conflict. DHCP is a must for any but the smallest networks.

Configuration information provided by DHCP

Although the primary job of DHCP is to assign IP addresses, DHCP actually provides more configuration information than just the IP address to its clients. The additional configuration information is referred to as *DHCP options.* The following is a list of some common DHCP options that can be configured by the server:

- ✔ The router address, also known as the Default Gateway address
- ✔ The expiration time for the configuration information
- ✔ Domain name
- ✔ DNS server address
- ✔ WINS server address

DHCP servers

A DHCP server can be a server computer located on the TCP/IP network. Fortunately, all modern server operating systems have a built-in DHCP-server capability. To set up DHCP on a network server, all you have to do is enable the server's DHCP function and configure its settings. In the section "How to Configure a Windows DHCP Client," I show you how to configure a DHCP server for Windows 2003.

A server computer running DHCP doesn't have to be devoted entirely to DHCP unless the network is very large. For most networks, a file server can share duty as a DHCP server. This is especially true if you provide long leases for your IP addresses. (I explain the idea of leases later in this chapter, in the section, "How long to lease?")

Many multifunction routers also have built-in DHCP servers. So if you don't want to burden one of your network servers with the DHCP function, you can enable the router's built-in DHCP server. An advantage of allowing the router to be your network's DHCP server is that you rarely need to power down a router. In contrast, you occasionally need to restart or power-down a file server to perform system maintenance, to apply upgrades, or to do some needed troubleshooting.

Understanding Scopes

A *scope* is simply a range of IP addresses that a DHCP server is configured to distribute. In the simplest case, where a single DHCP server oversees IP configuration for an entire subnet, the scope corresponds to the subnet. However, if you set up two DHCP servers for a subnet, you can configure each with a scope that allocates only one part of the complete subnet range. In addition, a single DHCP server can serve more than one scope.

You must create a scope before you can enable a DHCP server. When you create a scope, you can provide it with the following properties:

- ✔ A scope name, which helps you to identify the scope and its purpose.

- ✔ A scope description, which lets you provide additional details about the scope and its purpose.

- ✔ A starting IP address for the scope.

- ✔ An ending IP address for the scope.

- ✔ A subnet mask for the scope. You can specify the subnet mask with dotted decimal notation or with CIDR notation.

- ✔ One or more ranges of excluded addresses. These addresses won't be assigned to clients. (For more information, see the section "Feeling excluded?" later in this chapter.)

- ✔ One or more reserved addresses. These are addresses that will always be assigned to particular host devices. (For more information, see the section "Reservations suggested" later in this chapter.)

- ✔ The lease duration, which indicates how long the host will be allowed to use the IP address. The client will attempt to renew the lease when half of the lease duration has elapsed. For example, if you specify a lease duration of eight days, the client will attempt to renew the lease after four days have passed. This allows the host plenty of time to renew the lease before the address is reassigned to some other host.

- ✔ The router address for the subnet. This value is also known as the *Default Gateway address.*

- ✔ The domain name and the IP address of the network's DNS servers and WINS servers.

Feeling excluded?

We all feel excluded once in awhile. With a wife and three daughters, I know how that feels (hey, in that case, it's a guy thing). Sometimes, however, being excluded is a good thing. In the case of DHCP scopes, exclusions can help you to prevent IP address conflicts and can enable you to divide the DHCP workload for a single subnet among two or more DHCP servers.

An *exclusion* is a range of addresses not included in a scope, but falling within the range of the scope's starting and ending addresses. In effect, an exclusion range lets you punch a hole in a scope: The IP addresses that fall within the hole won't be assigned.

The following are several reasons for excluding IP addresses from a scope:

- ✔ The computer that runs the DHCP service itself usually must have a static IP address assignment. As a result, the address of the DHCP server should be listed as an exclusion.

- ✔ You may want to assign static IP addresses to your other servers. In that case, each server IP address should be listed as an exclusion. (However, reservations are often a better solution to this problem, as described in the next section.)

Reservations suggested

In some cases, you may want to assign a specific IP address to a particular host. One way to do this is to configure the host with a static IP address so the host doesn't use DHCP to obtain its IP configuration. However, two major disadvantages to that approach exist:

- ✔ TCP/IP configuration supplies more than just the IP address. If you use static configuration, you must manually specify the subnet mask, Default Gateway address, DNS server address, and other configuration information required by the host. If this information changes, you have to change it not only at the DHCP server, but also at each host that you've configured statically.

- ✔ You must remember to exclude the static IP address from the DCHP server's scope. Otherwise the DHCP server won't know about the static address and may assign it to another host. Then comes the problem: You'll have two hosts with the same address on your network.

A better way to assign a fixed IP address to a particular host is to create a DHCP reservation. A *reservation* simply indicates that whenever a particular host requests an IP address from the DHCP server, the server should provide it the address that you specify in the reservation. The host won't receive the

IP address until the host requests it from the DHCP server, but whenever the host does request IP configuration, it will always receive the same address.

To create a reservation, you associate the IP address that you want assigned to the host with the host's MAC address. Accordingly, you need to get the MAC address from the host before you create the reservation. You can get the MAC address by running the command `ipconfig /all` from a command prompt. (If that fails because TCP/IP has not yet been configured on the computer, you can also get the MAC address by running the System Information command, which is Start⇨All Programs⇨Accessories⇨System Tools⇨System Information.)

How long to lease?

One of the most important decisions that you'll make when you configure a DHCP server is the length of time to specify for the lease duration. The default value is eight days, which is appropriate in many cases. However, you may encounter situations in which a longer or shorter interval may be appropriate.

- ✔ The more stable your network, the longer the lease duration can safely exist. If you only periodically add new computers to the network (or replace existing computers), you can safely increase the lease duration past eight days.

- ✔ The more volatile the network, the shorter the lease duration should be. For example, imagine a wireless network in a university library, used by students who bring their laptop computers into the library to work for a few hours at a time. For this network, a duration as short as one hour may be appropriate.

Don't configure your network to allow infinite duration leases. Although some administrators feel that this cuts down the workload for the DHCP server on stable networks, no network is permanently stable. Whenever you find a DHCP server that's configured with infinite leases, look at the active leases. I guarantee you'll find IP leases assigned to computers that no longer exist.

Managing a Windows Server 2003 DHCP Server

The exact steps to follow when you configure and manage a DHCP server depend on the network operating system or router you're using. The following procedures show you how to work with a DHCP server in Windows Server 2003. The procedures for other operating systems are similar.

Setting up a DHCP server

If you haven't already installed the DHCP server on the server, call up the Manage Your Server application (choose Start⇨Administrative Tools⇨ Manage Your Server), click Add or Remove a Role, select DHCP Server from the list of roles, then click Next and complete the New Scope Wizard to create the first scope for the DHCP server. This wizard asks you to enter a name and description for the scope. Then, it asks for the basic IP address range information for the scope, as shown in Figure 25-1.

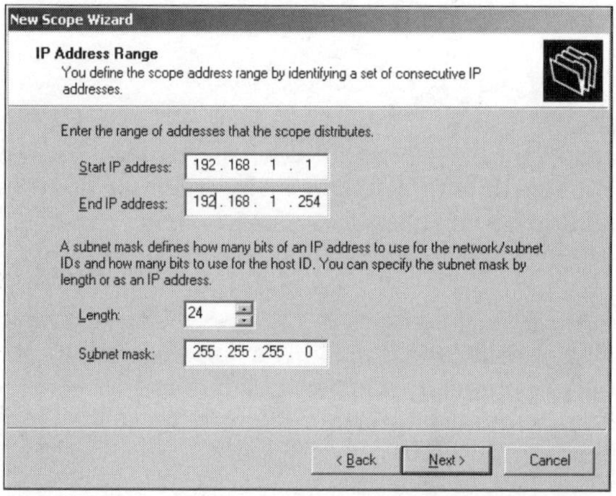

Figure 25-1: Specifying the scope's address range and subnet mask.

Once you've entered the starting and ending IP addresses for the range and the subnet mask used for your network, click Next. The wizard then asks for any IP addresses you want to exclude from the scope, the lease duration (the default is 8 days), the IP address of your gateway router, the domain name for your network, and the IP addresses for the DNS servers you want the client computers to use. When you complete the wizard, the DHCP server will be properly configured. It won't start running, however, until you authorize it as described in the next section.

Managing a DHCP server

You can bring up the DHCP management console by choosing Start⇨ Administrative Tools⇨DHCP, or by clicking Manage This DHCP Server in the Manage Your Server application. Either way, the DHCP management console appears, as shown in Figure 25-2.

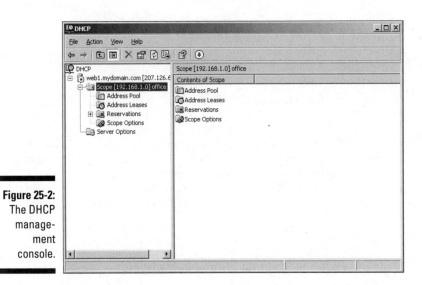

Figure 25-2:
The DHCP
manage-
ment
console.

From the DHCP console, you have complete control over the DHCP server's configuration and operation. The following paragraphs summarize some of the things that you can do from the DHCP console:

- You can *authorize* the DHCP server, which allows it to begin assigning client IP addresses. To authorize a server, select the server, choose Action⇨Manage Authorized Servers, and click Authorize.

- To add another scope, right-click the server in the tree and choose the New Scope command from the menu that appears. This brings up the New Scope Wizard so you can create a new scope.

- To activate or deactivate a scope, right-click the scope in the tree and choose the Activate or Deactivate command.

- To change scope settings, right-click the scope and choose the Properties command. This brings up the Scope Properties dialog box which lets you change the scope's starting and ending IP addresses, subnet mask, and DNS configuration.

- To change the scope exclusions, click Address Pool under the scope in the tree. This will list each range of addresses that's included in the scope. You can add or delete a range by right-clicking the range and choosing the Delete command from the menu that appears. You can also add a new exclusion range by right-clicking Address Pool in the tree and choosing Add New Exclusion from the pop-up menu.

- To view or change reservations, click Reservations in the tree.

- To view a list of the addresses that are currently assigned, click Address Leases in the tree.

How to Configure a Windows DHCP Client

Configuring a Windows client for DHCP is easy. The DHCP client is automatically included when you install the TCP/IP protocol, so all you have to do is configure TCP/IP to use DHCP. To do this, bring up the Network Properties dialog box by choosing Network or Network Connections in the Control Panel (depending on which version of Windows the client is running). Then, select the TCP/IP protocol and click the Properties button. This brings up the TCP/IP Properties dialog box. To configure the computer to use DHCP, check Obtain an IP Address Automatically and Obtain DNS Server Address Automatically.

Renewing and Releasing Leases

Normally, a DHCP client attempts to renew its lease when the lease is halfway to the point of being expired. For example, if a client obtains an eight-day lease, it attempts to renew the lease after four days. If necessary, you can renew a lease sooner by issuing the ipconfig /renew command at a command prompt. (You may want to do this if you've changed the scope's configuration or if the client's IP configuration isn't working correctly.)

You can also release a DHCP lease by issuing the ipconfig /release command at a command prompt. When you release a lease, the client computer no longer has a valid IP address. This is shown in the output from the ipconfig /release command:

```
C:\>ipconfig /release

Windows IP Configuration

Ethernet adapter Local Area Connection:

        Connection-specific DNS Suffix  . :
        IP Address. . . . . . . . . . . . : 0.0.0.0
        Subnet Mask . . . . . . . . . . . : 0.0.0.0
        Default Gateway . . . . . . . . . :
```

Here you can see that the IP address and subnet masks are set to 0.0.0.0 and the Default Gateway address is blank. When you release an IP lease, you can't communicate with the network by using TCP/IP until you issue an ipconfig /renew command to renew the IP configuration or restart the computer.

Part VI
The Part of Tens

The 5th Wave — By Rich Tennant

"It's okay. One of the routers must have gone down and we had a brief broadcast storm."

In this part . . .

*I*f you keep this book in the bathroom, the chapters in this section are the ones that you'll read most. Each chapter consists of ten (more or less) things that are worth knowing about various aspects of networking. Without further ado, here they are, direct from the home office in sunny Fresno, California.

Chapter 26

Ten Big Network Mistakes

*J*ust about the time you figure out how to avoid the most embarrassing computer mistakes (such as using your CD drive's tray as a cup holder), the network lands on your computer. Now you have a whole new list of dumb things you can do, mistakes that can give your average computer geek a belly laugh because they seem so basic to him. Well, that's because he's a computer geek. Nobody had to tell *him* not to fold the floppy disk — he was born with an extra gene that gave him an instinctive knowledge of such things.

Here's a list of some of the most common mistakes made by network novices. Avoid these mistakes and you deprive your local computer geek of the pleasure of a good laugh at your expense.

Skimping on Cable

If your network consists of more than a few computers or has computers located in different rooms, you should invest in a professional-quality cable installation, complete with wall-mounted jacks, patch panels, and high-quality hubs. It is tempting to cut costs by using the cheapest hubs and by stringing inexpensive cable directly from the hubs to each computer on the network. But in the long run, that approach will actually prove to be more expensive than investing in a good cable installation in the first place.

Here are just a few of the reasons it pays to do the cabling right in the first place:

- ✔ A good cable installation will last much longer than the computers it services. A good cable installation can last 10 or 15 years, long after the computers on your network have been placed on display in a computer history museum.

- ✔ Installing cable is hard work. No one enjoys going up in the attic, poking his or her head up through ceiling panels and wiping fiberglass insulation out of his or her hair, or fishing cables through walls. If you're going to do it, do it right so you don't have to do it again in just a few years. Build your cable installation to last.

- ✔ Your network users may be satisfied with 100Mbps networking now, but it won't be long before they demand gigahertz speed. And who knows how fast the next wave of networking will be? If you cut costs by using plain Cat5 cable instead of more expensive Cat5e cable, you'll have to replace it later.

- ✔ You might be tempted to skip the modular wall jacks and patch cables and instead just run the cable down the wall, out through a hole, and then directly to the computer or hub. That's a bad idea because the wires inside the network cable are solid wire, which is designed to last for a long time — provided it doesn't get handled much. If you run solid-wire cable directly to a computer, the wire will be stressed each time someone unplugs the cable. Even just dusting behind the computer (which some people actually do) can jostle the cable. Sooner or later, one of the wires inside the cable will break. Patch cables are made with stranded rather than solid wire, so they can tolerate a lot of handling without breaking. And if a patch cable does fail, you can replace it yourself for just a few dollars.

For more information about professional touches for installing cable, see Chapter 9.

Turning Off or Restarting a Server Computer While Users Are Logged On

The fastest way to blow your network users' accounts to kingdom come is to turn off a server computer while users are logged on. Restarting it by pressing its reset button can have the same disastrous effect.

If your network is set up with a dedicated file server, you probably won't be tempted to turn it off or restart it. But if your network is set up as a true peer-to-peer network, where each of the workstation computers — including your own — also doubles as a server computer, be careful about the impulsive urge to turn your computer off or restart it. Someone may be accessing a file or printer on your computer at that very moment.

Before turning off or restarting a server computer, find out whether anyone is logged on. If so, politely ask him or her to log off.

Also, remember that many server problems don't require a server reboot. Instead, you can often correct the problem just by restarting the particular service that's affected.

Deleting Important Files on the Server

Without a network, you can do anything you want to your computer, and the only person you can hurt is yourself. (Kind of like the old "victimless crime" debate.) Put your computer on a network, though, and you take on a certain amount of responsibility. You must find out how to live like a responsible member of the network society.

That means you can't capriciously delete files from a network server just because you don't need them. They may not be yours. You wouldn't want someone deleting your files, would you?

Be especially careful about files that are required to keep the network running. For example, some versions of Windows use a folder named `wgpo0000` to hold e-mail. If you delete this folder, your e-mail is history. Look before you delete.

Copying a File from the Server, Changing It, and Then Copying It Back

Sometimes working on a network file is easier if you first copy the file to your local hard drive. Then you can access it from your application program more efficiently because you don't have to use the network. This is especially true for large database files that have to be sorted to print reports.

You're asking for trouble, though, if you copy the file to your PC's local hard drive, make changes to the file, and then copy the updated version of the file back to the server. Why? Because somebody else may be trying the same thing at the same time. If that happens, the updates made by one of you — whoever copies the file back to the server first — are lost.

Copying a file to a local drive is an okay thing to do, but not if you plan on updating the file and copying it back.

Sending Something to the Printer Again Just Because It Didn't Print the First Time

What do you do if you send something to the printer and nothing happens? *Right answer:* Find out why nothing happened and fix it. *Wrong answer:* Send it again and see whether it works this time. Some users keep sending it over and over again, hoping that one of these days, it'll take. The result is rather embarrassing when someone finally clears the paper jam and then watches 30 copies of the same letter print.

Unplugging a Cable While the Computer Is On

Bad idea! If for any reason you need to unplug a cable from behind your computer, turn your computer off first. You don't want to fry any of the delicate electronic parts inside your computer, do you?

If you need to unplug the network cable, you should wait until all the computers on the network are off. This is especially true if your network is wired with Thinnet coax cable; it's not such a big deal with twisted-pair cable.

Note: With Thinnet cable, you can disconnect the T-connector from your computer as long as you don't disconnect the cable itself from the T-connector.

Assuming That the Server Is Safely Backed Up

Some users make the unfortunate assumption that the network somehow represents an efficient and organized bureaucracy worthy of their trust. Far from the truth. Never assume that the network jocks are doing their jobs backing up the network data every day, even if they are. Check up on them. Conduct a surprise inspection one day: Burst into the computer room wearing white gloves and demand to see the backup tapes. Check the tape rotation to make sure that more than one day's worth of backups are available.

If you're not impressed with your network's backup procedures, take it upon yourself to make sure that you never lose any of your data. Back up your most valued files to floppy disks frequently — or, better yet, to a CD-RW disc.

Connecting to the Internet without Considering Security Issues

If you connect a non-networked computer to the Internet and then pick up a virus or get yourself hacked into, only that one computer is affected. But if you connect a networked computer to the Internet, the entire network becomes vulnerable. Therefore beware: Never connect a networked computer to the Internet without first considering the security issues. How will you protect yourself and the network from viruses? How will you ensure that the sensitive files located on your file server don't suddenly become accessible to the entire world? How can you prevent evil hackers from sneaking into your network, stealing your customer file, and selling your customer's credit-card data on the black market?

For answers to these and other Internet-security questions, see Chapter 23.

Plugging in a Wireless Access Point without Asking

For that matter, plugging any device into your network without first getting permission from the network administrator is a big no-no. But Wireless Access Points (WAPs) are particularly insidious. Many users fall for the marketing line that wireless networking is as easy as plugging one of these devices into the network. Then, your wireless notebook PC or hand-held device can instantly join the network.

The trouble is, so can anyone else within about ¼ mile of the wireless access point. That means that you must employ extra security measures to make sure hackers can't get into your network via a wireless computer located in the parking lot or across the street.

If you think that's unlikely, think again. Several underground Web sites on the Internet actually display maps of unsecured wireless networks in major cities. For more information about securing a wireless network, see Chapter 10.

Thinking You Can't Work Just Because the Network Is Down

A few years back, I realized that I can't do my job without electricity. Should a power failure occur and I find myself without electricity, I can't even light a candle and work with pencil and paper because the only pencil sharpener I have is electric.

Some people have the same attitude about the network: They figure that if the network goes down, they may as well go home. That's not always the case. Just because your computer is attached to a network doesn't mean that it won't work when the network is down. True — if the wind flies out of the network sails, you can't access any network devices. You can't get files from network drives, and you can't print on network printers. But you can still use your computer for local work — accessing files and programs on your local hard drive and printing on your local printer (if you're lucky enough to have one).

Always Blaming the Network

Some people treat the network kind of like the village idiot who can be blamed whenever anything goes wrong. Networks do cause problems of their own, but they aren't the root of all evil.

If your monitor displays only capital letters, it's probably because you pressed the Caps Lock key. Don't blame the network.

If you spill coffee on the keyboard, well, that's your fault. Don't blame the network.

If your toddler sticks Play-Doh in the floppy drive, kids will be kids. Don't blame the network.

Get the point?

Chapter 27

Ten Networking Commandments

*B*lessed is the network manager who walks not in the counsel of the ignorant, nor stands in the way of the oblivious, nor sits in the seat of the greenhorn, but delights in the Law of the Network and meditates on this Law day and night."

— Networks 1:1

And so it came to pass that these Ten Networking Commandments were passed down from generation to generation, to be worn as frontlets between the computer geeks' eyes (taped on the bridges of their broken glasses) and written upon their doorposts. Obey these commandments, and it shall go well with you, with your children, and with your children's children.

1. Thou Shalt Back Up Thy Hard Drive Religiously

Prayer is a good thing, but when it comes to protecting the data on your network, nothing beats a well-thought-out schedule of backups followed religiously. (If this were an actual network Bible, a footnote here would refer you back to related verses in Chapter 15.)

II. Thou Shalt Protect Thy Network from Infidels

Remember Colonel Flagg from *M*A*S*H,* who hid in trashcans looking for Commies? You don't exactly want to become him, but on the other hand, you don't want to ignore the possibility of getting zapped by a virus or your network being invaded by hackers. Make sure that your Internet connection is properly secured with a firewall, and do not allow any Internet access that circumvents your security.

To counter virus threats, use network-aware antivirus software to ensure that every user on your network has up-to-date virus protection. And teach your users so they will know how to avoid those virus threats that manage to sneak past your virus protection.

III. Thou Shalt Keepeth Thy Network Drive Pure and Cleanse It of Old Files

Don't wait until your 200GB network drive is down to just one cluster of free space before you think about cleaning it up. Set up a routine schedule for disk housekeeping, where you wade through the files and directories on the network disk to remove old junk.

IV. Thou Shalt Not Tinker with Thine Network Configuration Unless Thou Knowest What Thou Art Doing

Networks are finicky things. After yours is up and running, don't mess around with it unless you know what you're doing. It may be tempting to log in to your firewall router to see if you can't tweak some of its settings to squeeze another ounce of performance out of it. But unless you know what you're doing, be careful! (Be especially careful if you think you *do* know what you're doing. It's the people who think they know what they're doing — and think no more about it — who get themselves into trouble!)

V. Thou Shalt Not Covet Thy Neighbor's Network

Network envy is a common malady among network managers. If your network is humming along fine at 100 Mbps, don't covet your neighbor's 1000Mbps network. If you run NetWare 6, resist the urge to upgrade to 6.5 unless you have a really good reason. And if you run Windows 2000 Server, fantasizing about Windows Server 2003 is a venial sin.

You're especially susceptible to network envy if you're a gadget freak. There's always a better switch to be had or some fancy network-protocol gizmo to lust after. Don't give in to these base urges! Resist the devil, and he will flee!

VI. Thou Shalt Schedule Downtime before Working upon Thy Network

As a courtesy, try to give your users plenty of advance notice before you take down the network to work on it. Obviously, you can't predict when random problems strike. But if you know you're going to patch the server on Thursday morning, you earn points if you tell everyone about the inconvenience two days before rather than two minutes before. (You'll earn even more points if you patch the server Saturday morning. Tell your boss you'll take next Thursday morning off to make up for it.)

VII. Thou Shalt Keep an Adequate Supply of Spare Parts

There's no reason that your network should be down for two days just because a cable breaks. Always make sure that you have at least a minimal supply of network spare parts on hand. (As luck would have it, Chapter 28 suggests ten things you should keep in your closet.)

VIII. Thou Shalt Not Steal Thy Neighbor's Program without a License

How would you like it if Inspector Clouseau barged into your office, looked over your shoulder as you ran Excel from a network server, and asked, "Do you have a liesaunce?"

"A liesaunce?" you reply, puzzled.

"Yes of course, a liesaunce, that is what I said. The law specifically prohibits the playing of a computer program on a network without a proper liesaunce."

You don't want to get in trouble with Inspector Clouseau, do you? License that application.

IX. Thou Shalt Train Thy Users in the Ways of the Network

Don't blame the users if they don't know how to use the network. It's not their fault. If you're the network administrator, your job is to provide training so the network users know how to use the network.

X. Thou Shalt Write Down Thy Network Configuration upon Tablets of Stone

Oral tradition works well as a supplement to real Bibles, but network documentation should be written down. If you cross the river Jordan, who else will know diddly-squat about the network if you don't write it down somewhere? Write down everything, put it in an official binder labeled *Network Bible,* and protect the binder as if it were sacred.

Your hope should be that 2,000 years from now, when archaeologists are exploring caves in your area, they find your network documentation hidden in a jar and marvel at how meticulously the people of our time recorded their network configurations.

They'll probably draw ridiculous conclusions such as we offered sacrifices of burnt data packets to a deity named TCP/IP and confessed our transgressions in a ritual known as "logging," but that makes it all the more fun.

Chapter 28

Ten Things You Should Keep in Your Closet

When you first network your office computers, you need to find a closet where you can stash some network goodies. If you can't find a whole closet, shoot for a shelf, a drawer, or at least a sturdy cardboard box.

Here's a list of what stuff to keep on hand.

Duct Tape

It helped get the crew of *Apollo 13* back from their near-disastrous moon voyage. You won't actually use it much to maintain your network, but it serves the symbolic purpose of demonstrating that you realize things sometimes go wrong and you are willing to improvise to get your network up and running.

If you don't like duct tape, a little baling wire and chewing gum will serve the same symbolic purpose.

Tools

Make sure that you have at least a basic computer toolkit, the kind you can pick up for $15 from just about any office-supply store. You also should have wire cutters, wire strippers, and cable crimpers that work for your network cable type.

Extra Cable

When you buy network cable, never buy exactly the amount you need. In fact, buying at least twice as much cable as you need isn't a bad idea, because that way half the cable is left over in case you need it later — and you will. Something will go wrong, and you'll suspect a cable problem, so you'll need extra cable to replace the bad cable. Or you may add a computer or two to the network and need extra cable.

If your network is glued together with preassembled 25-foot lengths of cable, having at least one 25-foot segment lying around in the closet is a good idea.

Extra Connectors

Don't run out of connectors, either. If you use twisted-pair cabling, you'll find that connectors go bad more often than you'd like. Buy the connectors in lots of 25, 50, or 100 at a time so you have plenty of spares lying around.

If your network still uses Thinnet cable, keep a few spare BNC connectors handy, plus a few T-connectors and a few terminators. Terminators have been known to mysteriously disappear. Rumor has it that they are sucked through some kind of time vortex into the distant future, where they're refabricated and returned to our time in the form of Arnold Schwarzenegger.

Patch Cables

If you wired your network the professional way — with wall jacks in each office — keep a few patch cables of various lengths in the closet. That way, you won't have to run to the store every time you need to change a patch cable. And trust me, you will need to replace patch cables from time to time.

Twinkies

If left sealed in their little individually wrapped packages, Twinkies keep for years. In fact, they'll probably outlast the network itself. You can bequeath 'em to future network geeks, ensuring continued network support for generations to come.

Extra Network Cards

Ideally, you want to use identical network cards in all your computers. But if the boss's computer is down, you'd probably settle for whatever network card the corner network street vendor is selling today. That's why you should always keep at least one spare network card in the closet. You can rest easy knowing that if a network card fails, you have an identical replacement card sitting on the shelf, just waiting to be installed — and you won't have to buy one from someone who also sells imitation Persian rugs.

Obviously, if you have only two computers on your network, justifying spending the money for a spare network adapter card is hard. With larger networks, it's easier to justify.

The Complete Documentation of the Network on Tablets of Stone

I've mentioned several times in this book the importance of documenting your network. Don't spend hours documenting your network and then hide the documentation under a pile of old magazines behind your desk. Put the binder in the closet with the other network supplies so that you and everyone else always know where to find it. And keep backup copies of the Word, Excel, Visio, or other documents that make up the network binder in a fireproof safe or at another site.

Don't you dare chisel passwords into the network documentation, though. Shame on you for even thinking about it!

If you do decide to chisel the network documentation onto actual stone tablets, consider using sandstone. It's attractive, inexpensive, and easy to update (just rub out the old info and chisel in the new). Keep in mind, however, that sandstone is subject to erosion from spilled Diet Coke. Oh, and make sure that you store it on a reinforced shelf.

The Network Manuals and Disks

In the land of Oz, a common lament of the Network Scarecrow is, "If I only had the manual." True, the manual probably isn't a Pulitzer Prize candidate, but that doesn't mean you should toss it in a landfill, either. Put the manuals for all the software you use on your network where they belong — in the closet with all the other network tools and artifacts.

Likewise the disks. You may need them someday, so keep them with the other network stuff.

Ten Copies of This Book

Obviously, you want to keep an adequate supply of this book on hand to distribute to all your network users. The more they know, the more they stay off your back. Sheesh, 10 copies may not be enough — 20 may be closer to what you need.

Chapter 29

Ten Network Gizmos Only Big Networks Need

*P*eople who compile statistics on things — such as the ratio of chickens to humans in Arkansas and the likelihood of the Mets losing when the other team shows up — report that more than 40 percent of all networks have fewer than ten computers and that this percentage is expected to increase in coming years. A Ross Perot-style pie chart would be good here, but my editor tells me I'm running long, so I have to pass on that.

The point is that if you're one of the lucky 40 percent with fewer than ten computers on your network, you can skip this chapter altogether. Here, I briefly describe various network gizmos that you may need if your network is really big. How big is big? There's no hard-and-fast rule, but the soft-and-slow rule is that you should look into this stuff when your network grows to about 25 computers.

The exceptions to the soft-and-slow rule are as follows: (1) Your company has two or more networks that you want to hook together, and these networks were designed by different people who refused to talk to each other until it was too late; (2) your network needs to connect computers that are more than a few hundred yards apart, perhaps in different buildings or via the Internet.

Repeaters

A *repeater* is a gizmo that gives your network signals a boost so the signals can travel farther. It's kind of like the Gatorade stations in a marathon. As the signals travel past the repeater, they pick up a cup of Gatorade, take a sip, splash the rest of it on their heads, toss the cup, and hop in a cab when they're sure no one is looking.

You need a repeater when the total length of a single span of network cable is larger than the maximum allowed for your cable type:

Cable	Maximum Length
10Base2 (coax)	185 meters or 606 feet
10/100BaseT (twisted-pair)	100 meters or 328 feet

For coax cable, the preceding cable lengths apply to cable segments, not individual lengths of cable. A segment is the entire run of cable from one terminator to another and may include more than one computer. In other words, if you have ten computers and you connect them all with 25-foot lengths of thin coax cable, the total length of the segment is 225 feet. (Made you look! Only nine cables are required to connect ten computers — that's why it's not 250 feet.)

For 10BaseT or 100BaseT cable, the 100-meter length limit applies to the cable that connects a computer to the hub or the cable that connects hubs to each other when hubs are daisy-chained with twisted-pair cable. In other words, you can connect each computer to the hub with no more than 100 meters of cable, and you can connect hubs to each other with no more than 100 meters of cable.

You can use a repeater to connect two groups of computers that are too far apart to be strung on a single segment. When you use a repeater like this, the repeater divides the cable into two segments. The cable length limit still applies to the cable on each side of the repeater.

Here are some points to ponder when you lie awake tonight wondering about repeaters:

- ✔ Repeaters are used only with Ethernet networks wired with coax cable. 10/100BaseT networks don't use repeaters.

  Actually, that's not quite true: 10/100BaseT does use repeaters. It's just that the repeater isn't a separate device. In a 10/100baseT network, the hub is actually a multiport repeater. That's why the cable used to attach each computer to the hub is considered a separate segment.

✔ Some 10/100BaseT hubs have a BNC connector on the back. This BNC connector is a Thinnet repeater that enables you to attach a full 185-meter Thinnet segment. The segment can attach other computers, 10BaseT hubs, or a combination of both.

✔ A basic rule of Ethernet life is that a signal cannot pass through more than three repeaters on its way from one node to another. That doesn't mean you can't have more than three repeaters or hubs, but if you do, you have to carefully plan the network cabling so that the three-repeater rule isn't violated.

✔ A two-port 10Base2 repeater costs about $200. Sheesh! I guess that's one of the reasons fewer people use coax cable these days.

✔ Repeaters are legitimate components of a by-the-book Ethernet network. They don't extend the maximum length of a single segment; they just enable you to tie two segments together. Beware of the little black boxes that claim to extend the segment limit beyond the standard 185-meter limit for Thinnet. These products usually work, but playing by the rules is better.

Managed Switches

A *managed switch* is a 10BaseT or 100BaseT switch that allows you to monitor and control various aspects of the switch's operation from a remote computer. Here are some of the benefits of managed switches:

✔ Managed switches can keep network usage and performance statistics, so you can find out which parts of your network are heavily used and which are not.

✔ A managed switch can alert you when something goes wrong with your network. In fact, the management software that controls the switch can even be configured to send you e-mail or dial your pager when a network error occurs.

✔ You can reconfigure a managed switch from any computer on the network, without having to actually go to the switch.

Inexpensive switches do not include management features. An unmanaged switch is fine for a small network, but for larger networks, you should invest in managed switches. A typical managed switch can cost two or three times as much as an equivalent unmanaged switch, but for larger networks, the benefits of switch management are well worth the additional cost. However, if your network has only one or two switches, you probably don't need management.

Bridges

A bridge is a device that connects two networks so they act as if they were one network. Bridges are used to partition one large network into two smaller networks for performance reasons. You can think of a bridge as a kind of smart repeater. Repeaters listen to signals coming down one network cable, amplify them, and send them down the other cable. They do this blindly, paying no attention to the content of the messages they repeat.

In contrast, a bridge is a little smarter about the messages that come down the pike. For starters, most bridges have the capability to listen to the network and automatically figure out the address of each computer on both sides of the bridge. Then the bridge can inspect each message that comes from one side of the bridge and broadcast it on the other side of the bridge only if the message is intended for a computer that's on the other side.

This key feature enables bridges to partition a large network into two smaller, more efficient networks. Bridges work best in networks that are highly segregated. For example (humor me here — I'm a Dr. Seuss fan), suppose that the Sneetches networked all their computers and discovered that, although the Star-Bellied Sneetches' computers talked to each other frequently and the Plain-Bellied Sneetches' computers also talked to each other frequently, rarely did a Star-Bellied Sneetch computer talk to a Plain-Bellied Sneetch computer.

A bridge can partition the Sneetchnet into two networks: the Star-Bellied network and the Plain-Bellied network. The bridge automatically learns which computers are on the Star-Bellied network and which are on the Plain-Bellied network. The bridge forwards messages from the Star-Bellied side to the Plain-Bellied side (and vice versa) only when necessary. The overall performance of both networks improves, although the performance of any network operation that has to travel over the bridge slows down a bit.

Here are a few additional things to consider about bridges:

- As I mentioned, some bridges also have the capability to translate the messages from one format to another. For example, if the Star-Bellied Sneetches build their network with Ethernet and the Plain-Bellied Sneetches use Token Ring, a bridge can tie the two together.

- You can get a basic bridge to partition two Ethernet networks for about $500 from mail-order suppliers. More sophisticated bridges can cost as much as $5,000 or more.

- If you've never read Dr. Seuss's classic story of the Sneetches, you should.

- If you're not confused yet, don't worry. Read on.

Gateways

No, not the Bill Gates way. This kind of gateway is a superintelligent router, which is a superintelligent bridge, which is a superintelligent repeater. Notice a pattern here?

Gateways are designed to connect radically different types of networks together. They do this by translating messages from one network's format to another's format, much like the Universal Translator that got Kirk and Spock out of so many jams. (Ever notice how all those planets with gorgeous females never seemed to have a word for *kiss,* so Kirk had to demonstrate?)

Gateways usually connect a network to a mainframe or minicomputer. If you don't have a mainframe or minicomputer, you probably don't need a gateway.

Keep the following points in mind:

✔ Gateways are necessary only because of the mess that computer manufacturers got us into by insisting on using their own proprietary designs for networks. If computer manufacturers had talked to each other 20 years ago, we wouldn't have to use gateways to make their networks talk to each other today.

✔ Gateways come in several varieties. My favorite is ornamental wrought iron.

It's a RAID!

In most small networks, it's a hassle if a disk drive goes south and has to be sent to the shop for repairs. In some large networks, a failed disk drive is more than a hassle: It's an outright disaster. Big companies don't know how to do anything when the computer goes down. Everyone just sits around, looking at the floor, silently keeping vigil 'til the computers come back up.

A *RAID system* is a fancy type of disk storage that hardly ever fails. It works by lumping several disk drives together and treating them as if they were one humongous drive. RAID uses some fancy techniques devised by computer nerds at Berkeley. These computer nerds guarantee that if one of the disk drives in the RAID system fails, no data is lost. The disk drive that failed can be removed and repaired, and the data that was on it can be reconstructed from the other drives.

Here are a few additional thoughts on RAID:

- ✔ *RAID* stands for *Redundant Array of Inexpensive Disks,* but that doesn't matter. You don't have to remember that for the test.

- ✔ A RAID system is often housed in a separate cabinet that includes its own RAID disk controller. It's sometimes called a disk subsystem. (Note that some server computers have RAID systems built in, however.)

- ✔ In the coolest RAID systems, the disk drives themselves are *hot-swappable.* That means that you can shut down and remove one of the disk drives while the RAID system continues to operate. Network users won't even know that one of the disks has been removed because the RAID system reconstructs the data that was on the removed disk, using data from the other disks. After the failed disk has been replaced, the new disk is brought online without a hitch.

Server Farms

Large networks with multiple servers often have their servers bunched together in one room; the result is known as a *server farm* (no, there's no E-I-E-I-O protocol). If you have more than two or three servers, you might want to consider some or all of the following methods of dealing with them:

- ✔ You can use inexpensive wire shelving to hold your servers. You can also get special wire shelves designed to hold keyboards, monitors, and processors, providing easy access to cabling. For a more professional look, you can get customized LAN-management furniture designed to hold multiple server computers in just about any configuration you need.

- ✔ If you have limited space, you can use a device known as a *KVM switch* to connect several server computers to a single keyboard, monitor, and mouse. (*KVM* stands for *keyboard, video, and mouse.*) That way, you can control any of the servers from the same keyboard, monitor, and mouse by turning a dial or pressing a button on the KVM switch.

- ✔ To save even more space, you can get rack-mounted servers instead of servers built in standard computer cases. Rack-mounted servers can be attached to the same standard 19-inch racks that rack-mounted hubs and patch panels mount to.

- ✔ A recent trend in server farms is the use of *blade servers.* These are complete servers that fit on a single card, which can be mounted vertically in a special rack-mounted case designed to hold several servers.

Gigabit Ethernet

Most small networks operate just fine with standard 100BaseT Ethernet connections. However, if your network is large enough to merit a high-speed backbone connection, you may want to look into Gigabit Ethernet. Gigabit Ethernet is a relatively new version of Ethernet, which runs at 1000 Mbps instead of 100 Mbps.

Gigabit Ethernet, also known as 1000BaseX, was initially designed to operate over fiber-optic cables but will eventually be able to work over Category-5 UTP cable as well. That's one of the reasons you should take care to install only top-quality Category-5 cable and keep the cable lengths under 100 meters.

Of course, Gigabit Ethernet is more expensive than 10BaseT or 100BaseT. A Gigabit Ethernet switch can cost several thousand dollars, and you need one at each end of the backbone.

Storage Area Networks

A *storage area network,* also called *SAN,* is designed for managing very large amounts of network storage — in some cases, downright huge amounts. A SAN consists of three components: storage devices (possibly hundreds of them), a separate high-speed network (usually fiber-optic) that directly connects the storage devices to each other, and one or more SAN servers that connect the SAN to the local area network. The SAN server manages the storage devices attached to the SAN and allows users of the LAN to access the storage.

Setting up and managing a Storage Area Network is a job for a SAN expert. If you're interested, you can find more information about storage area networks at the home page of the Storage Networking Industry Association at www.snia.org.

Protocol Analyzer

A *protocol analyzer* is a device that attaches to your network and examines all of the packets that are zipping along inside the cables. In the hands of a seasoned pro, a protocol analyzer can help diagnose all kinds of networking problems — performance problems, security breaches, broken connections, and so on.

Gadgets that used to be in this chapter

Over the years, as I've revised this book to keep up with current technology, I've had the privilege of dropping items from this chapter. I've dropped some items because they aren't even used in large networks anymore. Others I've dropped because their cost has come down so dramatically that they are now used in even the smallest networks or because their usefulness has grown to the point that they're essential for almost every network.

Here are a few of the goodies that I've retired from this chapter:

✔ **Fast Ethernet.** When 100Mbps Ethernet was new, it was expensive enough that only large organizations could justify it. Now it's dirt-cheap. Even the least expensive network cards and components support 100BaseT. So I've retired Fast Ethernet from this chapter. (Gigabit Ethernet is another story. Most networks are fine with 100 Mbps; only really large networks need 1,000 times that much speed.)

✔ **Switches.** In the old days, inexpensive 10BaseT networks used cheap hubs, and switches were used only for large networks where network performance was a driving factor. However, the price of switches has come down so much lately that I now recommend you build all 10BaseT networks using switches rather than hubs.

✔ **Routers.** Routers were once required only for large networks. However, now that broadband Internet access is the norm, many small networks — even networks with just two or three computers — use inexpensive routers to connect to the Internet.

✔ **Firewalls.** Again, because of the proliferation of cheap and fast Internet access, I can no longer say that only large networks need firewalls. Nowadays, *any* network that has a broadband Internet connection needs a firewall.

✔ **Superservers.** This is one of my favorite archaic buzzwords. Once upon a time, computer makers coined this phrase to refer to big servers with multiple processors that could handle work that used to require several servers. The idea was that network servers would become more like the mainframe computers of old, where a single computer handled the workload for an entire organization. Fortunately, this idea didn't catch on. (Imagine if somebody pulled the plug . . .)

I almost dropped RAID from this chapter this time around. As the price of disk drives continues to drop, RAID is becoming more and more common on smaller networks. Even inexpensive servers you can order over the Internet from companies such as Dell can be configured with built-in RAID.

But to use a protocol analyzer, you need a low-level understanding of how networking works. You need to understand about protocols, the differences between the Data Link and MAC Layers of the OSI Model, and the details that lurk inside the packets that make up your network traffic.

So although a protocol analyzer can be a nifty tool, it's usually found only in the hands of network technicians who work with large networks.

Chapter 30

Ten Layers of the OSI Model

. . . .

. . . .

*O*SI sounds like the name of a top-secret government agency you hear about only in Tom Clancy novels. What it really stands for, as far as this book is concerned, is *Open System Interconnection,* as in the Open System Interconnection Reference Model, also known as the OSI Reference Model or OSI Model (depending on how pressed for time you are).

The OSI Model breaks the various aspects of a computer network into seven distinct layers. These layers are kind of like the layers of an onion: Each successive layer envelops the layer beneath it, hiding its details from the levels above. (The OSI Model is also like an onion in that if you start to peel it apart to have a look inside, you're bound to shed a few tears.)

The OSI Model is not itself a networking standard in the same sense that Ethernet and TCP/IP are. Rather, the OSI Model is a framework into which the various networking standards can fit. The OSI Model specifies what aspects of a network's operation can be addressed by various network standards. So, in a sense, the OSI Model is sort of a standard's standard.

The first three layers are sometimes called the *lower layers.* They deal with the mechanics of how information is sent from one computer to another over a network. Layers 4 through 7 are sometimes called the *upper layers.* They deal with how applications relate to the network through application programming interfaces.

Layer 1: The Physical Layer

The bottom layer of the OSI Model is the Physical Layer. It addresses the physical characteristics of the network, such as the types of cables used to connect devices, the types of connectors used, how long the cables can be, and so on. For example, the Ethernet standard for 100BaseT cable specifies the electrical characteristics of the twisted-pair cables, the size and shape of the connectors, the maximum length of the cables, and so on.

Another aspect of the Physical Layer is that it specifies the electrical characteristics of the signals used to transmit data over cables from one network node to another. The Physical Layer doesn't define any particular meaning for those signals other than the basic binary values 0 and 1. The higher levels of the OSI model must assign meanings to the bits transmitted at the Physical Layer.

One type of Physical Layer device commonly used in networks is a *repeater*. A repeater is used to regenerate signals when you need to exceed the cable length allowed by the Physical Layer standard or when you need to redistribute a signal from one cable onto two or more cables.

An old-style 10BaseT hub is also Physical Layer device. Technically, a hub is a *multi-port repeater* because its purpose is to regenerate every signal received on any port on all of the hub's other ports. Repeaters and hubs don't examine the contents of the signals that they regenerate. If they did, they would be working at the Data Link Layer, and not at the Physical Layer. Which leads us to . . .

Layer 2: The Data Link Layer

The *Data Link Layer* is the lowest layer at which meaning is assigned to the bits that are transmitted over the network. Data-link protocols address things such as the size of each packet of data to be sent, a means of addressing each packet so that it's delivered to the intended recipient, and a way to ensure that two or more nodes don't try to transmit data on the network at the same time.

The Data Link Layer also provides basic error detection and correction to ensure that the data sent is the same as the data received. If an uncorrectable error occurs, the data-link standard must specify how the node is to be informed of the error so it can retransmit the data.

At the Data Link Layer, each device on the network has an address known as the *Media Access Control address,* or *MAC address.* This is the actual hardware address, assigned to the device at the factory.

You can see the MAC address for a computer's network adapter by opening a command window and running the `ipconfig /all` command, as shown in Figure 30-1. In this example, the MAC address (identified as the *physical address* in the output) of the network card is `00-50-BA-84-39-11`.

Figure 30-1: Displaying the MAC address of your network adapter.

```
G:\WINDOWS\System32\cmd.exe                                    _|□|×

C:\>ipconfig /all

Windows IP Configuration

        Host Name . . . . . . . . . . . . : doug
        Primary Dns Suffix  . . . . . . . :
        Node Type . . . . . . . . . . . . : Unknown
        IP Routing Enabled. . . . . . . . : No
        WINS Proxy Enabled. . . . . . . . : No

Ethernet adapter Local Area Connection:

        Connection-specific DNS Suffix  . : we1.client2.attbi.com
        Description . . . . . . . . . . . : D-Link DFE-530TX+ PCI Adapter #2
        Physical Address. . . . . . . . . : 00-50-BA-84-39-11
        Dhcp Enabled. . . . . . . . . . . : Yes
        Autoconfiguration Enabled . . . . : Yes
        IP Address. . . . . . . . . . . . : 192.168.1.100
        Subnet Mask . . . . . . . . . . . : 255.255.255.0
        Default Gateway . . . . . . . . . : 192.168.1.1
        DHCP Server . . . . . . . . . . . : 192.168.1.1
        DNS Servers . . . . . . . . . . . : 204.127.198.19
                                            63.240.76.19
        Lease Obtained. . . . . . . . . . : Sunday, June 13, 2004 8:28:14 PM
        Lease Expires . . . . . . . . . . : Monday, June 14, 2004 8:28:14 PM

C:\>
```

One of the most import functions of the Data Link Layer is to provide a way for packets to be sent safely over the physical media without interference from other nodes attempting to send packets at the same time. Ethernet uses a technique called CSMA/CD to accomplish this.

Switches are the most commonly used Data Link Layer devices in most networks. A *switch* is similar to a hub, but instead of regenerating incoming signals of every port, a switch examines the MAC address of every incoming packet to determine which port to send the packet to.

Layer 3: The Network Layer

The *Network Layer* handles the task of routing network messages from one computer to another. The two most popular Layer-3 protocols are IP (which is usually paired with TCP) and IPX (normally paired with SPX for use with Novell and Windows networks).

One important function of the Network Layer is *logical addressing*. As you know, every network device has a physical address called a MAC address, which is assigned to the device at the factory. When you buy a network interface card to install in a computer, the MAC address of that card is fixed and can't be changed. But what if you want to use some other addressing scheme to refer to the computers and other devices on your network? This is where the concept of logical addressing comes in; a logical address lets gives a network device a place where it can be accessed on the network — using an address that you assign.

Logical addresses are created and used by Network Layer protocols such as IP or IPX. The Network Layer protocol translates logical addresses to MAC addresses. For example, if you use IP as the Network Layer protocol, devices on the network are assigned IP addresses such as `207.120.67.30`. Because the IP protocol must use a Data Link Layer protocol to actually send packets to devices, IP must know how to translate the IP address of a device into the correct MAC address for the device. You can use the `ipconfig` command to see the IP address of your computer. The IP address shown in that figure is `192.168.1.100`.

Another important function of the Network layer is *routing* — finding an appropriate path through the network. Routing comes into play when a computer on one network needs to send a packet to a computer on another network. In this case, a Network Layer device called a *router* forwards the packet to the destination network. An important feature of routers is that they can be used to connect networks that use different Layer-2 protocols. For example, a router can be used to connect a local area network that uses Ethernet to a wide area network that runs on a different set of low-level protocols, such as T1.

Layer 4: The Transport Layer

The Transport Layer is the basic layer at which one network computer communicates with another network computer. The Transport Layer is where you'll find one of the most popular networking protocols: TCP. The main purpose of the Transport Layer is to ensure that packets move over the network reliably and without errors. The Transport Layer does this by establishing connections between network devices, acknowledging the receipt of packets, and resending packets that are not received or are corrupted when they arrive.

In many cases, the Transport Layer protocol divides large messages into smaller packets that can be sent over the network efficiently. The Transport Layer protocol reassembles the message on the receiving end, making sure that all packets contained in a single transmission are received and no data is lost.

Layer 4a: The Lemon-Pudding Layer

The Lemon-Pudding Layer is squeezed in between the rather dry and taste-less Transport and Session Layers to add flavor and moistness.

Layer 5: The Session Layer

The Session Layer establishes *sessions* (instances of communication and data exchange) between network nodes. A session must be established before data can be transmitted over the network. The Session Layer makes sure that these sessions are properly established and maintained.

Layer 6: The Presentation Layer

The Presentation Layer is responsible for converting the data sent over the net-work from one type of representation to another. For example, the Presentation Layer can apply sophisticated compression techniques so fewer bytes of data are required to represent the information when it's sent over the network. At the other end of the transmission, the Transport Layer then uncompresses the data.

The Presentation Layer also can scramble the data before it's transmitted and unscramble it at the other end, using a sophisticated encryption technique that even Sherlock Holmes would have trouble breaking.

Layer 7: The Application Layer

The highest layer of the OSI model, the Application Layer deals with the tech-niques that application programs use to communicate with the network. The name of this layer is a little confusing because application programs (such as Excel or Word) aren't actually part of the layer. Rather, the Application Layer represents the level at which application programs *interact with the network,* using programming interfaces to request network services. One of the most commonly known used application layer protocols is HTTP, which stands for HyperText Transfer Protocol. HTTP is the basis of the World Wide Web.

Index

• *O* •

• R •

radio spectrum bands, 133–134
radio waves
  antennas and, 133
  bands of the radio spectrum, 133–134
  defined, 131
  frequencies, 131–132
  wavelength, 132–133
RAID (Redundant Array of Inexpensive
    Disks), 373–374, 376
RAM. *See* memory
range of wireless networks, 135–136
RConsoleJ tool (NetWare), 284–285
Readme file (NetWare), 276
rebooting. *See* restarting
receiving e-mail
  attachments, 52–53, 57, 216
  in Outlook (Windows), 56–57
  tips, 52–53
Reconnect at Logon option, 29
Red Hat Linux distribution
  Network Configuration program,
    307–308
  overview, 300
  Samba Server Configuration tool,
    312–313
Redundant Array of Inexpensive Disks
    (RAID), 373–374, 376
reference books and magazines, 169–170,
    240–241, 297, 368
releasing DHCP leases, 352
Relnotes.asp file, 248
Remember icon, 6
Remote Manager tool (NetWare),
    282–283
renewing DHCP leases, 352
repeaters, 124–126, 370–371
replying to e-mail messages, 56
reservations (DHCP), 348–349

resetting passwords
  NetWare, 288
  Windows Server 2003, 259–260
resource sharing. *See also specific
    resources*
  independence lost by, 18–19
  Internet connection, 12, 326
  local versus network resources, 21–22
  My Network Places (Windows) and,
    26–27
  naming resources, 23
  overview, 12
restarting
  client computers, 231–233
  Linux networks, 308–309
  logged on users and, 356–357
  network services, 233–234
  problems cleared up by, 224, 232
  problems restarting, 232–233
  servers, 234–235
RG-58 cable, 106. *See also* coaxial cable
ring topology, 104
RJ-45 connectors, 113–115
roaming, 140
rogue access points, 144, 359
routers, 127–128, 326–328, 376

• S •

Samba file- and printer-sharing
  installing, 310
  overview, 309–310
  Red Hat configuration tool, 312–313
  starting and stopping, 311
SAN (storage area network), 375
scheduled tasks, performance and, 198
scopes
  DHCP, 347–349
  group account, 261
scripts for logging on, 186, 288–295

Notes

Notes

Notes

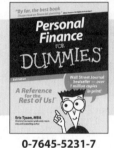

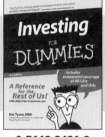
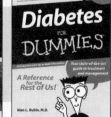

FOR DUMMIES®

A world of resources to help you grow

HOME, GARDEN & HOBBIES

Feng Shui FOR DUMMIES
A Reference for the Rest of Us!
0-7645-5295-3

Gardening FOR DUMMIES
2nd Edition
A Reference for the Rest of Us!
0-7645-5130-2

Guitar FOR DUMMIES
A Reference for the Rest of Us!
0-7645-5106-X

Also available:

Auto Repair For Dummies
(0-7645-5089-6)

Chess For Dummies
(0-7645-5003-9)

Home Maintenance For Dummies
(0-7645-5215-5)

Organizing For Dummies
(0-7645-5300-3)

Piano For Dummies
(0-7645-5105-1)

Poker For Dummies
(0-7645-5232-5)

Quilting For Dummies
(0-7645-5118-3)

Rock Guitar For Dummies
(0-7645-5356-9)

Roses For Dummies
(0-7645-5202-3)

Sewing For Dummies
(0-7645-5137-X)

FOOD & WINE

Cooking FOR DUMMIES
2nd Edition
A Reference for the Rest of Us!
0-7645-5250-3

Cookies FOR DUMMIES
A Reference for the Rest of Us!
0-7645-5390-9

Wine FOR DUMMIES
2nd Edition
A Reference for the Rest of Us!
0-7645-5114-0

Also available:

Bartending For Dummies
(0-7645-5051-9)

Chinese Cooking For Dummies
(0-7645-5247-3)

Christmas Cooking For Dummies
(0-7645-5407-7)

Diabetes Cookbook For Dummies
(0-7645-5230-9)

Grilling For Dummies
(0-7645-5076-4)

Low-Fat Cooking For Dummies
(0-7645-5035-7)

Slow Cookers For Dummies
(0-7645-5240-6)

TRAVEL

Italy FOR DUMMIES
2nd Edition
A Travel Guide for the Rest of Us!
0-7645-5453-0

Hawaii FOR DUMMIES
2nd Edition
A Travel Guide for the Rest of Us!
0-7645-5438-7

Las Vegas FOR DUMMIES
2nd Edition
A Travel Guide for the Rest of Us!
0-7645-5448-4

Also available:

America's National Parks For Dummies
(0-7645-6204-5)

Caribbean For Dummies
(0-7645-5445-X)

Cruise Vacations For Dummies 2003
(0-7645-5459-X)

Europe For Dummies
(0-7645-5456-5)

Ireland For Dummies
(0-7645-6199-5)

France For Dummies
(0-7645-6292-4)

London For Dummies
(0-7645-5416-6)

Mexico's Beach Resorts For Dummies
(0-7645-6262-2)

Paris For Dummies
(0-7645-5494-8)

RV Vacations For Dummies
(0-7645-5443-3)

Walt Disney World & Orlando For Dummies
(0-7645-5444-1)

Available wherever books are sold. Go to www.dummies.com or call 1-877-762-2974 to order direct.

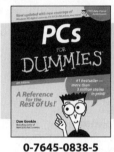

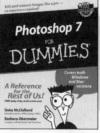